LUCIUS ANNAEUS SENECA, politician, philosopher and man of letters, was born at Cordoba in Spain around 4 BC. Brought to Rome at an early age, he rapidly rose to prominence due to his brilliance as a public speaker. His fame, however, was resented by the imperial family. Barely surviving a death sentence issued by Caligula (AD 37–41), Seneca was exiled in AD 41 to the barren island of Corsica by Caligula's successor, Claudius. After eight years he was recalled by Agrippina the Younger, the ambitious new wife of Claudius and mother of Nero. Seneca was made *praetor* and assigned the task of grooming her young son for the throne. In AD 54 Agrippina accelerated Claudius' death and installed Nero, now aged sixteen, over Claudius' son and legitimate heir Britannicus. Once merely Nero's tutor, Seneca suddenly became the emperor's chief political adviser. Despite the suspicious death of Britannicus in AD 55, the first five years of Nero's reign were regarded by no less a personage than the Emperor Trajan (AD 98–117) as a period of great prosperity – partly, no doubt, because of Seneca's guidance. Yet as Nero grew older he became resentful of those he viewed as his puppet-masters. In AD 59 he killed his mother in dramatic fashion; in AD 62 Burrus – the captain of the imperial bodyguard and Seneca's partner in guiding Nero's policy – died suspiciously. Seneca wisely attempted to distance himself from the imperial court by asking Nero to let him retire. Nero refused, and in AD 65 Seneca, implicated in a plot (probably falsely) to overthrow the emperor, was forced to take his own life.

In addition to his tragic oeuvre, Seneca wrote numerous philosophical works and letters that are deeply indebted to Stoic philosophy. The tragedies themselves greatly influenced the development of drama during the Middle Ages and Renaissance. After a period of neglect, Seneca's works are experiencing their own renaissance.

R. SCOTT SMITH was born in Baltimore, Maryland, in 1971 and was educated at Mary Washington College and then at the University of Illinois Urbana-Champaign. Since 2000 he has taught at the University of New Hampshire, where he is currently Associate Professor. He is co-author of *An Anthology of Classical Myth* (2004) and *Apollodorus'* Bibliotheke *and Hyginus'* Fabulae: *Two Handbooks of Greek Mythology* (2007), as well as articles on Seneca's philosophical and dramatic works.

SENECA

Phaedra and Other Plays

Translated and with an Introduction and Notes by
R. SCOTT SMITH

PENGUIN BOOKS

PENGUIN CLASSICS

Published by the Penguin Group
Penguin Books Ltd, 80 Strand, London WC2R ORL, England
Penguin Group (USA) Inc., 375 Hudson Street, New York, New York 10014, USA
Penguin Group (Canada), 90 Eglinton Avenue East, Suite 700, Toronto, Ontario, Canada M4P 2Y3
(a division of Pearson Penguin Canada Inc.)
Penguin Ireland, 25 St Stephen's Green, Dublin 2, Ireland (a division of Penguin Books Ltd)
Penguin Group (Australia), 250 Camberwell Road, Camberwell, Victoria 3124, Australia
(a division of Pearson Australia Group Pty Ltd)
Penguin Books India Pvt Ltd, 11 Community Centre, Panchsheel Park, New Delhi – 110 017, India
Penguin Group (NZ), 67 Apollo Drive, Rosedale, Auckland 0632, New Zealand
(a division of Pearson New Zealand Ltd)
Penguin Books (South Africa) (Pty) Ltd, 24 Sturdee Avenue, Rosebank, Johannesburg 2196, South Africa

Penguin Books Ltd, Registered Offices: 80 Strand, London WC2R ORL, England

www.penguin.com

This edition first published in Penguin Classics 2011
006

Translation, introduction and editorial matter copyright © R. Scott Smith, 2011
All rights reserved

The moral right of the translator and author of the introduction has been asserted

Set in 10.25/12.25 pt Postscript Adobe Sabon
Typeset by Palimpsest Book Production Limited, Falkirk, Stirlingshire
Printed in Great Britain by Clays Ltd, St Ives plc

ISBN: 978-0-140-45551-9

www.greenpenguin.co.uk

Contents

Acknowledgements   vii
Introduction   ix
Selected Further Reading   xxvii
A Note on the Translation   xxix

Preface to *Hercules Insane*   3
HERCULES INSANE

Preface to *Trojan Women*   55
TROJAN WOMEN

Preface to *Phaedra*   103
PHAEDRA

Preface to *Oedipus*   151
OEDIPUS

Preface to *Thyestes*   197
THYESTES

Preface to *Octavia*   241
OCTAVIA

Notes   281
Glossary   306

Acknowledgements

I have accrued many debts during the completion of this project, and, like Oedipus (Act V), I feel as though I should utter *non solvendo es* ('You cannot pay all of your debts!'). In lieu of plucking out my eyes, however, I can only offer the following acknowledgements. First and foremost, I would like to thank those scholars who graciously read over substantial parts of my manuscript and saved me from numerous errors and infelicities: Stephen Brunet, William M. Calder III, Thomas Kohn and Stephen M. Trzaskoma. Naturally, all remaining mistakes (may they be few!) are mine and mine alone. I should also like to thank The Center for the Humanities at the University of New Hampshire for their generous grant, which allowed me a semester off from teaching to bring the translations to completion, as well as Margarethe Billerbeck and John Fitch for their letters of support. I translated *Octavia* and much of *Trojan Women* during two three-week stints in the idyllic setting of the Fondation Hardt pour l'étude de l'Antiquité classique, which could not have been possible but for the financial assistance of the William A. Oldfather Research Fund at the University of Illinois at Urbana-Champaign. I must also acknowledge the work of my student swat team, who read over my translations and helped proofread the glossary: Jessica Charlesworth, Michael D'Angelo, Ali Gennaro and Andrew Holmes. Thanks also go to Peter Carson, my editor at Penguin, whose guidance, patience and prodding were essential to complete this project. Finally, I must acknowledge a debt I know I cannot repay, that to my darling wife Maggie, who not only read over every single word I wrote, making valuable suggestions all along the way and putting up with my incessant questions about English idiom, but who also gave me the daily strength needed to complete this Herculean task. All I can give in return is the dedication of this book – along with the promise that, now that it is published, we can talk about something other than Seneca's plays.

Introduction

I Seneca's Life

Lucius Annaeus Seneca (called Seneca the Younger to distinguish him from his father) was born sometime between 4 and 1 BC in Cordoba, a city in the Roman province of Baetica on the Iberian Peninsula. Both Seneca the Elder and his wife Helvia were provincial Roman citizens descended from Italian stock and wealthy enough to be included in the second-highest social order, ranked only behind the senatorial class. The elder Seneca, a successful businessman, spent much time in Rome, where he moved within literary circles and was himself a respected writer; he was the author of a history of the civil wars, now lost, and of surviving anthologies of rhetorical speeches that he collected for his three sons, the *Controversiae* ('Forensic Speeches') and *Suasoriae* ('Persuasive Speeches').

Desiring a first-rate education for his son Lucius, the elder Seneca brought him to Rome at an early age, but we do not have many firm details about Seneca's youth. We do know that by the late AD 30s the younger Seneca was – through the influence of his aunt – elected to a high public office, the quaestorship, and thereby became a senator. In the reign of Caligula (AD 37–41) he had achieved enough of a reputation as a public speaker to catch the notice of the emperor, who remarked that Seneca's speeches were 'mere classroom exercises' and 'sand without lime', today's equivalent of 'all style and no substance'. According to one romanticized account, the jealous emperor ordered Seneca to be executed because he had spoken brilliantly before the senate, and he was saved only by the timely intervention of one of Caligula's mistresses. This story – true or not – shows that

Seneca was already well enough known to attract the unwanted attention of the emperor.

Having escaped punishment under Caligula, Seneca was not so lucky with his successor, Claudius (AD 41–54). In the first year of Claudius' reign, Seneca was convicted of adultery with Caligula's sister Julia Livilla and exiled to the island of Corsica, where he spent the next eight years and wrote *Consolation to his Mother* and *Consolation to Polybius*. Since the charge – engineered by Claudius' third wife Messalina – was aimed primarily at removing Julia, Seneca may well have been innocent; even so, given Seneca's high-level connections and rising profile as an influential speaker, Messalina may have jumped at this opportunity to rid herself of a potential political obstacle – Seneca – at the same time.

Shortly after Messalina's death in AD 48 Claudius' fourth wife Agrippina persuaded the emperor to recall Seneca for the express purpose of tutoring her eleven-year-old son from her previous marriage, L. Domitius Ahenobarbus – later known as the Emperor Nero. Although Seneca was heavily influenced by Stoic philosophy and wrote several surviving philosophical treatises, Agrippina made it clear that Seneca was not to teach her son philosophy. Rather, he was to focus on rhetorical training, public speaking and grooming him for the emperorship, despite the fact that the legitimate heir to the throne was Claudius' biological son Britannicus. When in AD 54 Agrippina engineered Claudius' death and installed Nero, now sixteen, on the throne, Seneca's position suddenly changed from a prince's tutor to the emperor's adviser. The next year Nero, pressured by his mother to rid himself of his more legitimate rival, poisoned Britannicus. Seneca, of course, knew the truth but did not dare protest; perhaps his *De Clementia* ('On Clemency'), written shortly after this and addressed to the young Nero, was Seneca's way of responding to an impossible situation.

Despite this inauspicious start, for the first five years of Nero's reign Seneca – along with the captain of the imperial bodyguard, Burrus – guided Nero's hand admirably, balancing the young emperor's whims against the imperial ambitions of his mother. But in AD 59 Nero, yearning to slough off his mother's controlling presence, made two attempts on her life, succeeding in the second (more specifics may be found in the preface to *Octavia*). Soon after this Seneca's influence began to wane. Twice he attempted to extricate himself from the tightening web of imperial politics by asking Nero to allow him to retire, first after his associate Burrus' suspicious death in AD 62 and again in 64. Nero refused both times, but from 62 onwards Seneca increasingly refrained from public appearances and turned to the salve of philosophy; it is at this time that he wrote his *Spiritual Letters to Lucilius and Natural Investigations*, as well as other essays from the collection now called the *Dialogues*. Finally, in AD 65, after being falsely implicated in a failed conspiracy to murder Nero led by C. Calpurnius Piso, Seneca was ordered to commit suicide. His death by hemlock while conversing philosophically with friends recalls that of Socrates in 399 BC, as told in Tacitus' *Annals* (15.62–4).

II The Plays: the Basics

Ten plays have been handed down to us under the name Seneca: the tragedies *Hercules Insane*, *Trojan Women* (also called *Troad*), *Phoenician Women* (incomplete, also called *Thebaid*), *Medea*, *Phaedra* (also called *Hippolytus*), *Oedipus*, *Agamemnon*, *Thyestes*, *Hercules on Oeta* and the historical play *Octavia*. It is generally agreed that the last two are not by Seneca. *Hercules on Oeta*, painfully long and otiose, is stylistically unworthy of the 'genuine eight', and *Octavia*, for reasons outlined in the preface to that play, cannot have been written by him. These two plays, which draw heavily on Seneca's authentic works, were probably composed a generation or so after his death, perhaps in the Flavian period (AD 79–96); that Seneca's authentic works became models for these plays indicates their popularity immediately after his death. Although some critics still question the authenticity of individual plays[1] or the entire corpus,[2] the position adopted here is that of the scholarly majority: we have eight plays from Seneca's hand.

Given the stark difference between the bleak hopelessness of Seneca's plays and the generally optimistic tone found in his philosophical works, it is unsurprising that some have questioned whether both could have been written by the same person. Indeed, by late antiquity the idea developed that Seneca the Philosopher and Seneca the Tragedian were two distinct individuals. Yet there is little reason to doubt that the younger Seneca wrote tragedies. It is true that he does not mention them in his surviving philosophical works, but the historian of literature Quintilian, writing a generation after Seneca's death, quotes a line which he explicitly states was from Seneca's *Medea* (line 453; *Institutes of Oratory* 9.2.9). He further reports a debate that he heard 'while still a young man' between Seneca and the tragedian Pomponius Secundus over proper tragic diction (*Institutes of Oratory* 8.3.31). The chronology – Quintilian was born around AD 35 – hardly allows this Seneca to be the elder Seneca, who died in AD 39 or 40, and to assume this is a third, otherwise unknown Seneca adds unnecessary complexity.

A tantalizing statement comes from the historian Tacitus (*Annals* 14.52), who reports that Seneca began to compose *carmina* more frequently as Nero grew more fond of them. This word generally means 'poems/songs', but it may also specifically mean 'plays'. Nero, in fact, frequently assumed dramatic roles, 'sang tragedies' (Suetonius, *Nero* 21.3), and was dubbed *imperator scaenicus* ('the theatrical emperor') by Pliny (*Panegyric* 46.4). Suetonius and the historian Dio report that Nero had favourite roles: Orestes the Mother Killer, Blinded Oedipus, Hercules Insane, Oedipus the Exile, Thyestes, Heracles and Alcmaeon. The similarity between some of these roles and Seneca's plays has not unreasonably led some to claim that Seneca's dramatic production was, at least in part, encouraged by the emperor's interests.

We do not know when Seneca's plays were written or performed (if they were performed at all; see below, section IV). The earliest evidence of Seneca's plays circulating comes from a graffito in Pompeii that quotes *Agamemnon* (line 730), but this only tells us that this one play must predate the volcanic eruption of Vesuvius that buried the city in AD 79. It is also fairly certain that the author of the satirical *Apocolocyntosis* ('The Ascension of the Pumpkinhead Claudius into Heaven'), probably Seneca himself, parodied *Hercules Insane* (and perhaps

Trojan Women) in that work. Since *Apocolocyntosis* was written shortly after Claudius' death in October AD 54, that play must have been written sometime before that event. How long before, however, is anyone's guess. Many have suggested that Seneca wrote them during his exile (AD 41–48) because he would have had the leisure to compose them, but this is nothing more than conjecture. They could easily have been youthful compositions, as was Julius Caesar's now lost *Oedipus*.

Beyond this nothing certain can be said. Allusions to historical events, while suggestive, prove nothing about exact dates. On the other hand, a study of Seneca's verse technique allows us to construct a provisional relative chronology.[3] According to this study the plays fall into three distinct groups: 1) early plays: *Oedipus, Phaedra, Agamemnon*; 2) middle plays: *Medea, Trojan Women, Hercules Insane*; 3) late plays: *Thyestes, Phoenician Women*. This hypothesis is attractive for a number of reasons. First, *Phoenician Women* is incomplete; perhaps Seneca died before finishing the play. Second, *Thyestes*, considered by many to be Seneca's best play, should be a mature work. Third, only *Oedipus* and *Agamemnon* have polymetric odes, that is, odes that vary in metre from line to line; on this interpretation, these plays were experimental early plays before Seneca settled on odes based on more regular lyric metres.

III The Plays: the Dramatic Context in Greece and Rome

Seneca's plays are the only Latin tragedies to survive complete. Although we know that tragedies were written and performed continuously from 240 BC, when Livius Andronicus translated and staged a Greek play for the *Ludi Romani* ('The Roman Shows'), all of these plays have wholly perished or are preserved in only a few (usually short) fragments. Thus, we have only the barest traces of the extensive oeuvres of the early republican playwrights Naevius, Ennius, Pacuvius and Accius, which were regarded as classics both by Cicero (106–43 BC), who quotes from them liberally, and Quintilian. From the late Republic we have, for instance, Horace and Vergil's high praise of Asinius

Pollio's tragedies (*carmina*); although Vergil ranked them equal to Sophocles' plays, they, along with those of his contemporaries, have not survived. From the early empire we are also at a loss. The tragedies that Quintilian notes for their excellence – Varius' *Thyestes*, Ovid's *Medea* and Pomponius' works – have all but vanished. We know even less about the parallel genre of *praetextae*, historical dramas on Roman themes, which arose early in Rome and were performed at public festivals alongside Greek tragedies. Unless the *Octavia* is a *praetexta*, which is uncertain (see the preface to that play), all we have are fragments that allow only the most hypothetical reconstruction of that genre's nature and aims.

Because of the deplorable state of the evidence, it is difficult to ascertain how Seneca's plays fit into the wider genre of Roman tragedy. What is certain is that Seneca, like his predecessors, looked to Greek myth and, whether directly or indirectly, to the tragedies of the three great fifth-century Athenian playwrights, Aeschylus, Sophocles and Euripides (hereafter referred to as 'Greek tragedy'). In six cases we can compare Seneca's plays directly with an extant Greek play. Seneca's *Agamemnon*, like Aeschylus' play of the same name, covers the return and death of Agamemnon. Seneca's *Oedipus*, like Sophocles' version, dramatizes Oedipus' journey to self-discovery and self-blinding. Seneca's *Phaedra/Hippolytus*, *Hercules*, *Trojan Women* and *Medea* deal with the same episodes as Euripides' plays of the same names. Only in the case of *Thyestes* do we lack an extant Greek predecessor, although a reasonable case can be made that it dramatizes the same episode as Sophocles' lost *Atreus*.

Because of this similarity, it was once conventional wisdom that Seneca worked directly from a specific Greek play that served as his model. Seneca's plays, however, show great divergence in plot and in the direction of the dramatic movement from the Greek tragedies. Seneca's *Hercules*, for instance, unlike Euripides', begins with a prologue by the goddess Juno – a change that imparts greater unity to the drama. Seneca's characterization of a nervous Oedipus is vastly different from Sophocles' confident protagonist, and Tiresias must conduct a range of sacrifices to divine the god's will, whereas in Sophocles he simply *knows* what the god wishes. Seneca's *Trojan Women*, while recounting the horrifying death of Astyanax like his predecessor Euripides, also weaves the sacrifice of Polyxena into the narrative fabric of the play and gives it equal billing. In the last case some scholars have claimed that Seneca simply grafted Sophocles' lost *Polyxena* onto Euripides' *Trojan Women*. The problem with this approach is that it is based on the *a priori* assumption that Seneca's plays are derivative and without originality. Yet, Seneca's plays are no less original than those of his Greek predecessors, who were themselves drawing on pre-existing mythological stories and the dramatic works of other poets.

In an important study Richard Tarrant firmly debunked the view that Seneca wrote with the Greek originals at hand by demonstrating how dependent Seneca's dramaturgy was on dramatic developments that occurred *after* Euripides' death.[4] For example, unlike Greek tragedy, Seneca's plays adhere, with perhaps one exception (*Oedipus*), to a five-act division punctuated by choral odes. This dramatic structure evolved as the role of the chorus diminished as a functioning part of the dramatic action. The late plays of Euripides already saw a diminution of the chorus' role; his younger contemporary Agathon was said to have made choral odes nothing more than *embolima*, songs between acts. By the late fourth century BC the five-act structure had become customary in both comedy and tragedy; in the comedy *Dyskolos* ('Cranky Old Man') by Menander (343–291 BC?), we find a five-act division and, instead of choral odes, there is only the marker *chorou* ('[place] of the chorus'). Presumably, the choral odes were to be written separately and inserted into the play.

Tarrant also noted that Seneca's use of the chorus was markedly different from that of Greek tragedy. Because the *orchestra*, the 'dancing place' for Greek choruses, was by Seneca's day used for senatorial seating, the chorus would have been confined to the stage. Its size was, therefore, probably smaller, say three to six rather than the standard twelve or fifteen in Athenian tragedy,[5] and the chorus could (and often did) exit between acts when not demanded on stage for other reasons (Greek choruses stayed in the orchestra throughout the play). A reduced chorus would have been even more necessary if the performance was held in a private venue (see below). Tarrant also demonstrated that the long entrance monologues and asides commonly found in Seneca's plays do not have analogues in Greek tragedy. Indeed, Lycus' extensive entrance monologue in Act II of *Hercules Insane* and Andromache's internal debate set as an aside in Act III of *Trojan Women* would have seemed remarkable to a fifth-century Athenian audience.

Seneca, then, was probably following contemporary dramaturgical practices rather than retreating to those of Greek tragedy. Seneca's verse, too, is deeply influenced by the great Augustan poets Horace, Vergil and Ovid. Seneca writes his dialogue and speeches in the smooth iambic trimeter that developed during that time, and Seneca's choral odes (in both metre and content) are deeply indebted to Horace's *Odes*. Seneca also owed much to Vergil's great epic the *Aeneid*. For instance, Juno's opening speech in *Hercules Insane* recasts Juno's speech to the Fury Allecto in *Aeneid* 7, and Theseus' description of the underworld (Act III) recalls *Aeneid* 6. The influence of Ovid on Seneca is pervasive; Seneca frequently reshapes mythical stories in Ovid's *Metamorphoses* and commonly echoes that poet's language, and his *Phaedra* is indebted to Ovid's fictitious letter from Phaedra to Hippolytus (*Letters from Heroines* 4).

It is imperative to keep in mind that first-century Rome was vastly different from fifth-century Athens, and that the theatre will reflect those differences. Athenian tragedies were put on at public expense and performed in front of a city-wide audience at a religious festival in honour of Dionysus. In other words, they were democratic and religious, just like the culture from which they sprang. Seneca's tragedies were neither state-sponsored nor performed at a religious festival (as far as we know), and they were written in the empire, when the majority of the power rested in the hands of one man, the emperor. Although public performance of the Athenian sort cannot be ruled out entirely, Seneca's plays were probably aimed at a smaller, more elite audience, meant to be performed in an intimate, perhaps private venue – closer to our modern theatre halls than the theatre of Dionysus in Athens, which seated some 15,000 spectators. The proliferation of theatres in cities throughout the Roman empire

after Augustus' accession might suggest that public presenta-
tions of tragedies were common, but tragedy (and comedy) had
to compete against newer forms of entertainment that used the
stage: mime and pantomime. The former was a vigorous one-act
performance by actors who did not wear masks, usually on an
everyday theme, often vulgar or obscene, perhaps something
like a vaudeville show. Pantomime was an interpretive dance,
usually of a tragic episode, by a silent masked dancer accompanied by an individual singer or a chorus. Introduced in 22
BC, it became an instant success and was the favourite form of
entertainment of many emperors. Indeed, this, and not tragedy,
may have been the kind of tragic performance of which Nero
was fond.

IV The Nature of Seneca's Plays

When approached by readers conditioned by long exposure to
Greek tragedy, Seneca's plays will appear static, dark, brooding
and overly obsessed with violence and bloodshed. Greeks do
not show death onstage; Seneca is keen to dramatize violence.
Seneca's Medea murders her children onstage; in Euripides' play
this occurs offstage. Jocasta kills herself onstage with a sword
in Seneca's *Oedipus*; in Sophocles' version she hangs herself
offstage. In Euripides' *Hippolytus* Phaedra hangs herself offstage;
Seneca's Phaedra kills herself with a sword onstage over Hippolytus' dead body. Euripides' Hercules kills his wife and sons
offstage; Seneca's does so onstage. The narration of offstage
violence is just as vivid. Consider the stunning account of Atreus'
ritual sacrifice of Thyestes' children (*Thyestes*, Act IV), the report
of Hippolytus' brutal death (*Phaedra*, Act IV), or the description
of Astyanax's and Polyxena's deaths (*Trojan Women*, Act V).
The dramatization of death onstage disregards the instructions
of Horace, who wrote two generations earlier (*Poetic Technique*
185–6), 'do not have Medea butcher her children before the
audience's eyes or have vile Thyestes cook human flesh on stage.'
But episodes bordering on – or crossing over the line of – the
grotesque are not unusual for the early empire. Ovid's description of Philomela's amputated tongue attempting to crawl back

to its owner (*Metamorphoses* 6.557–60) should remind us that Seneca's shocking and grotesque scenes were fashionable at the time.

Though Seneca's plays are permeated with violence, their author's real preoccupation is with psychological forces, especially those that trigger violence. Atreus is consumed with anger; Phaedra with desire; Hercules with aggression; Hecuba with sorrow; Oedipus with guilt. Although all tragedy involves psychology to some degree, Seneca's characters are remarkably self-reflective and introspective, searching inwardly to analyse their own actions and the motivations for those actions. Greek characters, by contrast, show their motivations and emotions in dialogue with other characters. Seneca's plays, therefore, have less dialogue and more self-revealing monologues aimed at exploring the psychological constitution of the characters performing the action. Particularly striking examples of this externalization of thought and psychology may be found in the monologues of Phaedra (*Phaedra*, Act II), Atreus (*Thyestes*, Act II), Oedipus (*Oedipus*, Act I), Helen (*Trojan Women*, Act IV) and Lycus (*Hercules Insane*, Act II).

The focus on emotions – in particular the disastrous effects of anger and lust – brings us into the orbit of Stoic philosophy, to which Seneca was deeply indebted in his moral and ethical works. Indeed, the Stoics were highly interested in human psychology, and this no doubt contributed to Seneca's fixation on the psychological make-up of his characters. We also find other Stoic ideas expressed, primarily in the choral odes, such as the meditation of the true king in *Thyestes* (Ode II), and that on fate in *Oedipus* (Choral Interlude in Act V). But it would be a mistake to insist, on any level, that Seneca's plays are simple vehicles for philosophical messages. Nothing could be farther from the truth. Indeed, the world view of the plays is decidedly un-Stoic; moral chaos predominates and evil frequently triumphs over good. We are quite far away from the world governed by the providentially beneficent Stoic god.

One result of Seneca's fixation on emotions (Stoic or not) is that his plays often seem uninterested in action and plot development. In other words, Seneca's characters spend more time brooding over their actions than they do acting. The power of Senecan tragedy, therefore, is derived more from the power of its language than from the development of the dramatic action. Muscular and vibrant, Seneca's language is always front and centre. This is not to say that Seneca was unconcerned with plot, characterization or the unity of his plays, but that he was, first and foremost, a craftsman of words and argument, a verbal virtuoso if you will, and it was only natural that this virtuosity came to the fore when he composed his tragedies. Rhetorical training had always been a necessary part of an aristocratic education in Republican Rome, aiming at preparing a young man to speak persuasively in the senate or in a public oration. But by the early empire, when political power was concentrated in the hands of the emperor, the aims of a rhetorical education had shifted substantially. Although it was still necessary in the political arena, rhetorical facility increasingly became an index of one's position within the *literary* and *cultural* elite of Rome.

Given this cultural backdrop, it is unsurprising that Seneca's plays, like other literature of his time, revel in the fullness, complexity and cleverness of language. This can be seen in his pithy, epigrammatic style, one that attempts to capture in a single line a complex thought or the irony of a situation. Thus, as Hecuba states pointedly, Priam 'is denied cremation even as Troy burns' (*Trojan Women*, Act I); later (Act IV) those same fires become wedding torches, as Andromache exclaims at the thought of Polyxena's sham wedding to Achilles, 'Look! Troy's fires will illuminate this unprecedented wedding!' Seneca's rhetorical flair can also be seen in the arguments between characters, where verbal punches are thrown in rapid succession as each attempts to outmanoeuvre the other (see especially Lycus vs Megara and Amphitryon in *Hercules Insane*, Act II; Pyrrhus vs Agamemnon in *Trojan Women*, Act II; Atreus vs his Adviser in *Thyestes*, Act II). By contrast, rhetoric can also inform copiously argued points as well; see such lengthy exchanges as the debate between Phaedra and her Nurse on the nature of Love (*Phaedra*, Act II), Hippolytus' justification of his life in the woods (Act III), Oedipus' account of his actions against his wife's criticism of cowardice (*Oedipus*, Act I) or Helen's sophistic defence-speech

(*Trojan Women*, Act IV) – the last, certainly, would not seem out of place in the law courts of Rome. Rhetoric informs the whole of Seneca's tragedies.

Rhetorically explosive, Seneca's language can be, and often is, powerful, brilliant and dramatically effective. At times, however, that same language can appear – at least to more modern aesthetic tastes – bombastic and excessive. So it seemed to the German literary critic A. W. Schlegel, who in 1809 denounced Seneca so scathingly as a dramatist that it took more than a century and a half for him to be rehabilitated. In Schlegel's purely aesthetic view, Seneca's tragedies were nothing more than rhetorical exercises, inferior purveyors of artificiality paling in comparison with the great Greek originals; that is, stale imitations of the vibrant, democratic tragedies of Aeschylus, Sophocles and Euripides. Friedrich Leo, the great German editor of Seneca's plays in the late nineteenth century, followed Schlegel's lead. He, too, regarded the plays as nothing more than 'rhetorical exercises fashioned into the shape of a drama' and was prepared to give up all of Seneca's tragedies for just Ovid's *Medea*. This privileging of Greek plays over their Roman counterparts continued well into the twentieth century and even abides today – consider how infrequently Seneca is read in modern classrooms compared to his Greek predecessors. But over the past fifty years both scholars and directors alike have increasingly valued the dramatic potential of Seneca's plays.[6] No longer evaluated solely by the (admittedly high) standards of Greek tragedy, Senecan tragedy has re-emerged from the shadows to take its rightful place in the history of theatre (see next section). We now regard them as original compositions with something important to say, not as neglected stepchildren of greater parents.

We have saved for the end a question as knotty as the riddle of the Sphinx: were Seneca's plays performed in antiquity? This is indeed a vexed issue, and one that will probably never be answered satisfactorily because of the nature of the evidence. The view that Seneca's plays were never meant to be performed prevailed throughout the nineteenth and twentieth centuries – a function of Schlegel's and Leo's criticism of the plays – and still has its adherents today, although it is now the minority opinion. Critics who tend to this view usually argue that Seneca's plays were written not for performance but for recitation, and some even argue that they were meant only to be read. There is some evidence that recitation-dramas were popular from the first century BC through at least the second century AD, but the evidence is not as clear-cut as some would suppose. What exactly a recitation-drama entailed – even whether it involved a single speaker or multiple speakers – is not known. Perhaps it was as T. S. Eliot imagines it (in his introduction to Thomas Newton's collection of Seneca's tragedies): 'the characters in a play of Seneca behave more like members of a minstrel troupe sitting in a semi-circle, rising in turn to do his "number".' Even if recitation-dramas were the dominant form of tragedy in this period, there is still no external evidence that Seneca's plays were necessarily written with that aim in mind – just as there is no evidence that they were performed.

We simply do not know, and will probably never know, whether the plays were staged in antiquity. The real question is whether Seneca composed them expecting a full performance. Here we have only the evidence of the plays themselves. On the one side, we must consider the static nature of the plays, difficulty staging certain scenes (in particular, the sacrifice and examination of the entrails in *Oedipus*, Act II), internal inconsistencies, and the attention to individual scenes at the expense of the whole. On the other side, there are many scenes that beg for performance, and some which *require* stage action to be sensible. One example must suffice: when Thyestes reacts to the appearance of his sons' heads and hands in the gripping end of *Thyestes*, there is no verbal cue to explain his reaction; the scene presupposes stage action – the presentation of his sons' heads and hands – that is not cued in the text. Since no obstacle to staging is insurmountable today, or was in the Renaissance or even in antiquity, this last point seems to me decisive: Seneca meant his plays to be realized on stage.[7]

V Seneca and Early Modern Tragedy

If Seneca's plays were not performed in antiquity, his Renaissance successors, who viewed his plays as eminently playable, were certainly unaware of that fact. From the late fifteenth century on Seneca's plays were performed in the original Latin in schools, universities, Inns of Court, and in European theatres. Even earlier, Albertino Mussato in 1315 looked to the metre, structure and subject matter of Seneca's plays (particularly *Thyestes*) when he composed his 'angry tragedy' *Ecerinis*, the first known Renaissance tragedy, for the University of Padua. Editions of Seneca's tragedies, already circulating in Europe in the thirteenth century, proliferated in the centuries that followed; anthologies of Seneca's best passages and lines were also abundantly available. Seneca's plays were taught in schools, along with Lucan and Martial, for the purpose of finding something worthy of imitation. The plays were individually translated into English (rendered mainly in fourteeners) between 1559 and 1567, later published together in Newton's famous edition of 1581. Even Elizabeth I attempted a translation of *Hercules on Oeta*. In England, but even more so in France and Italy, Seneca's influence on the tragic traditions that emerged was deep-rooted and pervasive.

A selected list of dramatists influenced by Seneca will give a sense of his abiding influence. Among French playwrights there are most famously Corneille and Racine, who adapted Seneca's *Medea* and *Phaedra* respectively, but whose other plays are also deeply indebted to Seneca in form and style. In Italy Cinthio, Dolce, and Groto imitated Seneca's rhetorical drama and his dramatization of violence, horror and blood. In England the earliest plays – Sackville and Norton's *Gorboduc* (performed 1561), Wilmot's *Tancred and Gismund* (performed 1568) and Hughes' *The Misadventures of King Arthur* (1587) – consciously imitated Seneca's plays even as their authors looked to English history for subject matter. Senecan influence is also evident in later playwrights in greater or lesser measure. To name but a few: Marlowe (*Tamburlaine the Great*, 1587–8; *Edward II*, 1592), Kyd (*The Spanish Tragedy*, c. 1587); Shakespeare (*Titus Andronicus*, 1590; *Richard III*, 1591; *Hamlet*, 1601; *King Lear*, 1604–5); Marston (*Antonio and Mellida, Antonio's Revenge*, c. 1600); Jonson (*Sejanus*, 1603); and Chapman (*Revenge of Bussy D'Ambois*, 1610).

At the core of Seneca's influence was his reputation as a dramatic stylist, a poet worth emulating, and a font of moral ideals. A brief survey of sixteenth-century criticism reveals the special status Seneca had among educated theatre critics. Giraldi Cinthio, the author of *Orbecche* (performed 1541), a play deeply indebted to Seneca's tragedies, opined that Seneca had surpassed the Greek achievement (*Discourses*, 1543) 'in wisdom, in weightiness, in grace, in majesty, in expression'. Bartolomaeo Ricci (*On Imitation*, 1545) praises the 'weightiness of the tragedies', which was 'produced first and foremost by the power of his expression'. The humanist J. C. Scaliger (*Poetics*, 1561) judged Seneca equal to the Greeks in the majesty of his plays and superior to Euripides in the brilliance of his style. Compare Thomas Newton's frequently cited words from his introduction to *Seneca His Tenne Tragedies* (1581):

> [his] whole wrytinges, penned with a peerelesse sublimity and loftinesse of Style, are so farre from countenauncing Vice, that I doubt whether there bee any amonge all the Catalogue of Heathen wryters, that with more gravity of Philosophicall sentences, more waightynes of sappy words, or greater authority of sound matter beateth down sinne, loose lyfe, dissolute dealinge, and unbridled sensuality: or that more sensibly, pithily, and bytingly layeth downe the guerdon of filthy lust, cloaked dissimulation and odious treachery.

The notion that Seneca was a moralist, that his tragedies were cautionary tales against human vice, runs counter to (most) modern interpretations of the plays, which rightly do not view them as simple vehicles for moralizing. But it was precisely Seneca's apparent moral message, combined with the weightiness of his poetry, that appealed so powerfully to early playwrights.

But that is not all. The very conception of early English tragedy, of its structure and nature, is deeply indebted to Seneca. Even if we admit the importance of other native dramatic forms (e.g., chronicles, biblical cycles, morality plays), and the influence of European drama, itself indebted to Seneca, Seneca's crucial role in shaping the tragic tradition is undeniable. In some cases his influence is clear and direct. Seneca's five-act division, found in the earliest imitative plays, became canonical;[8] his dramaturgy, in particular self-meditative monologues and asides, also helped shape the tragic form. Playwrights frequently borrowed lines from Seneca's Latin, translated or adapted a passage for a new context, or alluded to scenes in Seneca's text. Less direct, perhaps, but no less clear, is Seneca's influence on the shaping of the revenge play (the plays listed above are almost all of this type) and the introduction of a ghost (as in *Thyestes* or *Octavia*) announcing the revenge; in this vein are Andrugio in Marston's *Antonio's Revenge*, Hamlet's father in Shakespeare's *Hamlet* and the multiple ghosts in Chapman's *The Revenge of Bussy D'Ambois*. So, too, English tragedy's meditations on power through the characterization of megalomaniacal tyrants. Piero in *Antonio's Revenge* is modelled directly on Atreus in *Thyestes*, and the Shakespearean characters of Richard III, Macbeth and Lear are all descendants of the tyrannical characters in Senecan tragedy – mediated, to be sure, through other influences and by Shakespeare's own genius. Seneca's dramatized violence, if not the main source, certainly reinforced the English predilection for violence and death on the stage.

Seneca's impact on later tragedy, then, can be direct or indirect. Or, put another way, some playwrights consciously imitated Seneca, while others unconsciously adopted Senecan structure, ideas, rhetorical strategies, characterization, etc., that had already become embedded in the increasingly rich tradition of English tragedy. An unfortunate consequence of this is that identifying a specific influence often becomes quite hard, especially as one moves forward in time. Whether a ghost announcing revenge in play X, or a tyrannical king in play Y, or a philosophical medita-tion on fate in play Z – all typical of Seneca's plays – is indebted to his tragedies is an exceedingly difficult question to answer. Often the answer is 'yes', but this 'yes' comes with the caveat that debts to Seneca are often filtered through and conditioned by later English tragedy. We would do well to remember J. W. Cunliffe's warning in *The Influence of Seneca on Elizabethan Tragedy*: 'As English tragedy advances, there grows up an accumulation of Senecan influence within the English drama in addition to the original source, and it becomes increasingly difficult to distinguish between the direct and indirect influence of Seneca. In no case is the difficulty greater than that of Shakespeare' (p. 66). But discerning when a specific Senecan motif, scene, characterization or idea came into English tragedy is less important than recognizing the fact that certain Senecan motifs, scenes, characterizations or ideas were deemed important enough to be perpetuated.

This discussion has been necessarily brief. Readers who wish to learn more about the specific influences of Seneca on English tragedy are encouraged to consult the works by Boyle, Miola and Cunliffe in the bibliography below.

NOTES

1. F. Ahl's *Two Faces of Oedipus* and his translation of Seneca's *Phaedra* (Ithaca and London, 1986).
2. T. Kohn, 'Who Wrote Seneca's Plays?', *The Classical World* 96 (2003), pp. 271–80.
3. J. G. Fitch, 'Sense-Pauses and Relative Dating in Seneca, Sophocles and Shakespeare', *American Journal of Philology* 102 (1981) 289–307.
4. R. J. Tarrant, 'Senecan Drama and Its Antecedents', *Harvard Studies in Classical Philology* 82 (1978) 213–63.
5. W. M. Calder III, 'The Size of the Chorus in Seneca's *Agamemnon*', *Classical Philology* 70 (1975) 32–5.
6. See the list of seventy-four performances worldwide from 1993 to 2007 compiled by Katharina Kagerer and Wilfried Stroh at W. Stroh, 'Staging Seneca: The Production of Troas as a Philological Experiment', in Fitch 2008: 216–20.
7. Recently, Fitch has put forth an intermediate position, namely, that only certain scenes were written with the stage in mind ('Playing Seneca' in Harrison 2000: 1–12). This position has the merit of explaining why Seneca's individual scenes seem more successful than the tragedies as unified wholes, and it offers a solution to the vexed question why some scenes seem to require performance, while others seem to preclude it. But it is unsatisfactory in that it presupposes two modes of composition, one aimed at the stage and another at mere recitation or reading. There is no evidence for such a fragmented mode of writing.

8.   Some have argued that this five-act structure was taken from the
     Roman comedy writer Terence, who, like Menander and Seneca,
     observes a five-act structure. But that the earliest English plays
     retain the choral odes between acts seems to me to prove definit-
     ively that Seneca was the model and not Terence, whose plays do
     not have choral odes.

Selected Further Reading

Ahl, F., *Two Faces of Oedipus: Sophocles' Oedipus Tyrannus and Seneca's Oedipus* (Ithaca, 2008).

Boyle, A. J. (ed.), *Seneca Tragicus: Ramus Essays on Senecan Drama* (Berwick, Victoria, 1983).

—, *Tragic Seneca: An Essay in the Theatrical Tradition* (London, 1997).

—, *An Introduction to Roman Tragedy* (London, 2006).

Calder, W. M., 'Seneca: Tragedian of Imperial Rome', in *Theatrokratia*, ed. R. S. Smith (Hildesheim 2005) 311–26.

—, 'The Rediscovery of Seneca Tragicus at the End of the XXth Century', in *Theatrokratia*, ed. R. S. Smith (Hildesheim 2005) 403–17.

Cunliffe, J. W., *The Influence of Seneca on Elizabethan Tragedy* (London, 1893; repr. Hamden, Conn., 1965).

Davis, P. J., *Seneca: Thyestes* (London, 2003).

Erasmo, M., *Roman Tragedy: Theatre to Theatricality* (Austin, Texas, 2004).

Fitch, J. G. (ed.), *Seneca* (Oxford, 2008).

Harrison, G. W. M. (ed.), *Seneca in Performance* (London, 2000).

Littlewood, C. A. J., *Self-Representation and Illusion in Senecan Tragedy* (Oxford, 2004).

Mayer, R., *Seneca: Phaedra* (London, 2002).

Miola, R. S., *Shakespeare and Classical Tragedy: the Influence of Seneca* (Oxford, 1992).

Pratt, N. T., *Seneca's Drama* (Chapel Hill, 1983).

Rosenmeyer, T. G., *Senecan Drama and Stoic Cosmology* (Berkeley, 1989).

Segal, C., *Language and Desire in Seneca's Phaedra* (Princeton, 1986).

Staley, G. A., *Seneca and the Idea of Tragedy* (Oxford, 2010).

Sutton, D. F., *Seneca on the Stage* (Leiden, 1986).

Wilson, M., *The Tragedy of Nero's Wife: Studies on the Octavia Praetexta* (Auckland, 2003).

Editions and Commentaries Used in This Translation

Billerbeck, M., *Seneca Hercules Furens* (Leiden, 1999).

Boyle, A. J., *Octavia Attributed to Seneca* (Oxford, 2008).

Coffey, M. and Mayer, R. (eds.), *Seneca Phaedra* (Cambridge, 1990).

Fantham, E., *Seneca's Troades* (Princeton, 1982).

Ferri, R., *Octavia: A Play Attributed to Seneca* (Cambridge, 2003).

Fitch, J. G., *Seneca's Hercules Furens* (Ithaca, 1987).

—, *Seneca Tragedies*, Loeb Classical Library, 2 vols (Cambridge, Mass., 2002, 2004).

—, *Annaeana Tragica: Notes on the Text of Seneca's Tragedies* (Leiden, 2004).

Keulen, A. J., *L. Annaeus Seneca Troades* (Leiden, 2001).

Tarrant, R. J., *Seneca's Thyestes* (Atlanta, 1985).

Töchterle, K., *Lucius Annaeus Seneca: Oedipus* (Heidelberg, 1994).

Zwierlein, O., *L. Annaei Senecae Tragoediae* (Oxford, 1986).

A Note on the Translation

Seneca's tragedies, like all ancient plays, are elaborate poems set in dramatic form. The dialogue and speeches are mainly in iambic trimeter, which is roughly equivalent to six iambic feet, one foot longer than Shakespeare's pentameter but with a similar pulse. The choral odes are usually set pieces in a lyric metre taken from Horace, the great Augustan lyric poet. Because of the power of Seneca's poetry, it was with some reluctance that I decided to render the speeches and dialogue into elevated prose and render the choral odes into formal poetic metre. This decision made sense for many reasons. First, it was a space-saving measure. Second, modern plays are not written in verse; a prose translation would be more familiar to most readers. Third, I wanted to stress the difference between the choral odes and the acts of the plays; this was most easily accomplished by setting the choral odes off visually and aurally from the rest of the play.

The choral odes, however, deserve to be rendered into formal poetic metre, not prose. I wanted there to be an identifiable pulse, one that gave continuity to the piece and would be recognizable in a dramatic performance. After some experimentation, I settled on the following: a four-beat iambic line for the common anapaestic songs; a modified English Sapphic metre for odes in Sapphic metre; anapaestic lines for Asclepiads; and loose three-beaters for glyconics. In the case of the polymetric odes in *Oedipus* (choruses II and III), which vary in metre line by line, rather than force the content into some fixed metrical form, I allowed myself complete freedom and took the opportunity to experiment with English form and rhythm – all with the aim of representing Seneca's own experimentation.

From many years' experience teaching ancient drama I have come to realize that readers are often at a loss how to deal with choral odes because of their alien nature. To alleviate the strangeness of these often beautiful pieces, I have added titles to give a sense of the overall subject, but readers must not mistake these for Seneca's own. Likewise, I have added stage directions, even though there are none indicated by the manuscripts. By doing so I proclaim my belief that Seneca's plays were written for the stage and are eminently actable – as evidenced by numerous performances in the Renaissance and the recent interest in staging Seneca's tragedies on the modern stage.

Finally, Seneca's plays frequently allude to the rich mythological tradition the Romans inherited from the Greeks. Rather than burden the text with countless footnotes, I have included a glossary of proper names at the end. While I have tried to be comprehensive in terms of myth, I elected not to include every geographic reference in Seneca's long catalogues of places, notably those found in Chorus III of *Trojan Women* and in Hippolytus' song in *Phaedra*, Act I. Because of the peculiar nature of *Octavia* I felt it was prudent to keep the notes keyed to the names in the text rather than include them in the glossary – hence the greater number of notes to that play.

HERCULES INSANE

Preface to *Hercules Insane*

Born of Jupiter and the mortal Alcmena in Thebes, Hercules was relentlessly persecuted by his jealous stepmother Juno (Greek Hera), who saw Hercules' mere existence as a slight to her position as Jupiter's wife and a constant reminder of her husband's faithlessness. His name (Greek Herakles, 'Glory of Hera'), in fact, reveals how tightly bound Hercules was to the goddess who tormented him – even before he was born. When Alcmena went into labour, Juno, anticipating Hercules' imminent birth, tricked Jupiter into swearing an oath that the next descendant of Perseus born would become king of Mycenae. She then summoned Ilithyia, the goddess of childbirth, and ordered her to delay the birth of Hercules (grandson of Perseus) and to hasten that of Eurystheus (another grandson of Perseus), who was born several months premature.

Juno's persecution of Hercules continued after his birth. When he was still an infant, Juno sent twin serpents into his crib; these he crushed with his infant hands, heralding his greatness. When Hercules had become a young man, performed many early deeds and taken Megara as his wife, Juno drove Hercules insane, which led to the deaths of his wife and sons (an episode that Seneca, like Euripides before him, transfers to immediately after his labours). Juno was also responsible for his twelve labours. Because of Jupiter's untimely oath, Hercules was forced to serve his inferior Eurystheus, who ordered him to perform twelve seemingly impossible labours – all of which he successfully accomplished, much to Juno's chagrin. Most Greek heroes were known for one great exploit (e.g., Perseus and Medusa or Jason and the Golden Fleece); the fact that Hercules accomplished *twelve* labours – not to mention numerous other side-deeds – is a function of his status as the greatest and most famous Greek hero.

Despite his undeniable greatness, the ancient Greeks and Romans had no single conception of Hercules. For some he was a conquering hero, a civilizing force that brought peace to the world by eliminating evil forces. For others he was the paragon of virtue, the long-suffering hero who by dint of his noble deeds was awarded immortality. For still others he was nothing more than a brutish lout, prone to drunkenness and wanton violence. Hercules, then, was an ambivalent hero, or perhaps better a *polyvalent* hero, one that represented various ideals or flaws and that could be exploited by writers and artists in a variety of ways.

Seneca, therefore, had a choice as to *what kind* of Hercules to dramatize, and his characterization of the hero is central to an understanding of the play. Seneca's Hercules fully reflects the ambivalence present in Greek myth. On the positive side, Hercules is aggressive, relentless, and *powerful*; he brings peace by destroying evil forces that threaten human harmony and wellbeing. On the negative side, he is aggressive, relentless and *violent*; he accomplishes his tasks by brute strength, and this frequently involves destruction. Even before Hercules arrives onstage, we come to know both sides of his character through the speeches of Juno (negative), Amphitryon and Megara (positive). In all three, however, Hercules' *aggression* and *destructiveness* is emphasized. In horror, Juno describes Hercules' demolition of the sacred barrier that separates the living from the dead, and fears that he will next destroy that which separates gods and humans. She worries that he will wreck Olympus and rule as the king of a devastated realm. Amphitryon and Megara, in turn, pray that Hercules will break through the earth to save them, recalling earlier occasions of Hercules' barrier-breaking, such as his violent cleaving apart of the Straits of Gibraltar to allow Ocean to flow in, and the breaking apart of the Thessalian mountains to provide an exit for the swollen Peneus river.

When Hercules finally arrives onstage (Act III) and learns of Lycus' usurpation of the throne, his aggression is writ large before the audience's eyes. So eager is he to dispatch yet another evil king – this is what he *does*, after all – that he does not even have time to embrace his father, wife or children. He pushes them away instead! Comparison with Euripides' *Heracles* here is instructive. In Euripides' version, Hercules shows tenderness towards his family upon his return, making his subsequent descent into madness all the more shocking, unexpected and touching. In Seneca's version, such tenderness has no place, for Hercules' madness and violence against his family are simply extensions of the hero's already violent and aggressive nature. Later, in Act IV, when Amphitryon cautions Hercules that he should wash his hands clean of Lycus' blood before sacrificing – a central tenet in religious ritual – Hercules refuses, responding brusquely, 'How I wish I could have drained that hateful man's blood over the altar as a libation to the gods!' The play, as Fitch well puts it, 'explores the *continuity* between the sane and insane mind' (1987: 30). Because of this continuity (effected by the addition of Juno's prologue) Seneca's play is far more unified than Euripides' version, which falls into two dissociated halves, the first dramatizing the timely return of Hercules and his killing of Lycus, the second the onset of his madness and his killing of his family.

In antiquity the title was probably *Hercules*. The addition of the tag *Insane* was likely added later to distinguish it from the other play about Hercules that was incorporated into the Senecan corpus, the inauthentic *Hercules on Oeta* (not translated in this volume), which dramatizes Hercules' apotheosis.

Characters

JUNO, *queen of the gods, sister and wife of Jupiter*
AMPHITRYON, *mortal father of Hercules*
MEGARA, *Theban wife of Hercules, daughter of Creon*
LYCUS, *usurper of the Theban throne*
HERCULES, *son of Jupiter and Alcmena*
THESEUS, *Athenian king, friend of Hercules*
CHORUS *of Theban citizens*
Three SONS *of Hercules and Megara* (Mute)
ATTENDANTS *of Lycus* (Mute)

ACT I

[JUNO *enters from one of the wings*]

JUNO: Sister! The Thunder-god's *sister* – that is all I am now. What other name do I have left? Forsaken as wife, I've abandoned Jupiter, always someone else's lover, and left the lofty vaults of heaven. What else could I do? I've been driven from heaven to make room for his whores, forced to live here, on earth. Whores possess the skies now. [*Pointing skyward*] Look, the Great Bear¹ inhabits the quadrant high above the icy northern pole, a heavenly constellation that guides Greek ships. And here, where the day grows longer in spring, Taurus shines bright, the bull that once carried Tyrian Europa through the sea-waves. There, the daughters of Atlas, the wandering Pleiades, unfurl their band of stars, a constellation feared by sailors at sea. Here, Orion menaces the gods with his sword, here golden Perseus has his own stars. Here shine the twin sons of Tyndareus, the Gemini, a luminous constellation; and there, the twins for whom the wandering land stood still.² And not only did Bacchus and Bacchus' mother reach heaven,³ but to make sure that no quadrant of heaven would be without reminders of his scandalous affairs, the world wears the Garland of Ariadne, Bacchus' mistress from Cnossus!

But those are old grievances. This one land, this dreadful, uncivilized land of Thebes, teems with irreverent mothers – how often it has made me a stepmother!⁴ Alcmena may triumph over me, ascend to heaven, and take possession of my throne. Her son may obtain immortality and the stars his father promised him – that mighty son whose conception cost the world a day, when Phoebus, ordered by Jupiter to keep

his rays sunk beneath Ocean's waters, was slow to lift his
shining light from the eastern sea.[5] Even so, my hatred of him
will never subside or abate: my anger will always live on, ever
fresh, ever violent. My burning resentment will never allow
peace between us. No, I will wage war upon him until the end
of time.

But what kind of war can I bring to bear against him? Every
terrible monster the hostile earth creates, every frightening,
terrifying, death-dealing, savage-looking, vicious creature the
sky and sea produce – Hercules breaks and tames them all.
He always prevails, growing even stronger from these trials.
He feasts on my wrath. He turns my hatred into his glory. My
cruel commands have only served to prove his paternity and
to provide him the means to increase his fame! Every land
that the Sun looks upon from daybreak to sunset, when it
darkens the two Ethiopian races with its nearby flame,[6]
worships his indomitable courage. The whole world tells
stories of him . . . as a god! I have no more monsters at my
disposal. It is less of a task for Hercules to perform my
commands than it is for me to give them! He revels when he
hears my bidding. What cruel challenge can that tyrant Eurystheus issue that would possibly harm Hercules, who lays waste
to everything in his path? After all, he carries the terrifying
creatures he faced and slew as weapons – he comes armed
with the Lion and Hydra![7]

Not even the wide earth gives enough scope for his daring.
See, he has broken through the underworld gates of infernal
Jupiter[8] and is now carrying the spoils of that conquered king
back to the world above. It was not enough for him just to
return. No, he had to wreck the barrier that separates the
living from the dead. I myself looked on with my own eyes as
he tore through and dispelled the darkness of hell and over-
powered Dis. Then he even boasted to his father that he had
despoiled his brother's realm![9] Why doesn't he just go and
lead off Dis himself, the king of a realm equal to Jupiter's,
bound and burdened with chains? Why does he not storm the
dark realm below and set himself up as lord and master there?
Behold, he has uncovered the Stygian world below! He has

laid bare the path to hell's abyss, and now the sacred, unknown world of dread death lies open for all to see.

And now? He's celebrating his triumph over me, proud and defiant after tearing open the prison of the dead, parading the grim hellhound throughout the cities of the Argolid, *my* cities,[10] hoisting it aloft with the hand that disdains me. I watched as daylight flickered and the sun quailed at the sight of Cerberus. Even I felt the shiver of fear come over *me*, and as I gazed at the triple heads of that vanquished monster, I shuddered to think of what I had ordered him to do.

But these complaints are trivial. We must now turn our worries towards heaven, for fear that the man who conquered the kingdom of hell may seize hold of the kingdom of heaven. He will snatch the sceptre from his own father's hands! His ascent to heaven will not be gentle like Bacchus'. He will demolish all that stands in his way – he is willing to rule over heaven even if it lies in ruins! His confidence swells from his earlier tests of strength. He learned that he had the might to conquer heaven by holding it up. When Hercules bent his neck beneath the weight of the world, he did not so much as flinch from the toil of bearing such a mass. The vault of heaven rested more stably upon Hercules' shoulders![11] He held aloft the starry firmament of heaven, wavering not at all, even as *I* pressed down with all my weight upon it.[12] He now seeks a path to heaven.

[*To herself*] Go on, angry Juno, go on, crush this over-reacher, meet him in battle, rip him apart with your bare hands! Why entrust such hatred to someone else? Send away the wild beasts; relieve Eurystheus from the wearying job of giving Hercules orders. Unleash instead the Titans, those brazen gods who tried to shatter Jupiter's dominion! Open up the caverns of Sicilian Etna and set free that massive Giant pinned beneath the mountain, whose shifting below the ground causes the Doric lands to convulse and quake![13]

Yet those he vanquished. Do you seek a match for Hercules, scion of Alcaeus? There is none – except Hercules himself. Then let him contend with himself. Let the Furies be roused from the deepest pits of Tartarus and summoned here; let their

fiery tresses spread flame and their cruel hands savagely crack
their snake-whips. Now go ahead, you brazen hero, go ahead
and aim for the palace of the heavenly gods. Now scorn your
human origins. You reckless man, do you think you have
escaped the realm of Styx, the land of ghosts? I will visit hell
upon you here; I will summon up the goddess who is buried
deep in the murk of hell, jailed beneath the prisons where the
guilty are banished after death, enclosed in a huge mountain
dungeon and hemmed in on all sides, Discord. I will unleash
all that remains in the depths of Dis' realm: hateful Villainy
will come, and raging Wickedness, who licks the blood of her
own family, Delusion and self-destructive Madness – these,
yes these, must be the instruments of my resentment, the agents
of my revenge.

Handmaidens of Dis, begin your destructive work, shake
your burning pine-torches furiously! Let Megaera lead forth
her fell serpentine army, hoisting in her grief-bringing hands
a torch seized from burning pyres, an enormous beam. On
with it! Gain your revenge for his desecration of your Stygian
realm. Inflame his heart, stoke his mind with flames more
violent than the fires that roil and churn within the volcanic
furnaces of Etna. Yet, before we can ensnare the mind of
Hercules and torment him into delirium, insanity, madness, I
myself must first lose my own mind. Juno, why do you remain
sane? Sisters! You must unhinge my mind first and shake me
from my wits, if I am to execute a scheme worthy of a stepmother.

My hopes and prayers must now change. I pray that
Hercules comes home and sees his children safe and sound,
and that he returns with his strength intact. At last I have
found a day when that accursed might of Hercules will benefit me. He defeated me. So what? Now let him conquer himself.
Let that man who returned from the dead now yearn for
death! Let the fact that he is Jupiter's son for once be advan-
tageous to me. I will stand beside him and steady his hand so
that the shafts from his bowstring fly straight and true. I will
steer the madman's weapons to their targets; at long last will
I assist Hercules in his battles. Then, when the deed is done,

let his father receive into heaven him and his bloodstained
hands.

Let the hostilities commence! The day dawns, and the Sun-
god rises, gleaming in the brilliant saffron cloak of dawn.

[JUNO *leaves*]

CHORUS I: Ode to Dawn

Few star-lights flicker, fainter now,
as heaven sinks and night retreats,
her wandering fires fleeing light's
rebirth, as Dawnstar marshals his
luminous troop of shining stars.
The icy northern constellation,
the seven stars of Arcas' Bear,
has turned its cart, heralding Dawn.[14]
The Sun has left the cobalt waves
behind and peeks over Oeta's heights;
the thickets famed for Cadmus' girls[15]
bleed crimson, splashed by daylight's shafts,
and Phoebus' sister flees for now.

Balanced upon a lofty branch,
the shrill-voiced Thracian mistress preens,[16]
her wings outstretched to greet the new
sun's rays amidst her chirping chicks –
her nestlings twitter, chirr and tweet,
a noisy choir proclaiming day.

Hard toil now stirs, and worries too:
men open doors to meet their tasks.
Now shepherds send their flocks to pasture
and gather fodder white with frost;
their bullocks, temples not yet graced
with horns, cavort in open fields,
while the mothers rest, replenishing
their teats, and frisky kids romp gaily
in meadows, roaming as they please.

Now sailors put their lives at risk,
trusting their ships to fickle winds
as breezes blow and swell the sails.

Now fishermen sit perched on rocks,
preparing hooks meant to deceive,
or, lying in wait, they breathlessly
survey their prey with steady hands,
as quivering fishes twitch their lines.

These are the lives of simple folk,
serene, content and blameless souls,
with peaceful homes and humble means.
But cities – this is where immense
anxieties and pressures roam.
Here some men sleeplessly attend
the heartless doors of mighty men,
while others endlessly amass
vast riches, gawking at their wealth,
still poor amidst their heaps of gold.
Some crave the people's love and fame,
like ships propelled by treacherous winds,
but the mob shifts more than the sea.
Some love the clamour of the courts,
contentious trials, the hue and cry,
selling their words and wrath for gain.

A peaceful life is known by few;
these understand time's rapid flight
and love the never-returning now.

Live on, live happy while you may!
Life hastens on with hurried steps;
with every winged day the wheel
of the racing year advances on.
Once the harsh Fates complete their spinning,
they never wind the life-threads back.
The human race now mindlessly

races to meet the doom that's near:
we freely head to the lakes of hell.
You are too fearless, Hercules,
too quick to visit gloomy ghosts.
Your fate, fixed long ago, will come –
no one may tarry when called to death
or may postpone his destined day:
once we are called, the urn is next.

Let Glory carry others' names
to distant lands, and Fame, that gossip,
exalt those men the world throughout,
lifting them equal to the stars.
Let others ride triumphantly
upon their lofty chariots.
For me, I pray I stay unknown,
safe and secure in a humble home.
The meek attain a ripe old age
and silver hair, and lowly homes
with little wealth remain secure,
their modest means intact and safe.
But unrelenting daring plummets,
falling and crashing hard below.

But here comes Megara, sad soul,
her hair unbound, her brood in tow,
and Amphitryon, slowed by old age.

ACT II

[*Enter* AMPHITRYON *and* MEGARA, *accompanied by her children. They take their place before the altar*]

AMPHITRYON: Great lord of Olympus, ruler of the cosmos, I beg you: at last put a limit on our great suffering, bring an end to our plight! No day dawns without worries. The end of one hardship is but a step towards the next. Straight upon my son's return another foe is found. Even before he sets foot inside our house, before we can celebrate his homecoming, he is ordered to face another hostile challenge. No pause, no moment to relax – except while the next order is being given. Juno has hounded him from the very beginning. Even his infancy was not spared! He overcame monsters before he learned what monsters were. When he was but a babe, twin crested snakes slithered towards him with hissing mouths, but he, that babe, crawled to meet them, gazing calmly, coolly, into the serpents' fiery eyes. He let the serpents wind their coils tightly around him, his expression ever serene, but with his tender hands he squeezed, crushing their necks swollen with venom and anger – a dress-rehearsal for the Hydra.

He chased and captured the swift Arcadian beast whose head was graced with glorious golden horns.[17] That great lion, the terror of Nemea, groaned as his life was squeezed out by his mighty arms. And what about the gruesome stalls of the Thracian herd of horses and the king that Hercules fed to them? Or the bristling Maenalian boar that used to haunt the thick-wooded ridges of Erymanthus, which shook Arcadia's forests when it charged? Or the bull that sent ripples of fear through the hundred cities of Crete? In the remote western regions, along the Spanish shores, he killed the triple-bodied cowherd and drove his plunder, a great herd of cattle, back from the land where the sun sets – now Cithaeron pastures the cattle that once grazed beside Ocean's waves. When he was ordered to traverse the southern regions that blaze beneath searing heatwaves, lands scorched by the raging midday sun, he broke the mountains apart, and by removing this barrier he made a wide pathway for Ocean to rush in.[18] After this he invaded the rich grove of the Hesperides and bore away the golden spoils guarded by a serpent who never sleeps. And what about the vicious monster of Lerna, its countless heads that dealt death from countless directions – did he not in the end overcome it with fire and teach it how to die? Did he not shoot down from the high clouds the Stymphalian birds, that flock which blotted out the day with the canopy formed by their wings? The unwed queen of the race of women living along the Thermodon river, whose beds never felt a male's body, did not overcome Hercules. Nor were his hands, always ready to take on a glorious challenge, ashamed to take on the foul labour of cleaning Augeas' stables.

What good has any of this done him? He is barred from the world he defended! The world senses that the man who brought it peace is now absent. Crimes that bring profit and prosperity are now called bravery. Good people are forced to obey criminals. Might makes right, and the force of law is crushed beneath the weight of fear. Right here in Thebes, before my own eyes, I saw sons perish in defence of their father's kingdom, felled by a ruthless hand. I saw the king himself, the last scion of Cadmus' noble house, slain, his glorious crown cut off along with his head.[19] Who has enough tears for the horrors of Thebes? This land, the fertile mother of so many gods – what a tyrant she fears! Thebes, from whose fields, from whose fertile folds a crop of young stalwart men was born, swords drawn and at the ready;[20] Thebes, whose walls Jupiter's son Amphion built by moving stones with the magical rhythm of his songs; Thebes, the city which the father of the gods left heaven to visit so often, the city which has welcomed gods, made them, and – if it is permitted to say it

– perhaps *will* make them: despite its glorious past Thebes now stands subjected beneath the yoke of a vile lord. Descendants of Cadmus, offspring of the Serpent Race, how far you have sunk! You shrink from a nobody, an exile barred from his own land and oppressive to ours. But the man who punished crimes on land and sea and smashed cruel sceptres with a hand of justice, now plays the slave in a faraway place and endures the oppression he kept others from enduring. An exile – an *exile*! – has seized possession of Thebes, Hercules' home. Lycus holds sway in Thebes.

But not for long. Hercules will soon be here and take his revenge. He will emerge suddenly, unexpectedly, under the shining stars above. He will either find a way, or make one. Hercules, may you arrive safe and sound and return to your loved ones; may you, a conquering hero, at last return to your conquered house!

MEGARA: Emerge from the shadows, my husband, use your might to break through the darkness. If you can find no path back to us, if the route is barred, rip open the earth and return through that gaping hole, even if it means releasing all that lurks beneath the dark night of hell! Return as you did once before, crashing through the mountain ridges of Tempe, demolishing them as you carved a steep passage for a swiftly rushing river, a mighty upheaval![21] You lowered your shoulders and drove into the mountains, forcing them apart, and once the obstacle was ruptured, that raging Thessalian river gushed forth along its new channel. Now, too, break through an impassable barrier, the one that separates the living from the dead. Come for your parents, your children, your country! Return all that ravenous time has stored away over countless epochs, drive before you the great hordes of the mindless dead[22] who stand in fear of the light. It would not be like you to bring back only the spoils you were ordered to bring!

But my words are too hopeful, my hopes too extravagant, I fear, since I know not what lies in store for us. Will that day ever come when I may embrace you, clasp your right arm and scold you for taking so long to return, for forgetting me? On that day, great leader of the gods, a hundred unbroken bulls

will offer their heads to you; on that day, Grain-goddess, all
of Eleusis will celebrate your mystery rites and hurl long
torches in secrecy;[23] on that day will I believe that all is right
in the world, that my brothers breathe again, and that my
father sits upon his rightful throne, prosperous and powerful.
But if some unyielding power keeps you barred from us, I am
prepared to follow you. Either return in all your might and
save us, or drag us to our deaths! You *will* drag us down; for
no god will ever lift up our broken lives.

AMPHITRYON: Dear daughter-in-law, united to our family's
blood by marriage, you have always been a faithful wife and
devoted mother, protecting the bed and brood of great-hearted
Hercules. So I beg you: turn your mind to better thoughts,
raise your spirits. Hercules will come, I'm certain of it, just as
he has returned from every other labour: a greater man.

MEGARA: People in dire straits readily believe what they *want*
to believe.

AMPHITRYON: No, they devise excessive fears for themselves
and cannot possibly imagine that things could turn out well.
Once you give in to fear, you only think the worst.

MEGARA: But he's buried deep beneath the earth, covered,
crushed by the weight of the whole world – what path does
he have to the world above?

AMPHITRYON: What path did he have when he travelled through
the scorching southern lands, through sands that billowed up
like the waves on a stormy sea, and through the sandy sea-
tides, twice waxing, twice waning? And when he was caught
fast in the Syrtes' shallows, his ship stuck on a sandbar, what
did he do? He left the ship behind and overcame the seas – on
foot!

MEGARA: Fortune's an unjust goddess. Rarely does she spare
men of the greatest courage. No one can throw himself at so
many dangers for so long and get away scot-free. If Disaster
passes someone by frequently enough, it's inevitable that he
will run into him sooner or later.

[*Enter* LYCUS *with his attendants from the wings*]

But wait – here comes the usurper Lycus now. See how savage,
how threatening a look he wears on his face, how his bearing

matches his violent character; look how he brandishes in his right hand the sceptre that rightfully belongs to my father!

LYCUS: [*to his attendants*] The rich lands of Thebes, all the fertile soil that stretches to mountainous Phocis, all that the Ismenus waters, all that Cithaeron gazes upon from its lofty peak, all that the Isthmus commands as it carves a slender path between two seas – I rule it all. This kingdom was no inheritance from my father. I was no lazy heir waiting for my birthright to come through. I do not have noble ancestors or a family tree graced with noble titles. But my prowess in war is renowned. Those who boast of a distinguished lineage are merely praising what *others* have done.

Yet the hand that holds a sceptre taken by force trembles from fear. Security lies wholly in steel; if you know that your subjects object to your rule, you need to keep your sword drawn to protect it. Ruling in someone else's stead is a precarious business. Yet there is one who can legitimize my position as king should she be joined to me in a royal marriage: Megara. Her distinguished lineage will give my fledgling reign the blush of legitimacy. I cannot imagine that she would reject this opportunity and spurn my bed. But if she does snub me in a fit of obstinacy, I'm prepared to eradicate Hercules' entire family root and branch. So what if the people speak disapprovingly of my actions? So what if they hate me? Thick skin is the most important quality a king can have. One must be able to live with unpopularity.

So let us see what happens: chance has given us an opportunity. There she is, her head covered in a sad veil, her dress drawn over her head. She stands beside the gods for protection – and Hercules' true sire clings to her side.[24] [*He approaches* AMPHITRYON *and* MEGARA]

MEGARA: [*aside*] What new evil does that villain, that bane and ruin of our family, have in store for us? What is he after now?

LYCUS: [*to* MEGARA] Good queen, descendant of a long line of kings, heiress of a distinguished family, kindly give me your ear. Hear out my words patiently – it will not take long. If mortals bore everlasting grudges, if rage once felt in the hearts

of men never abated, if conquerors always clung to power
only to have the conquered try to take it away, everything
would be devastated by warfare. Nothing would be left! Farmland would lie desolate, overgrown, in weeds. Buildings would
be torched, whole nations buried beneath deep ash. Restoring
peace is smart policy for the victors and, for the vanquished
– well, there is no choice, really. Come, join me in power. Let
us unite our hearts and souls. Take my hand. Take it as an
assurance of my sincerity. Why do you stand there glaring at
me, brooding in silence? Speak!

MEGARA: Me? Take *your* hand, stained as it is with the blood of
my father, drenched in the slaughter of my two brothers?
Sooner will the east extinguish the sun's fires and the west
relight them, sooner will snow trust flame, sooner will Scylla
join Sicily to Italy, sooner will the fleeting currents of furious
Euripus off Euboea's coast stand still! You took from me my
father, my kingdom, my brothers, my home, my country. What
remains for me? One thing, and I cherish it more than a brother
or a father, a kingdom or a home: my hatred of you! And to
my great, great disappointment, I must share *that* with all my
people – how small a portion of that hatred belongs to me!

So go ahead, lord it over us, puff out your chest, put on
those haughty airs: an avenging god always follows on the
heels of insolent men. Do you not know what happens to
the ruling families of Thebes? Do I need to remind you of
all the mothers who either suffered or committed horrific
crimes?[25] Or of Oedipus' double sin, when the names of
spouse, son and father were all confounded? Or of his twin
sons, their twin armies, their twin funerals?[26] And what about
that arrogant mother Niobe, Tantalus' daughter, who out of
grief turned into rigid rock on Phrygian Sipylus and still weeps
sadly for her loss? And don't forget the founder of Thebes
himself, Cadmus. He was cast out of Thebes, and as he
surveyed his new Illyrian kingdom, he raised his fearful,
crested head and left long tracks in his wake as he slithered
along. This, yes this, is the sort of destiny that awaits you. So
go ahead, play the despot to your heart's content. Soon the
usual fate of our kings will come calling on you.

LYCUS: Come now, stop seething, stop sputtering these wild threats! Learn from Hercules how to follow the orders of kings. Yes, I wield a sceptre taken by force, won by the very hand that holds it. Yes, my power is absolute and unchecked by any law – weapons always trump laws, after all. All the same, I should like to say a few words in my defence. You say that your father and brothers were slain in our bloody war. My response? War knows no limits and does not choose its victims. Once the sword is drawn, rage is not easily controlled. Wars, and the soldiers who fight them, revel in bloodshed. Next, you argue that your father was driven to fight by patriotism for his own country, I by shameless greed for power. Well, all that matters is the outcome of war, not the reasons for it. But let us put the past behind us. When conquerors put down their weapons, it is only right that the conquered put aside their hostility. I do not ask you to bow down to me as your king and worship me. And the very fact that you do not take your defeat lying down delights me. You are indeed worthy to be a king's wife. Let us be married.

MEGARA: The chill shiver of dread races through my lifeless body – what a horrifying proposal strikes my ears! I did not tremble with fear when peace was shattered and war erupted, when the din of battle echoed around Thebes' walls. I endured it all fearlessly. But this marriage makes me shudder. Now, for the first time, I feel like a captive. Go ahead, shackle my body with chains, threaten me with death by starvation, a slow, lingering death. No form of torture will break my loyalty. Hercules, I'll die first, ever and always your wife.

LYCUS: Such courage! Remember, your husband lies buried in hell.

MEGARA: He descended to hell so that he can attain heaven.

LYCUS: The burden of the vast earth weighs upon him!

MEGARA: No burden is too heavy for the man who held heaven aloft.

LYCUS: I'll force you –

MEGARA: Force only works on those unprepared to die.

LYCUS: Fine, then tell me what kingly gift I could give you for our new marriage.

MEGARA: Your death – or mine!

LYCUS: You will die for such madness!

MEGARA: Then I will rejoin my husband.

LYCUS: Is my power no match for that, that *slave* of yours?

MEGARA: Remember how many kings that slave has sent to death!

LYCUS: Why then does he serve a king and endure servitude?

MEGARA: Take away the harsh commands and you take away his heroism.

LYCUS: You think being exposed to beasts and monsters is heroism?

MEGARA: It is heroic to subdue what the rest of us dread.

LYCUS: That great boaster – lost in the shadows of Tartarus!

MEGARA: The path from earth to the stars is not smooth.

LYCUS: He aspires to dwell with the heavenly gods? Based on what paternity?

AMPHITRYON: Enough! Poor wife of great Hercules, say no more. It is for me to tell of the true father and lineage of Hercules, the descendant of Alcaeus. Consider the countless mighty deeds this remarkable man has accomplished. Consider how he pacified all the lands that the Sun-god sees from sunrise to sunset. Consider all the terrifying monsters he has vanquished, and recall how he defended the gods and stained the land of Phlegra with the blood of those who defied them.[27] Can you really doubt his lineage? Jupiter is his father! I am not fabricating some story here. Consider Juno's anger!

LYCUS: You are profaning Jupiter's name! Humans and gods cannot mix.

AMPHITRYON: A great many gods were created in just that way.

LYCUS: But were they slaves before they became gods?

AMPHITRYON: Did the Delian god not shepherd flocks in Pherae?[28]

LYCUS: Did he wander in exile over the whole earth?

AMPHITRYON: No, but his fugitive mother did before she gave birth to him on a wandering island![29]

LYCUS: Phoebus did not face savage monsters, fearsome beasts!

AMPHITRYON: Wasn't the first to stain Phoebus' arrows the Python?

LYCUS: What about the trials Hercules endured as a babe?

AMPHITRYON: Didn't the boy who was expelled from his mother's womb by lightning, Bacchus, soon take his position next to his lightning-hurling father? Well? Wasn't the god who steers the stars and roils the clouds himself hidden in a hollowed-out mountain cave as an infant?[30] Such births are always attended by worry. Being born a god always comes at great cost.

LYCUS: But if someone's visibly suffering, you know he is mortal.

AMPHITRYON: If someone's visibly brave, you cannot say he is suffering.

LYCUS: So we are supposed to call a man brave if he takes the lion skin off his shoulders and gives it as a present to a girl, if he puts aside his club and covers his body with an embroidered, shimmering Sidonian dress?[31] Are we to call a man brave if he slicks back his bristling hair with scented oils? If he moves those hands known for their manly exploits to the unmanly sound of the tambourine, all the while sporting an oriental turban upon his head?

AMPHITRYON: Was Bacchus embarrassed to appear feminine, to let his locks fall down his back? To shake his slender thyrsus in his tender hand as he stepped daintily, trailing a long robe adorned with oriental gold behind him? It's entirely reasonable for a hero to take a break from manly deeds after a long stretch of strenuous work.

LYCUS: Of course – just look at Eurytus' house that Hercules destroyed! Or the herd of maidens he humped like cattle![32] Neither Juno nor Eurystheus issued orders to do *this* – no, these labours Hercules did all on his own.

AMPHITRYON: You're not telling the whole story. His own deeds include Eryx, whose skull Hercules cracked using that savage king's own boxing gloves, and Libyan Antaeus, who joined Eryx in death. Busiris' altars, dripping with the slaughter of foreigners, drank deep the blood of their owner, his just deserts. His own work includes Cygnus, whom he forced to meet death, despite being impervious to bronze or steel, despite bearing no wound upon his body.[33] And do not forget Geryon, no single monster, but conquered by a single hand. You will

be counted among these soon enough – and *they* never tried
to debauch his marriage bed!

LYCUS: What Jupiter could do, a king can do. You once gave a
wife to Jupiter[34] and you will now give one to your king. Your
daughter-in-law here will learn by your example that it is
nothing new to bow to one's betters – even her husband will
approve! But if you stubbornly refuse to be coupled with me
beneath wedding torches, well, I'll produce a noble heir by
you, even if I have to use force!

MEGARA: Ghost of Creon! House of Labdacus! Wedding torches
of incestuous Oedipus! Give this marriage of mine the kind
of ending Theban marriages are wont to meet. Come, you
bloody brides of Aegyptus' sons, come with your murderous
hands still dripping with the bloodshed of your husbands.
There is one Danaid still missing from your number. Her place
will I take and complete your heinous crime!

LYCUS: Wilful bitch! Since you snub my marriage proposal and
threaten your king, you will soon know what absolute power
is capable of. Embrace the altars, but know this: no god will
save you from me, not even if Hercules should heave back the
whole world and make his way in triumph to the heavens
above. [*To his attendants*] Collect firewood, pile it high! Let
the temple burn down and collapse upon all of these who have
sought refuge here. Let both Hercules' wife and his whole
flock of sons be consumed on a single blazing pyre!

AMPHITRYON: I ask you one favour, Lycus, as Hercules' father.
Kill me first, as is only right.

LYCUS: Oh, come now, the king who uses only death as punishment doesn't know how to be a dictator. One has to impose
different punishments. You don't put miserable people to
death; you reserve that for the more fortunate. [*To his attendants*] While the logs are piled ever higher for this funeral pyre's
consuming flames, I will go make votive sacrifice to the lord
of the sea. [LYCUS *leaves by one of the wings*]

AMPHITRYON: Greatest power in heaven, father and lord of the
heavenly gods, you who terrify the earth with lightning-strikes,
check the wicked hand of this ruthless king! It's no use. Praying to the gods is useless. Son! Wherever *you* are, hear me!

What is this? Why does the temple suddenly shake, heaving
this way and that? Why does the ground rumble? A mighty
crash resonates from the depths of hell! We are answered! It
is the sound of Hercules approaching!

CHORUS II: Prayer for Hercules in Hell

O Fortune, how cruelly you treat valiant heroes,
unjust, the rewards you dole out for their merits!
Will Eurystheus rule in untroubled tranquillity,
while Hercules, son of Alcmena, must wrestle
fell monsters, with hands that once hoisted up heaven?
Like lopping off heads of the Hydra, so fertile,
or swindling three sisters and stealing their apples,
by forcing their vigilant dragon to slumber,
that sentinel guarding those valuable orchards?

He trekked to the Scythian nomads, far-drifters,
who wander as guests in the lands of their fathers;
he trod on his march over seas that were frozen,
an ice-covered wasteland, no crashing of breakers.
No waves to be found on this sea, only grim ice:
where vessels once ran under billowing canvas,
now footpaths are trod by the long-haired Sarmatians.
The sea now sits still, but will shift with the seasons:
in summer it hosts ships, but horsemen in winter.
There, she who commanded the husbandless nation,
whose delicate waist was concealed with a corselet
of gold, did remove from her body that trophy,
her shield, and the bands that protected her breasts, white
like snow, and she bowed down before him, her captor.

What drives you, bold Hercules, down to the chasm
of death along paths that allow no returning?
Why visit Proserpina's kingdom in hell?

There, too, neither northern nor westerly winds whip
up waves into sea-swells, great swollen breakers;

no starlight from Gemini, saviours of sailors,
Tyndareus' twins, will bring comfort in terror.
That sea is a wasteland of stillness and blackness,
and when pale-faced Death, with insatiable hunger,
has ushered innumerable throngs to those waters,
one boatman[35] will ferry across the great masses.

We pray you escape from hell's pitiless chokehold,
the Fates' irreversible spindles, unyielding.
When you were assailing old Nestor's town, Pylos,
the Death-king, that ruler of peoples unnumbered,
did meet you in war, his hands baleful and deadly,
and wielded a three-forked weapon before him.
This god you made flee with a wound so minute:[36]
the lord of grim death saw grim death and grew pale.
Break Fate's grip with violence! Unveil the bleak death-
     world,
throw light on its darkness. Yes, break the impassable
divide, make it furnish a path to the skies!

But one man could move the grim lords of the shadows,
unyielding, harsh gods, with his songs and entreaties,
when seeking his wife, fair Eurydice: Orpheus.
His songs had the power to slow racing rivers,
to move trees and birds and great stones on the earth,
and charging beasts stopped when his voice hit their ears.
Now strains unaccustomed were soothing the dead –
against the great silence his voice rang more clearly:
the Furies shed tears for the dead Thracian bride,
and gods, who yield not to soft weeping, shed tears;
hell's judges, severe when they scrutinize misdeeds,
brows furrowed and grim as they question defendants –
these, too, sat and wept for Eurydice's sorrows.
At last spoke the ruler of death, 'We are won over.
Go, seek the blue skies, but on this one condition:
Eurydice, follow your husband and trail him;
you, Orpheus, turn not your gaze to your wife
before the clear daylight reveals the broad heavens

and Spartan Taenarum's broad portal is near.'
But love, if it's true, will not stand for delay.
Impatience won out: he glanced, and she vanished.
What kings could be conquered by sweet-sounding songs,
these kings can be conquered by violence and might.

ACT III

[*Enter* HERCULES, *accompanied by* THESEUS *and carrying Cerberus*]

HERCULES: Lord of the nourishing light, glory of heaven, you who drive your fiery chariot on daily orbits, who lift your bright countenance above the lands that rejoice at the sight of you! Phoebus, shining god, forgive me if you have gazed upon anything forbidden. I was ordered to bring the world's hidden secrets to light. You, too, lord and father of the heavenly gods: hold your lightning bolt before you to shield your eyes! And you who rule over the seas in the second realm, head to the depths of the sea! And if any other god looks down upon earth from on high, let him, too, avert his eyes and keep his gaze on heaven for fear of polluting himself with this unnatural sight. Do not look upon this unholy monstrosity! Only two must look upon this fiend: the man who carried it out, and the goddess who ordered it done. The earth was not enough for Juno's anger; it was insufficient for my torture, insufficient for my toil. I have gazed upon places no one else could enter, places unknown to Phoebus' rays, the dark netherworld, the vast abyss awarded to the Jupiter they call infernal, the dread lord of hell. And I could have been king there – had the third realm pleased me at all. I conquered the murky gloom of eternal night, and all that is even more frightening than night, the cheerless gods and the Fates. I scorned death and returned. What else remains? I've seen hell. I've opened hell up. What else is left? Come now, Juno, you've already kept my hands inactive too long! What do you want conquered next?

[*Seeing his family at the altar surrounded by* LYCUS' *men*]
But why does a hostile force surround the temple? Why does
a dreadful line of armed soldiers blockade its sacred entrance?

AMPHITRYON: Do my eyes deceive me? Am I seeing what I want
to see, or has that world-conqueror, the great glory of Greece,
escaped the land buried in silence and cheerless gloom? Is that
really my son? My whole body is numb with joy! [*Embracing*
HERCULES] O son, Thebes' late-coming saviour, do I hold in
my embrace a man who has returned to the skies above, or
am I deceived in my joy and only clutch an empty phantom?
Is it really you? I recognize your muscles, your broad shoulders, your tall frame, your head held so high!

HERCULES: Father, why your unkempt appearance? Why is my
wife cloaked in mourning? Why are my sons covered in such
filth? What disaster weighs so heavily upon my house?

AMPHITRYON: Your father-in-law has been slain. Lycus now
possesses his kingdom. He intends to kill your sons, father
and wife.

HERCULES: Ungrateful land! Did no one come to the aid of
Hercules' family? Did the world I kept safe just watch as this
great crime was perpetrated? But why waste the day complaining? Our enemy must be put to death! Let my glorious heroic
record suffer this one blemish, that Hercules' final opponent
be someone as worthless as Lycus. I'm off to drain the lifeblood of my foe. Theseus, stay here in case some force attacks
unexpectedly. [*Pushing* AMPHITRYON *and* MEGARA *away*] I
am called to battle – no, father, no time for embraces, no time,
my wife. Lycus will soon be dispatched to announce to Dis
that I have already returned! [HERCULES *leaves with Cerberus,
the* CHORUS *trails off behind him*]

THESEUS: Queen, brighten those sad, sad eyes. And you, Amphitryon, stifle those streaming tears. Your son has returned
safely! If I know Hercules, Lycus will pay the penalty he owes
Creon. 'Will pay' is too slow – he is already paying. Even 'is
paying' is too slow. He has paid.

AMPHITRYON: May the god who has the power hearken to our
prayers and stand beside us in our time of need. Great-hearted
companion of my great son Hercules, recount for us his heroic

deeds, how long a journey it was to reach the gloomy ghosts, how Hercules forced the hellhound to wear unyielding chains.

THESEUS: You force me to recall events that make my skin crawl even though I am now safe. Scarcely yet do I trust this life-giving air. My eyes are weak; my vision is blurry and I can barely endure the daylight to which I have grown unaccustomed in my long absence.

AMPHITRYON: Overcome all the dread that still lingers deep within your breast, Theseus. Do not cheat yourself of the greatest profit of your toils, the sweet recollection of hardships overcome. Tell us your story. Tell of your shuddering ordeal.

THESEUS: I beseech all that is right and holy in the universe, and you, lord of the spacious realm that receives many, and you too, goddess, you for whom your mother vainly searched the whole world through:[37] may I be allowed to reveal what is rightfully hidden and concealed by the earth unpunished!

There is a lofty peak that rises from the Spartan landscape, where Taenarum with its dense forests presses hard upon the sea. Here lies the portal down to the hateful house of Dis, a deep cleft in a lofty crag, an immense cavern with enormous, yawning jaws, a wide passageway through which the throngs of dead pass. The path at first is not sunk in total darkness. A faint ray of the forsaken sun lights the way, but it is only a pale glimmer of diluted light, and it plays tricks on your eyes. It is like the light one encounters during the first signs of dawn or the last moments of twilight, when night is mixed with day. Beyond this, the path spreads out into vast expanses of empty space, such that the entirety of the buried human race can proceed unhindered. Descending is no difficult task. The path pulls you down with it: just as a river current often sweeps boats downstream against their will, so too do the gripping air and the greedy jaws of death's caverns draw you down the way, and the shadows clutch at you, never allowing you to turn around and retrace your steps.

The first thing you meet is a giant sweeping river: the Lethe silently glides along its peaceful course and takes cares away. But it also allows no chance of returning; it weaves its sluggish stream in a tapestry of twists and turns, just like the winding

Maeander with its unpredictable course, a great puzzle twisting back on itself then moving forwards, doubting whether to head for the sea or back to its source. Next lie the foul swamp-waters of the listless Cocytus. Here a vulture calls eerily, there a horned owl hoots balefully, and throughout the whole region the ominous shriek of the screech owl echoes. A dark, shivering forest rings the swamp, a thick curtain of black foliage dominated by towering yew trees. This is the haunt of Sleep; here grim-faced Hunger lies inert, a gaunt phantom of skin and bones, and Guilt hides his face in shame. Then come Fear and Dread, Death and gnashing Grief, Mourning cloaked in black, shivering Sickness, and War girt in steel; hidden in the farthest reaches is crippled Old Age, supporting his weight with a staff.

AMPHITRYON: Is there any fertile earth that produces grain or wine?

THESEUS: There you will find no lush green meadows, no ripe fields of grain gently undulating beneath Zephyr's breath, no trees offering fruit-bearing branches. It is nothing but a barren wasteland, a vast expanse of boggy, lifeless earth, eternally stale, eternally foul. The air is still and stagnant, a listless world blanketed by heavy, black night. Everything is shrouded in sadness. The land of the dead is more dreadful than death itself.

AMPHITRYON: What about the king who holds sway over the dark realm? From what seat does he oversee the weightless throngs of the dead?

THESEUS: In the dark recesses of Tartarus there lies a place engulfed by deep shadows and a syrupy mist. Here, from a single spring two very different streams flow: one, on which the gods swear oaths, is a sleepy river that silently ushers forth the sacred waters of the Styx. But the other, the Acheron, gushes forth violently, a mighty torrent propelling boulders downstream with its current, allowing no recrossing. The front of Dis' palace is ringed by this pair of rivers, and his whole residence sits shrouded beneath the shadows of a dark grove. The entranceway to the overlord's realm yawns over you, a giant, arching cavern that seems to want to swallow you; this

is the corridor the shades take, this is the gateway to the
kingdom of the dead. This opening is ringed by a great field
where Dis sits in judgment, scowling haughtily as he assigns
the newly arriving spirits their final abodes. The god projects
a majesty, a fell, dreadful majesty. His face is grim but resembles his brothers' and reflects his divine lineage. He has the
look of Jupiter, but when he hurls thunderbolts. The grimness
of the realm is in no small part owing to the king himself –
even fearsome creatures are afraid to meet his steely gaze.

AMPHITRYON: Is the story true that long-deserved punishments
are rendered unto the dead, that guilty souls, though they have
no memory of their crimes, are punished as is their due? Who
is the assessor of truth, the arbiter of justice?

THESEUS: No single inquisitor sits upon a lofty tribunal and
metes out long-awaited verdicts to trembling defendants. The
guilty face Minos of Cnossus in one court, Rhadamanthus in
another, and in a third Thetis' father-in-law Aeacus hears cases.
The punishment always fits the crime, which comes back to
haunt the offender; the guilty are afflicted with punishment
established by their own precedent. I saw murderous leaders
rotting in prison and violent dictators' backs scourged by their
subjects. But all those who wield absolute power peaceably
and, though master over life and death, keep their hands free
of crime and rule humanely, without bloodshed and sparing
their people's lives – after these men have measured out a long
span of years, a life of blessings, they either head for heaven
or for blessed eternal life in the lush fields of Elysium to act
as judges. All you kings, refrain from shedding human blood!
Your crimes will be punished, be sure, but in greater measure.

AMPHITRYON: The guilty – are they imprisoned in a special
place? And is it true, as men say, that the wicked are afflicted
with harsh punishments and never-ending torture?

THESEUS: Yes. A swiftly whirling wheel wrenches Ixion's limbs
and a massive rock weighs heavily upon Sisyphus' shoulders.
Old man Tantalus stands in the middle of a river, his throat
parched with thirst, and chases after the water; waves lap at
his chin, teasing him, and though he has been deceived so
many times before, he allows himself to believe – the stream

is so, so close! – but the water vanishes in his very mouth. Overhanging fruit likewise tortures his hunger. Tityus offers his winged friend an eternal feast upon which to feed. The daughters of Danaus carry full urns of water in vain, the son-killing daughters of Cadmus still wander in madness,[38] and a ravenous bird torments Phineus' tables.

AMPHITRYON: Now tell me about my son's valiant encounter. Was the hellhound he took from his uncle given freely as a gift, or did he have to wrest it from him?

THESEUS: A deathly crag hangs over sluggish, shallow waters, where the river stagnates and its streams become still. A grisly old man, unkempt, ghastly to look at, watches over it and shuttles terrified souls across. A long, tangled beard hangs down from his face and his tattered cloak is held together by a knot at his shoulder. His deep-set eyes radiate an eerie white glow. This ferryman guides the raft across the river himself with a long pole, a lonely figure amidst the emptiness.

He had dropped off his previous load and was putting onto shore to collect yet more souls when Hercules pushed through the retreating crowd of the dead and demanded passage. Charon shouted in a dreadful voice, 'Where are you going, you impetuous man? Advance no further. Stop!' But Alcmena's son brooked no delay and compelled the boatman by force. He subdued him with his own pole and boarded the boat. The skiff, capable of holding countless dead, sank down beneath the weight of one; the raft, now too heavy, settled deep into the water and on both sides drank in the Lethe as it rocked this way and that. The monsters Hercules had vanquished on earth cowered in fear: the savage Centaurs <gap in the text>[39] and his Lernaean labour, the Hydra, submerged its bountiful heads in the water and fled to the farthest banks of the Stygian swamp.

After this the palace of insatiable Dis comes into view. Here dwells the vicious hellhound, the realm's great watchdog, who terrifies the shadowy ghosts by whipping its triple heads back and forth and filling the whole cavern with mighty growls. Coiled snakes lick its heads, which are caked with gore; its manes are a row of bristling vipers, and its tail is a long, writhing,

hissing serpent. Its horrific form is matched by its fury: as soon
as it hears the slightest footstep, its hackles are raised, a line
of quivering snakes, and it perks up its ears to catch any sound,
ears that can hear even the movements of ghosts. When Jupiter's son drew closer to the cave, the hellhound sat there in
uncertainty, feeling a tinge of fear. But then, without warning,
it unleashed a fearsome barking, filling the silent land with
terror, and the serpents all over its body hissed threateningly.
The ear-splitting din, the harrowing, unholy sound released
from its three mouths terrified even the souls far away in
blessed Elysium. Hercules for his part loosened the fierce,
yawning jaws of the Nemean lion from his left shoulder and
held out the head to shield himself with its enormous pelt.
Brandishing the giant oak club in his right hand, he swung
with great fury, now here, now there, a ceaseless volley of
blows thumping the hound over and over. Broken and worn
down, it lost its menace, lowered all three heads, and withdrew
entirely from the cave. The royal couple seated upon the
throne felt the grip of fear take hold and bade Hercules to
lead the hound off. As for me, Hercules requested that they
hand me over too – a request they did not dare refuse.[40]

Hercules stroked the ponderous necks of the beast with
his hand as he bound it with adamantine chains. The hound
forgot that it was the sleepless guardian of the dark realm,
laid its ears back, and let itself be led away, acknowledging
Hercules as its master and lowering its muzzles in submis-
sion. Its serpentine tail lashed both of its flanks meekly. But
when we arrived at the mouth of Taenarum and the bright-
ness of day – a strange, unfamiliar sight – struck its eyes,
the subdued beast suddenly found its fight again and furiously shook the giant chains, straining this way and that.
He nearly knocked Hercules off his feet and all but carried
him back down face-first. Hercules then looked to my hands
for help. With our combined strength we dragged the hellhound back up to the world above as it raged furiously and
thrashed about, all in vain. When Cerberus met the bright
day and caught sight of the radiant expanses of glorious
heaven, it first squeezed its eyes tight and tried to drive out

the hateful day, then it turned its eyes away and drove its
heads fully to the ground. At last it found shelter – in
Hercules' shadow.

[*Enter* CHORUS, *followed by* HERCULES]

But look, here comes a festive crowd, cheering loudly, wear-
ing garlands of laurel on their temples. Listen! They're singing
the praises of great Hercules!

CHORUS III: Ode to Death

King Eurystheus, whose birth was brought in haste,
ordered you to journey to the bowels of the earth.
Only this remained to complete your labours,
to despoil the lord of the third dominion.
So you boldly entered the pitch-black portal,
the dread pathway that leads to grim-faced ghosts
far away through shadowy, fearsome forests.
Yet this path is packed with great thronging crowds,
crowds like those when city folk come in swarms
to new shows at a brand-new theatre;
crowds like those that throng to Olympian Zeus
when the fourth year renews his festival;
crowds like those that assemble at the equinox,
when the time comes round for the nights to lengthen,
when ascendant Libra, desiring sweet sleep,
holds in balance the Sun-god's chariot-team –
an assembly for the mystery rites of Ceres,
when initiates leave their homes in Athens
in great haste for Eleusis' night-time rites.
So immense were the crowds that drifted over
those hushed fields: old men limped by, slow with age,
sad-faced, sated and weary of their long lives;
those of better years sped along that path,
youthful women unyoked to men in marriage,
teens with hair unshorn on the verge of manhood,
babes who had just learned to say 'mama, mama'.
To dispel their fears, a parade of torches
leads the babes and scatters the night before them;[41]

dark must the rest journey through the shadows.
What grim thoughts, O souls of the dead, are yours,
when the light is gone, but it dawns on you that
you are buried beneath the heavy earth?
Gloom and emptiness and depressing shadows,
baleful hues of night and of death, a haunting,
stifling stillness beneath bleak, barren clouds.
Late may we be brought there, when old and grey;
no one comes too late to death's realm, the land whence
none return once inside its clutching embrace.
Why do men go dashing to meet their doom?
Death yields not; the full measure of mankind
roaming on this great earth will journey deathward
and set sail on that listless stream, Cocytus.
Death, for you does everything grow, whatever
lives between the rising and setting suns. Be
gentle, Death: we are sure to come, and soon.
Death, for you we are ready and waiting.
Slow though you approach, of our own we hasten:
lives, like candles, begin to melt when lit.

O happy day in Thebes,
a day of great thanksgiving!
Embrace the altars in joy,
sacrifice fattened victims!
Let young women, arm in arm
with men, perform their dances;
let farmers of the fertile earth
put down their ploughs and rest.
For Hercules' hand has wrought
peace from east to west
and where the midday sun
denies shade for the weary.
All the lands that are lapped
by Tethys' wide embrace
have been tamed by Hercules' toils.
Now he has crossed Tartarus'
lakes, tamed hell and returned.

No threat is left in the world;
for nothing lies beyond hell.
[*To* HERCULES *as he enters*]
For your sacrifice, place
upon your bristling brow
a wreath of your prized poplar.

ACT IV

HERCULES: By my avenging hand Lycus has been slain, his face meeting the earth as he fell. Then all those who were joined to that tyrant in a bond of friendship also joined him in death. Now in honour of my victory I must perform a sacrifice to my father and the other gods in heaven, slaughtering upon the altars the victims that they are due.

I pray to you first Pallas, bringer of war, my ally and supporter in my labours, in whose left hand the aegis with its petrifying face strikes awe and fear. May Bacchus be gracious, conqueror of Lycurgus and the red seas, bearer of the thyrsus and its spear-point concealed by green ivy, and the twin divinities, too, Phoebus and Phoebus' sister (the sister more suited to the bow, Phoebus to the lyre), and all my brothers who dwell on Olympus – except those brothers born of my stepmother. [*To his attendants*] Drive fattened flocks here and bring all the incense that the Indians harvest in their fields and the Arabs collect from their trees. Let rich smoke billow! My head will be wreathed by a garland of poplar; as for you, Theseus, shade your brow with a wreath of olive, the symbol of your land. Here I will worship the Thunder-god; you must go and venerate the founders of this city, the woodland cave of pitiless Zethus, the famed waters of Dirce, and the sacred hearth of our former king who hailed from Tyre.[42] [THESEUS *starts to leave, but stops short of leaving. To attendants*] Heap the incense on the flames!

AMPHITRYON: Son, you must first cleanse your hands, which still drip with the blood of your enemy.

HERCULES: How I wish I could have drained that hateful man's

blood over the altar as a libation to the gods. No more acceptable an offering can be poured on the altars, no choicer victim
sacrificed to Jupiter, than a wicked king.

AMPHITRYON: No, son, pray to your father to end your labours,
to grant our weary souls peace and rest at last.

HERCULES: I will utter solemn prayers worthy of Jupiter – and
me! May heaven and earth and sea remain in their rightful
places, and may the stars glide uninterruptedly along their
eternal courses. May the peoples on earth enjoy deep-seated
peace. May all steel be used only to work the fields, and all
swords remain in their sheaths. May no violent tempest whip
up the seas, no lightning bolt leap forth from Jupiter's hand
in anger, and no raging river, fed by the melting winter snows,
ravage fertile farmlands. May poisons vanish, may no lethal
herb swell with harmful toxins. May kings never turn out to
be cruel, pitiless tyrants. And if even now the earth is bound
to produce some evil thing, may it come quickly, and if she is
creating some monster, let it be mine!

[*Hallucinating*] But what's this? Shadows have laid siege to
the midday sun! Though there are no clouds, Phoebus passes
through the sky with his face shrouded. Who drives the light
away? Who pushes it back towards the east? Why does this
strange night rise with its darkling shroud? Why do so many
stars fill the heavens in daylight hours? Look! Our first labour,
the Lion, nearly fills the whole sky with its fiery radiance,
blazing with rage and preparing to strike with its jaws. It
will soon maul some constellation and carry it off. See how
it stands menacingly, its giant maw gaping wide? See how it
breathes fire? See how it shakes its flaming mane? It is preparing to leap, in a single bound, over all the constellations that
parade forth during the grievous autumn and the long winter
months and to pounce on the sign of spring, the Bull, and
break its neck!

AMPHITRYON: What malady has suddenly come upon you? Son,
why do you keep turning your fierce eyes here and there and
envision an imaginary sky with so troubled a look upon your
face?

HERCULES: Earth has been completely tamed, the swollen seas

have yielded, the kingdom of hell has felt our onslaught. Only heaven remains untouched by my hand – yes, this, this is a labour worthy of Hercules! Let me be borne high into the lofty regions of the sky's dome, let me reach for heaven! The stars – this is my father's promise to me. And if he refuses? Earth cannot hold Hercules and will at last render him unto the heavenly gods. See, the whole assembly of the gods calls me forth and opens wide the gates for my ascension – except for one goddess who forbids it. [*To an imaginary* JUNO] Will you not unlock the gates of heaven and let me in, or must I tear down the doors of defiant heaven?

You still hesitate? Then I will remove the chains that bind Saturn, yes, I will release my grandfather and unleash him against my two-faced father's pitiless rule. Let the Titans find their fury and ready themselves for war. I will lead them forth. I will hoist rocky crags with their forests on my shoulders; with my own hands I will wrench mountain ridges from their foundations along with the centaurs that dwell in them. With a pair of mountains will I make a pathway to heaven – Chiron will see his beloved Pelion resting beneath Ossa, and Olympus, the third step, will either reach heaven or else I will hurl it and send it crashing into heaven![43]

AMPHITRYON: Chase these wicked designs from your thoughts! You are not of right mind, great though you may be. Please, stop these mad urges!

HERCULES: What's this? The Giants in all their destructive power are stirring for war! Tityus has escaped the shadows of hell, his chest a mangled, empty cavity – but see how high he stands, so close to heaven! Cithaeron convulses, lofty Pallene shudders, and Tempe recoils in fear. One Giant has already seized Pindus' ridges, another Oeta's, while Mimas rages dreadfully. A flame-bearing Fury screeches, cracking her whip and pressing stakes charred in funeral pyres ever closer to the faces of her enemies. Tisiphone, a pitiless goddess, her head protected by a palisade of serpents, guards with outstretched torches the gates of hell left vacant by my abduction of the hellhound.

[*Espying one son*] Look! There lurks the offspring of our enemy – the fell seed of King Lycus – in hiding! Soon my hand will return you to your hateful father. My bowstring will unleash fleet arrows – it is for justice that Hercules' weapons are launched!

AMPHITRYON: What has his delusion, his madness come to? Oh god, he's bent back the horns of his massive bow and attached the string; he's opened the quiver and with great force lets fly a singing shaft. Oh! the arrow speeds right through the boy's neck, leaving the wound behind!

HERCULES: [*moving towards the central stage door*] Now I will root out the rest of his brood, tear up every hiding place! There can be no delay – a greater campaign awaits me in Mycenae, to demolish the massive Cyclopean walls with my bare hands. Let my massive club swing here and there, smash down the barrier, break through the doorposts, batter and dislodge the roof! Now the whole palace is in full view: I see that wicked man's son trying to hide! [*Enters temple*]

AMPHITRYON: [*near stage door*] Look, Hercules, your boy's at your knees, stretching out his hands in supplication, pleading with you in a terrified voice. O dreadful deed, so grim, so horrifying to see! He snatched the boy up as he was begging for his life and furiously spun him around two, three times and sent him spinning like a wheel against the wall. Oh, how awful a cracking sound his head made as his brains splattered all over the walls of the house. [MEGARA *enters from temple doors*] Now poor Megara flees like a madwoman from her place of hiding, clutching her youngest to her breast.

HERCULES: [*emerging from the stage door in pursuit of* MEGARA] Flee! Seek protection in the very arms of the Thunder-god if you wish! No matter where you hide, this hand of mine will hunt you down and drag you out!

AMPHITRYON: [*to* MEGARA] Where, poor woman, are you heading? What shelter, what hideout do you hope to find? No place is safe when Hercules is on a rampage! No, child, no – embrace him, try to calm him with soothing words and supplication.

MEGARA: [*embracing* HERCULES] Husband, please, spare me, I beg you. Look, it's me, your Megara! This is your son – he has your features in him, your build! Do you see how he stretches out his hands?

HERCULES: [*seizing* MEGARA] I've got my stepmother in my grasp! Come now, receive your punishment. Free Jupiter from his humiliating yoke to you. But first, before his mother's death, this little monster here must die. [*Exit* HERCULES *with* MEGARA *and baby into the temple*]

AMPHITRYON: What do you intend to do, you madman? Will you shed the blood of your family? Oh! The infant, terrified by his father's fiery gaze, perished before Hercules could deliver his blow: terror took away his life. Now Hercules is poising his massive club over his wife. Oh! He smashed her bones; her head is gone, obliterated, leaving her but a headless trunk. [*To himself*] How can you bear to watch this, old man? You cling too much to life! If you are sickened by sorrow, you have a ready way out – death! Come, Hercules, plunge your arrows into *my* chest! Turn that club stained with the bloodshed of monsters against *my* body. Rid yourself of me, your false father, the one blight upon your great name, the one who diminishes your great glory.

THESEUS:[44] Why, old man, do you throw yourself in the way of death? What is your mad purpose? Flee, go into hiding. Keep Hercules' hands free from this one misdeed!

HERCULES: [*emerging from the temple*] All is well – the whole house of that shameful king has been eradicated. Wife of all-powerful Jupiter, it is to your divinity that I have slaughtered this flock of sacrificial victims. I have happily fulfilled my vows, I have offered up gifts worthy of you. Soon Argos will provide other sacrificial victims.

AMPHITRYON: [*presenting himself on the altar*] You have not yet completed your sacrifice, son. Finish it off. Look here, another victim stands at the altar with neck presented for the fatal blow. I'm ready, I'm willing, I demand it! Strike! What's this? Do my eyes fail me? Is my vision blurred by tears of sorrow, or do I see the hands of . . . of Hercules shake? His eyes fall shut, caught in sleep's embrace, his neck lolls about, and his chin drops to his chest! His knees buckle, bringing the whole weight of his body crashing to the ground, just like a mountain ash cut down in a forest or a mass of rock sunk down into the sea as a foundation for a harbour.

[*Running to* HERCULES] Are you alive, son, or did the same
madness that sent your family to death send you to your doom
as well? No, it's only a deep sleep; his chest still moves up and
down. Give him time to rest. Hopefully, sleep will break that
powerful sickness's potency and its mastery over his heart.
Slaves, remove his weapons, so that if his madness returns he
will not have them.

CHORUS IV: Ode to Sleep

Let heaven mourn! Let mighty Zeus,
the lord of lofty heaven, mourn!
Let the lush earth and shifting sea
with its ebb and flow lift up their cries!
Sun-god, above all you must mourn,
who bathe the land and sprawling seas
with light as you send night away,
your handsome countenance ablaze.
For Hercules, like you, did travel
to earth's far edges, where you set
and rise; he saw your two abodes.
Set his mind free, great gods in heaven,
free him from such insanity!
Restore his sickened mind to reason!

O Sleep, who vanquish all our woes,
rest for the soul and restoration,
far sweeter time of human life;
O winged child of starry night,
O drowsy brother of brutal Death,
who mix false dreams with true, a faithful
and faithless guide of what's to come;
O port amid life's stormy waves,
O harbour for life's troubled times,
respite from light, dark Night's companion,
stealing over kings and poor alike,
how you prepare the human race,
tortured by thoughts of death and dying,

by showing them the long, long night.
Come, gently soothe this worn-out man,
restrain him, bind him in chains of sleep;
let slumber seize his unconquered limbs,
do not release his angry heart
until he finds his former mood.

Look, nightmares torture him – his chest
heaves violently, he turns and tosses:
so great a malady, so great
a bane cannot be cured with ease.
His empty hands unconsciously
grasp for the club that used to serve
as prop for his exhausted head,
frantic, vain spasms clutching air.
His fever holds on doggedly,
like violent waves and swollen seas
that roil and churn and seethe enraged
after the storm has lost its strength.

Dispel these raging waves from his mind,
let him again feel love and honour.
No, rather let his mind remain
unhinged in turmoil; let him stay
oblivious to his heinous sin.
Only your madness keeps you free
from guilt; for next to innocence
is ignorance that you have sinned.

Beat, beat your breast, let it resound
with mighty Herculean blows!
Your massive arms once hoisted heaven,
now lash them with avenging hands;
let heaven hear your awful wails,
let Proserpina, queen of hell,
perceive your mournful, haunting cries;
let Cerberus, hell's sentry, hear
your howls above the ringing din

of barking and the rattling noise
of massive chains that choke his neck.
Make hell's abyss, the sprawling seas,
and skies, which better felt your shafts,[45]
resound with mournful lamentation;
for breasts beset by monstrous ills
deserve not mild, but brutal blows –
one dirge to make three realms resound!

You too, stout arrows, weighing down
his quiver, faithful comrades all,
deadly ornaments about his neck,
cut deep into his untamed back!
You, sturdy club, must smite his breast
and shoulders with repeated blows –
the knots must dig into his flesh.
Such pain his weapons, too, must mourn.
   [*The bodies of the children are carried or wheeled out on
   a platform called the* exostra* *as the chorus addresses them*]
You never shared your father's fame:
you never cut down savage kings;
no Greek arena saw you trained
to use your bodies dexterously
and boldly box, bare-handed or gloved.
Your only training lay in bows
and arrows stored in Scythian quivers:
these shafts you fired straight and true,
but harmless were your targets, deer,
timorous deer that take to flight.
No boar or lion, no dangerous beast
yet felt your arrow's piercing sting.
Go forth, you blameless souls, go forth
into the Stygian port below,
brutally felled in youth's first bloom
by a father's folly, a ghastly crime.
Children, go forth, you ill-starred sons,
follow your father's famous footsteps.
Go forth and see the god he angered!

ACT V

HERCULES: [*awakening*] What place is this, what land, what stretch of earth? Where am I? In the east, beneath the rising sun, or under the Bear in northern skies? Could this be the western edge of the world, where earth meets Ocean? What air is this I breathe? What land is this upon which my tired body rests? I have returned to the land of the living, no doubt – but why do I see this house demolished, these bloodied bodies lying stretched out upon the ground? Or has my mind not yet rid itself of the ghostly images of hell? Do throngs of the dead still flit before my eyes even now, after my return? It shames me to admit it, but I am filled with terror – in the pit of my stomach I feel that some wickedness is at hand.

Where is my father? Where is my wife, that proud mother of a great flock of children? Why isn't my lion skin at my side? Where, where has it gone, that shield in times of danger and soft bedding for Hercules' sleep? Where are my arrows? Where is my bow? Who could have stolen my weapons from me while I still live? Who could have taken such great spoils? Who does not fear Hercules, even when asleep? I want to see my vanquisher, now! Summon up your fighting spirit, Hercules. Could it be that my father left heaven and produced another son, one whose conception required a night even longer than mine?

[*Recognizing the corpses*] What wickedness is this I see? My sons lie dead, their bodies beaten and bloody – my wife, slain! Did one of Lycus' supporters seize power? Who would dare to commit such crimes against Thebes now that Hercules has returned? All of you who dwell along the banks of the

Ismenus, in the fields of Attica and in the realm of Phrygian Pelops, that land lashed by the waves of twin seas – come to my aid, identify the perpetrator of such brutal slaughter! I will rain down my wrath indiscriminately; whoever conceals the enemy from me will become my enemy. Conqueror of Hercules, are you afraid to come out? Show yourself! Whether you are here to gain vengeance for the bloodthirsty Thracian and his savage team of horses,[46] or for Geryon's herd, or for the lords of Libya,[47] come at me! I will not shrink from the fight. Look, here I am, defenceless, unarmed. Go on, attack me using my own weapons!

But why won't Theseus look at me? Why won't my father? Why do they hide their faces? [*Approaching them*] Tears can wait. Tell me, who sent my whole family to death in one fell swoop? Father, why won't you answer? Theseus, *you* tell me. Theseus, please, I beg you, after all we've been through! Neither says a word to me; they bury their faces in shame, sobbing to themselves. In a time of such great calamity, what is there to be ashamed of? Did that reckless overlord of Argos' city, Eurystheus, visit such disaster upon us? Did Lycus upon his deathbed send a hostile army to ruin us? I beg you, father, if my deeds mean anything to you, if your sacred role as my father, second only to Jupiter, means anything to you, I beg you to tell me: who destroyed my family? Who preyed upon me?

AMPHITRYON: Let these evils pass in silence –

HERCULES: – and remain unavenged?

AMPHITRYON: Revenge often causes harm.

HERCULES: Who endures such wickedness submissively?

AMPHITRYON: People who fear worse.

HERCULES: Father, what could be worse? What greater catastrophe could one fear than this?

AMPHITRYON: Your misfortune – how little you realize!

HERCULES: Pity me, father! I'm stretching out my hands to you in supplication. What? He avoids my touch? [*Seeing the blood on his hands*] Here, here lurks the crime: where did this blood come from? Why is that deadly arrow dripping with a child's blood? It's tinged in the venom of the Lernaean Hydra! Now

I see my weapons' work. I no longer seek the man who did this – only I could have bent back the bow, only my hand could have arced the bowstring, and it barely yields to me at that. [*To* AMPHITRYON *and* THESEUS] I turn to you once again, father: is this wicked deed mine? No response: it must be mine.

AMPHITRYON: Though the grief is yours, the crime belongs to your stepmother. No one is at fault for this disaster.

HERCULES: [*invoking* JUPITER] Now, father, now vent your anger, release your thunderbolts from every quadrant of heaven! Though you have forgotten me, at least avenge your grandsons, late though your vengeance may be. Make the starry firmament rumble with thunder, hurl your fires from both poles! Bind me to the rough Caspian crags, let the rocks and ravenous birds tear at my flesh. Why let Prometheus' cliffs remain empty? Prepare a sheer cliff face above the tree line on the mighty mountaintop of the Caucasus so that I can feed birds and beasts alike. Or stretch me out between the Clashing Rocks at the narrows of the Scythian Sea, one arm on this side, the other on that, and when the time comes round for the rocks to collide and the opposing cliff faces crash forcefully into each other, sending the sea lying in between heavenward, I will lie there, a restless barrier between the mountains.

But why dream? I will amass a great pile of firewood here and cremate this wicked body of mine drenched in the blood of my family. Yes, yes, this must be my punishment. I will return Hercules to hell.

AMPHITRYON: His heart is not yet rid of its turbulent delirium – only the target of his anger has changed. He vents his rage against himself – the unmistakable symptom of madness.

HERCULES: Grim realm of the Furies! Dungeons of the dead! District reserved for the throngs of guilty souls! Earth, if some secret place of banishment lies beyond Erebus, the land of darkness, and remains unknown to Cerberus – and to me – I bid you bury me there! I go forth into the deepest recesses of Tartarus, this time never to return! O spirit of mine, you have always been too violent! Who could shed enough tears for you, children, as your slain bodies lie sprawled throughout the whole house? This face of mine, hardened as it is by troubles, does not know how to cry. Bring me my bow; bring me my arrows; bring me my massive club. For you, my boy, I will snap my shafts, while for you, son, I will break my bow. [*Referring to* MEGARA *and their infant son*] For your two ghosts my deathly club will burn. I will add the quiver filled with Lernaean arrows to your pyre. Yes, my weapons must pay the price. I will burn you, too, hands, you that cursed my weapons, you vile instruments of a stepmother!

AMPHITRYON: Who would call a mistake a crime?

HERCULES: Monstrous mistakes are tantamount to crimes.

AMPHITRYON: Now more than ever we need Hercules to be Hercules: endure the weight of this great disaster!

HERCULES: My madness has not eradicated all shame from my soul. I will not allow myself to send the whole world running to avoid being polluted by my presence. My weapons, Theseus! I demand that you give back the weapons that you took from me, and do it quickly. If I am of sound mind, place the weapons in my hands; but if madness remains, father, stay clear. I will find a way to die.

AMPHITRYON: By all the sacred ties of family, by the rights inherent in either name you call me, whether it is father or foster-father, by my white hair that virtuous men must respect – by all of this, Hercules, I beg you: show mercy to my lonely old age, these tired years of mine! You are the sole pillar of our fallen house, the one light for me in my great affliction. Do not take your life! I have never received any benefit from your labours. I have always been afraid for you, whether you were facing the hazards of the sea or monstrous creatures. Every savage king in the whole wide world, whether dealing death with his hands or on his altars,[48] causes me fear. As your father I think I deserve some reward for all my suffering during your continual absence: stay, let me hold on to you and look at that face I've longed to see.

HERCULES: There is no reason why I should linger any longer in this hateful light and hold on to this life. I have lost every valuable thing I possessed: my mind, weapons, reputation, wife, sons, all my good work – even my madness is gone. No

one on earth could purify my polluted soul. Death, death is
the only cure for this crime!

AMPHITRYON: You will kill your father!

HERCULES: I will kill myself so that I cannot.

AMPHITRYON: Right here, before your father's eyes?

HERCULES: I taught him to watch heinous deeds.

AMPHITRYON: No! Think about all those famous deeds sung
the whole world through. Pardon yourself for this, your sole
offence.

HERCULES: Could a man who has never pardoned another
pardon himself? All my praiseworthy actions were done under
orders. This one deed is all my own. Help me, father, whether
you are moved by fatherly love or by my awful destiny or by
the stain on my glorious heroism, bring me my weapons. I
must defeat Fortune with my own hands.

THESEUS: Though your father's appeals should prevail upon
you, be moved, too, by my tears. Rise up and shatter this
present adversity with your usual vigour. Now call up that
spirit of yours which can overcome any hardship. Now is the
time to exercise your great heroism: forbid Hercules from
giving in to his anger.

HERCULES: If I live, I have committed crimes. If I die, I have
suffered them. No time: I must purge the lands now. For far
too long already has a wicked monster been ranging before
my eyes, a savage, pitiless, violent monster. Come, Hercules,
undertake this daunting task, a labour greater than the twelve
that came before. Weakling! Do you hesitate now? How brave
you were but moments ago against boys and trembling mothers! [To THESEUS and AMPHITRYON] If my weapons are not
returned to me at once, I will cut down every lofty mountain
forest on Thracian Pindus, and burn down all the groves
sacred to Bacchus and the forested ridges of Cithaeron along
with my body, and I will bring every house in Thebes with
their masters and household idols, every temple with their
gods crashing down on my body and bury myself beneath the
city's ruins. And if the collapsed city walls are not heavy
enough to crush my stout shoulders, if the seven gates of
Thebes are not enough to cover and bury me, then I will heave

up this whole mass of earth, which sits at the centre of the cosmos and separates heaven and hell, and bring it crashing down upon my head!

AMPHITRYON: Here, I am returning them.

HERCULES: That is an utterance worthy of Hercules' father. [*Holding up an arrow*] Behold, the shaft by which my boy was slain.

AMPHITRYON: That arrow was fired by Juno, though the hands were yours.

HERCULES: This arrow will *I* now use.

AMPHITRYON: Look, my son, see how my heart pounds, how my breast trembles with fear!

HERCULES: The arrow's notched.

AMPHITRYON: [*on the brink of collapse*] Look, now you're committing a crime willingly, intentionally!

HERCULES: Tell me, what would you have me do?

AMPHITRYON: Nothing, for me at least. My grief can get no worse. You alone can save my son for me, but not even you can take him from me. [*Brandishing a sword*] I have escaped my greatest fear. You cannot make me miserable, but you can make me happy. Decide as you like, but be sure to remember when deciding that your reputation is at stake and depends upon what you do now: either you live or you kill again. This life-spirit of mine, fading, worn out by age and no less by suffering, hangs on by the slenderest thread. How can anyone be so slow to return life to his father? I will brook no further delay! I will plunge this sword deep into my decaying body. Here, they will say, lies the victim of sane Hercules.

HERCULES: Wait, father, please wait – check your hand. Come, heroic Hercules, give in to your father's command. Add this – that you live – to Hercules' list of labours. Theseus, lift up my tormented father's body from the ground. My impure hand shrinks from touching anything so pure.

AMPHITRYON: [*rising, taking* HERCULES' *hand*] No, I willingly clasp this hand of yours. Supported by your hand I will walk, and by bringing your hand to my sick breast will I drive away my pain and sorrow.

HERCULES: Into what land of exile will I go? Where can I hide?

In what land can I vanish and blot out my name? What river could cleanse these bloodstained hands of mine? The Tanais or the Nile or the violent Tigris racing through Persian lands? The raging Rhine or Tagus' torrents, swirling with Spanish treasure? Even if the icy Maeotis were to pour all of its northern seas over me, even if the whole of Ocean's western waters, the haunts of Tethys, were to wash over my hands, the deep stain of my family's blood will never be erased.

Into what lands will you withdraw, you butcher of your family? To the east? The west? My famed exploits have left me no place of exile. The whole earth shuns me. The stars have turned their courses and run crosswise. The Sun-god even looked upon Cerberus with less revulsion.

Faithful Theseus, my dear friend, help me seek out some far-off hiding place into which I can disappear. Since you are always the kindly judge of other people's crimes and offer the guilty compassion and redemption,[49] pay me back now for rescuing you: lead me back down to the shadows of hell, I beg you, and bind me with the chains that once held you. Yes, the world below will hide my guilty soul – yet even that place knows me.

THESEUS: My land awaits you. There the man-slaughtering hands of the War-god were purified and again took weapons to hand.[50] Yes, Hercules, you are called to the land where gods go to find redemption and return to innocence.

All leave

TROJAN WOMEN

Preface to *Trojan Women*

After fighting on the shores of Troy for ten long years, the Greeks finally took the city through the ruse of the Trojan Horse, thus bringing the Trojan War to a close. As the angry and embittered Greek soldiers ransacked the city during Troy's final night, they committed horrific atrocities under the cover of darkness. The lesser Ajax raped Cassandra as she clung to the sacred statue of Minerva, and Pyrrhus, the son of Achilles, brutally murdered the aged King Priam upon the altar of Jupiter while his wife Hecuba looked on. When dawn broke the next morning, nearly all of the Trojan men had been killed; a few had fled from the city. The women and children, rounded up and assembled on the shores, were held as captives until they could be assigned to their new Greek masters.

This is the setting for Seneca's play, which dramatizes the grief of the Trojan women as two further atrocities perpetrated by the Greeks unfold: the sacrifice of Polyxena to Achilles' ghost and the hurling of Astyanax from the city walls. Seneca's play is, as far as we can tell, the only one from antiquity that combines these two episodes into one dramatic whole, and this may be his innovation. Euripides' *Trojan Women* is set after the sacrifice of Polyxena and foregrounds Astyanax' death. In that same playwright's *Hecuba*, Polyxena's death is dramatized, but it is paired with that of her brother Polydorus and is set in Thrace, not at Troy. Sophocles' *Polyxena*, of which we have only a few fragments, seems to have dramatized only Polyxena's death (although in it Achilles' ghost appeared on stage and demanded Polyxena's death, a scene which may have been in Seneca's mind when he composed Talthybius' speech in Act I). One of Seneca's

Latin predecessors, who were enamoured with the Trojan cycle
more than any other Greek myth, may have joined the two
episodes, or have been following a lost Greek play that had
already done so, but because their plays are almost wholly lost,
we cannot know for sure.

Seneca's attempt to weave these two episodes together means
that the play is somewhat dissociated – a 'flaw' that critics have
sometimes brought to bear against it. It is true that it has less
unity than Euripides' *Trojan Women*, where Hecuba's presence
onstage throughout the play unifies the whole as the women are
taken away one by one and Astyanax is killed and buried. In the
place of unity, however, there is symmetry. Acts II and IV of
Seneca's play involve the fate of Polyxena. These two acts, in
turn, frame Act III, which dramatizes Andromache's unsuccessful attempt to hide her son Astyanax from the Greeks. It is only
in Act V that the two strands come together, when the Messenger reports the twin deaths in a single gripping narrative.

Symmetry is not confined to the architecture of the play.
Seneca also creates temporal symmetry between pre- and post-
war events. Both Polyxena's sacrifice and Astyanax' death are
constructed in such a way as to evoke the memory of a specific
pre-war episode. Polyxena's death thus becomes the post-war
analogue of Agamemnon's pre-war sacrifice of his daughter Iphigenia at the Greek port of Aulis. Just as Iphigenia's sacrifice
secures the Greeks' passage to Troy, Polyxena's sacrifice will
secure the Greeks' passage back from Troy (this is ironic,
however, since the audience knows that most Greeks will suffer
catastrophe en route or upon their return). Likewise,
Andromache's failed attempt to hide her son Astyanax from the
Greeks and Ulysses' unravelling of her ruse are all calculated to
recall his uncovering another mother's ruse, namely, Thetis'
unsuccessful attempt to keep the young Achilles from fighting
at Troy (and from certain death) by hiding him among the maidens
at Lycomedes' court.

Seneca, in fact, incorporates much of the Trojan Cycle into
his play, frequently alluding to the mythical events found in those
Greek epic poems that, along with Euripides' tragedies mentioned
above, form the backdrop to his play. Chief among these is

Homer's *Iliad*. To take one instance, the argument between Agamemnon and Pyrrhus in Act II of Seneca's play not only structurally recalls that between Agamemnon and Achilles in *Iliad* 1 (more symmetry), it is also filled with allusions to specific famous episodes found in the epic (Books 9, 16, 20 and 24). Although less visible, Homer's *Odyssey* and the Homeric *Aethiopis* are also present. By writing multiple episodes of the Trojan War into this one play, Seneca emphasizes the fact that the diaspora of the Trojan women is the heartbreaking culmination of a long and brutal conflict in which no one really wins.

Characters

HECUBA, *Trojan, widow of Priam*
TALTHYBIUS, *Greek, herald of Agamemnon*
PYRRHUS, *Greek, son of Achilles*
AGAMEMNON, *Commander of the Greek Army*
CALCHAS, *Greek prophet*
ANDROMACHE, *Trojan, widow of Hector*
OLD MAN, *Trojan, guardian of Astyanax*
ASTYANAX, *Trojan, son of Hector and Andromache*
ULYSSES, *Greek general*
HELEN, *Greek, wife of Menelaus and Paris' widow*
POLYXENA, *Trojan, daughter of Priam and Hecuba* (Mute)
MESSENGER
CHORUS *of captive Trojan women*
GREEK SOLDIERS (Mute)

ACT I

SCENE: The shores of Troy. The time is the morning after the sack of Troy. The smouldering ruins of the city lie in the background.

[HECUBA *stands alone on stage*]

HECUBA: All of you who put your trust in power, playing lord and master in a mighty palace, fearing not the fickle gods but blindly trusting your good luck, look at me, [*gesturing behind her*] look here, at Troy! Never, never has Fortune presented greater illustrations of how perilous is the perch upon which the lofty stand. Troy, the pillar of mighty Asia, the exquisite achievement of the gods' toil,[1] has been toppled and now lies in ruins. Many allies came to aid Troy in war: Thracian Rhesus, who drank the frigid waters of the seven-mouthed Tanais,[2] Ethiopian Memnon, who first greeted the reborn day where the warm Tigris meets the crimson sea, and Amazon Penthesilea, who, looking out over her neighbours, the nomadic Scythians, once thundered across the shores of Pontus with her squadrons of cavalry.[3] Troy was razed despite them all. The towers of Pergamum are fallen. Look, the walls, those once glorious, soaring walls, now lie in heaps on the charred remains of houses. The palace is engulfed in flames. Assaracus' great mansion smoulders. Even so, the flames do not keep the conquerors' greedy hands at bay – Troy is pillaged even as she burns. Billowing smoke blots out the skies, and the sun, as if engulfed in a thick cloud, casts a mournful pall over us, fouled by the ashes that once were Troy.

The victors remain insatiable in their anger. They survey the city of Ilium that long clung to life. They mark out their targets with their eyes. They repay Troy for the ten-year siege with unbridled savagery. But as they gaze at Troy's demise, an uneasy shiver comes over them; although the conquered city lies right there before their eyes, they refuse to believe it could have been conquered. With predatory hands they ransack Dardanus' city, carrying off so much plunder that not even their thousand ships can hold it all.

I swear by the gods hostile to me, by the ashes of my country, by you, my dear Priam, benevolent ruler of the Phrygians, who now lie buried beneath the whole kingdom of Troy, by your ghost, my dear son Hector, who kept Troy standing so long as you yourself stood among the living, and by you, my great flocks of sons, you ghosts of lesser glory – you are all my witnesses: this whole disaster, the doom that Cassandra, the maddened prophetess of Phoebus Apollo, predicted would happen in her god-inspired harangue, though the god kept her from being believed – all of this I, Hecuba, dreamed first when I was pregnant.[4] I did not keep my fearful visions secret; no, I played the part of an unheeded prophetess long before Cassandra ever spoke. It was not the crafty Ithacan Ulysses or his night-time companion Diomedes or deceitful Sinon who cast firebrands against you, my people. I lit the fire that burns you now.

But why do you, old woman who cling too long to life, lament the downfall of your ruined city? Unfortunate woman, turn your mind to more recent woes. The calamity of Troy's fall is already a thing of the past. I watched on in horror as the king was slaughtered, a foul and monstrous deed committed on the very altars of the gods; the fierce warrior Pyrrhus, the descendant of Aeacus, seized the king by the hair, savagely twisted his head back, baring his neck, and pushed his wicked sword deep into his throat, burying it completely in the wound. Priam welcomed the death-blow, but when the sword was pulled out, the blade came out of the old man's neck without a drop of blood upon it.

Whose violent passions would not have softened, who would not have refrained from carrying out such a cold-blooded murder at the sight of an old man approaching the finishing line of human life? Or at the thought that the gods above would witness this crime? Or out of respect for a fallen kingdom? Priam, that father of so many would-be kings, lies unburied and is denied cremation even as Troy burns. Yet all

of this suffering is not enough for the gods: even now Priam's
daughters and his sons' wives are being awarded to Greek
masters as the urn casts lots. [*Gesturing to herself*] Yes, even
I will join them – worthless prize that I am! One Greek promises himself Hector's widow, one hopes for Helenus' wife,
another for Antenor's. There's even one who wants to share
your bed, Cassandra. But they all dread me – my lot is the
only one the Greeks dread winning.

    [*Enter* CHORUS]

    Friends, my band of captive Trojan women, why have you
stopped your lamentation? Pound your chests, resume your
wailing – offer Troy these last rites as is due. For far too long
now Ida, the fell mountain home of that ruinous judge Paris,
should have been resounding with your cries of mourning.

CHORUS I: TROY'S MOURNING

No inexperienced band are we,
unused to mourning or to tears.
Affliction we have known for years
unbroken, since Paris set foot
in Sparta, a Trojan guest in Greek
lands, and sailed off upon the ship
built of the sacred pines that grow
in the groves of mother Cybele.
Ten winters since have Ida's peaks
grown white with snow, her slopes made bare
to fashion pyres for fallen men.
Ten summers since have harvesters
along Sigeum's fields cut down
their crops while fearing for their lives.
No day has passed without despair;
each day, new sorrows call for tears.

Repeat, repeat your mournful cries,
and you, poor queen, lift up your hand:
you will we follow, a worthless band –
well-versed are we in misery.

HECUBA

   Companions of my luckless lot,
   my loyal band, unbind your hair,
   allow your locks to veil your necks,
   and daub your cheeks with Trojan ash,
   still warm; fill up your hands – this alone
   are we allowed to take from Troy.
   Expose your shoulders, my captive band;
   let your dresses fall about your hips,
   secure the folds and bare your torsos.
   Do you conceal your breasts for him,
   your fallen husband, out of shame?
   A captive needs no modesty.
   Now tie your shawls around your waists
   and free your hands to pound, to pound,
   to pound your breasts incessantly.
   This mournful look befits us so,
   a band of women fit for Troy.
   Repeat your practised lamentations,
   wail louder than you have before –
   for it is Hector that we mourn.

CHORUS

   We have unbound our once lush hair,
   ragged from mourning many deaths;
   unfettered locks now shroud our necks,
   our faces wear Troy's searing ash.
   Our dresses fall to bare our bodies,
   hitched at the waist to veil our legs.
   Our naked breasts now call for blows –
   unleash your pain, unleash your fury,
   make the Rhoetean shores resound
   with wails, give mountain-dwelling Echo
   no time to mimic final words
   or repeat the dirge's final strains;
   no, force her to return in full
   your howls for Troy – let the whole sea
   and heaven hear. Be vicious, hands,
   be vicious: pound your breasts, pound hard,

pound them with violence and fury!
We crave a wail beyond the norm –
for it is Hector that we mourn.

HECUBA

For you, Hector, I strike my arms,
I strike my shoulders till they bleed;
for you I beat my head with fists,
for you a mother's breasts are bloodied,
torn by her vicious fingernails.
I will reopen every scar,
renew the wounds I scratched into
my body at your funeral,
letting a bloody river flow.
You were the pillar of our country,
you fended off its doom; in our
exhaustion you protected us,
you were our bulwark; ten long years
Troy stood supported by your arms.
Troy fell with you; the final day
of Hector was his country's last.

Now turn your mourning to another,
pour out your tears for Priam's fate.
For Hector has received his due.

CHORUS

O aged lord of Phrygia,
who was twice captured by the Greeks,[5]
receive our tears, our lamentation!
Troy always suffered doubly while
you reigned as king: twice did Greek rams
assault and batter down its walls;
twice did the city feel the sting
of Hercules' ill-fated bow.[6]
A long parade of death preceded
yours, father, all of Hecuba's
great brood, that flock of would-be kings.
Now on Sigeum's shores you lie,
a headless corpse, an offering

cut down for mighty Jupiter,
your family's last fatality.

HECUBA

Another now deserves your tears.
My Trojan band, you must not mourn
for Priam's death, my husband's end:
let all proclaim, 'Priam is blessed!'
He journeys down to join the dead,
but freedom has he found in death –
he will not bear Greek servitude,
nor bend his neck beneath their yoke,
nor gaze on Atreus' two sons,
nor treacherous Ulysses' face,
nor be displayed as spoils of war
in Greek parades of victory.
His hands, his sceptre-wielding hands
will not be bound behind his back
or feel the pinch of golden chains
as Agamemnon leads him through
the spacious Mycenaean streets,
a pageant shameful for a king.[7]

[HECUBA *leaves*]

CHORUS

'Priam is blessed!' we all proclaim:
he took his kingdom with him when
he passed away, and now he strolls,
untroubled, through Elysium's groves,
surveying pious souls in search
of Hector, fortunate in death.
'Priam is blessed!' Yes, every man
is blessed who, perishing in war,
takes all that's perished with him.

[*Enter* TALTHYBIUS]

TALTHYBIUS: All we Greeks do is wait in port! It doesn't matter
whether we're setting out or going home.

CHORUS: What prevents the Greek ships from sailing off? Tell
us, what god keeps you from heading home?

TALTHYBIUS: My mind shudders, my body shivers at the thought
of what I saw. Visions too great to be true! You would have
hardly believed it. I hardly believe it. But I saw it, I saw it with
my own eyes. The Sun-god had just started to tinge the moun-
taintops with his morning light, night was just turning to day
when suddenly the ground rumbled and convulsed deep below.
Treetops swayed violently and the lofty, sacred grove thundered with mighty crashes and the sound of splintering. The
upheaval was not confined to the land, either: the sea felt the
presence of its kinsman Achilles and its waters began to swell.
Then, suddenly, the ground split in two. It was a giant cavity,
laying bare the enormous, dark caverns of hell. The yawning
crater offered a pathway to the upper world and lifted up
Achilles' tomb.

The ghost of the Thessalian general, awesome and menacing, suddenly darted from his tomb. He looked just like he
did when he laid waste to the Thracian army as he practised
for the destruction of Troy; or when he struck down Neptune's
boy Cygnus, that young man with gleaming white hair; or
when he went raging through the battle-lines, hewing down
men in violent slaughter and clogging the Xanthus with
corpses, forcing the god to creep along his bloodied channel
as he looked for a way through the carnage; or when he stood
on his chariot, exulting in victory, and drove his team onward,
dragging Hector behind him and Troy towards its doom. He
was enraged, and his thunderous voice filled the whole shore:
'Go ahead, you do-nothings, go ahead and take with you the
war prizes that are owed to my ghost! Go ahead, you ingrates,
launch your ships! Sail over my seas! The Greeks appeased
Achilles' wrath once before, and it cost them dearly.[8] It will
now cost them dearly again. Polyxena must be betrothed to
my ashes and sacrificed by Pyrrhus' hand. Her blood must
drench my tomb.'

After he spoke these words, he left the light to return to the
darkness. As he plunged into the earth, making his way back
to Dis' realm, he joined the earth together and sealed off the
enormous cavern. The waters were again tranquil and calm.

The winds had lost their menace. The sea murmured peacefully as waves rolled gently in. Above the murmur you could
make out a chorus of sea-gods, the Tritons, singing a wedding
hymn beneath the deep blue sea.

[TALTHYBIUS *and the* CHORUS *leave*]

ACT II

SCENE: The Greek camp, in front of Achilles' tomb.

[*Enter* PYRRHUS *and* AGAMEMNON, *attended by Greek soldiers and* CALCHAS]

PYRRHUS: [*to* AGAMEMNON] While you were merrily preparing to set sail on your voyage home, did Achilles just happen to slip your mind? Did you forget that it was his might, and his might alone, that toppled Troy? The delay Troy enjoyed after his death was nothing more than the time it took for the city to decide which way to fall! Even if you are willing to grant his demands, and are quick to do so, it is too late – all of the Greek generals are already carrying off their war prizes! This is the least you could do for all his courageous deeds. Or did he not earn it? When his mother ordered him to sit out the war so that he could live an easy life deep into old age, surpassing the years of old man Nestor, did he not tear off that sham disguise, his mother's tricks, and reveal himself to be a man by taking up weapons?[9] Telephus, stubborn ruler of an unwelcoming kingdom, was the first to stain Achilles' untested hand with blood – the blood of royalty no less! – when that king tried to stop him from entering Mysia, land of ferocious warriors. But he later learned that Achilles' powerful hand was also gentle.[10] He sacked the city of Thebe and captured its king, Eetion, who watched on as his kingdom fell. Achilles likewise demolished the city of Lyrnessus nestled under a towering mountain. So, too, that land famous for Briseis' capture, and Chryse, causing disputes among kings,[11] and far-famed Tenedos, and Scyros, fertile land nourishing Thracian flocks on lush pasturage, and Lesbos, which divides the Aegean Sea, and Cilla, city dear to Phoebus Apollo – not to mention all those cities washed by the floodwaters of the Caicus when it swells into a torrent in springtime.

Think about all the nations he exterminated, the great terror he caused, those countless cities strewn about the land as if wrecked by a massive tornado. All of this would be the crowning glory, the crowning achievement for someone else – for Achilles it was just his journey here! Just consider how mighty he was, how great were the wars he fought while he was preparing for this war. Even if I were to pass over his other mighty exploits, would Hector's death not be enough all by itself? My father conquered Troy. All you did was demolish its empty shell. Joy and pride wash over me when I recount my great father's celebrated deeds and accomplishments here: he slew Hector in front of his father's eyes, Memnon in front of his uncle's.[12] Dawn, Memnon's mother, mourned, and as a sign of her gloom she ushered in a gloomy day, her once rosy face now ashen and colourless. Achilles was horrified when he saw the precedent he set with his victory: he learned that even men born of goddesses die. Then he cut down Penthesilea, that savage Amazon woman, his final triumph.

You owe Achilles. And if you assess his services honestly, you owe him even a young Greek woman from Mycenae or Argos if he were to demand it. You still hesitate? Have you suddenly grown a conscience, suddenly become merciful? Do you think it savage to sacrifice Priam's daughter to Peleus' son? Remember, you sacrificed your own for Helen![13] I'm not asking you to do anything new. You set the precedent long ago.

AGAMEMNON: All you young men have a common fault: you can't control your impulses. But whereas others' unbridled passion is owed to their youth, yours, Pyrrhus, is inherited from your father. Once before I calmly put up with the insolent threats of one of Aeacus' high and mighty descendants,[14] and I can do it again. The more power you have, the more you have to endure patiently.

But why shower that illustrious general's noble ghost with ill-omened bloodshed? You should learn first what conquerors should do and what the conquered should endure. You will

not wield power long if you exercise it violently, but if you
exercise it with restraint, it will last. The more Fortune exalts
you and increases your power among men, the more you must
remain humble in your prosperity, fearing a sudden change
in luck, putting no trust in gods that give you all you want
and more. I have learned through conquering that it takes
only a moment for the mighty to fall. Does Troy's fall make
us overconfident and overweening? Remember, we Greeks
now stand where Troy just stood!

Fine, I'll admit that there were times that I was unrestrained
with my power, that I let myself get too arrogant and overconfident. But that arrogance was checked by one thing: Fortune
– and the fact that she could have raised someone else to that
lofty position instead of me. Do you make me proud, Priam?
No, you make me fearful. How can I of all people regard kingship as anything other than a meaningless title with seductive
but empty glory and having my temples graced by an illusory
crown? All of this fickle chance will take from me, I know it,
and it might not take a thousand ships or ten years to do it.
Fortune does not always wait so long to pounce on her victims.

I'll make another confession, though I fear it may offend
my fellow Greeks. Though I wanted to rout the Phrygians and
conquer them, I wish I could have done it without destroying
Troy completely and razing it to the ground. But when it comes
to angry men and blazing swords, especially when victory is
won in the darkness of night, how can a general control them?
It's not possible. Those shameful and savage acts committed
last night?[15] Chalk them up to the Greeks' long suffering and
the cover of darkness. Rage works itself into a frenzy under
the cloak of night, and the victor's sword, once it gets a taste
of blood, lusts uncontrollably for more. Whatever's left of this
fallen city must be preserved. It has suffered more than enough
punishment. As for sacrificing a royal princess and offering
her up as a funeral gift, as for drenching the ashes of the dead
with blood and calling such a heinous murder a wedding – this
I will not allow. I'm responsible for the actions of all my men.
Not preventing a crime when you are able to is tantamount
to giving the order.

PYRRHUS: So Achilles' ghost will receive no war prize?

AGAMEMNON: Of course he will: everyone across the world will sing his praises, and even unknown lands will hear tell of his great name. But if ashes are appeased by bloodshed, go slaughter the sleek-necked cattle in Phrygia's herds. No mother would need tears for this. What you intend to do – what kind of custom is that? When has a human life been forfeited as an offering to the dead? Save your father from hostility and loathing. You're asking us to honour his shade with bloody retribution!

PYRRHUS: How fearless you are when success raises your spirits! How spineless you become at the first rattle of danger, you tyrant of kings! Is your heart now all aflame with sudden desire, with a new bout of lust? Will you, a single man, rob us of our war prizes countless times? No, with this hand of mine I will offer Achilles the victim he is owed. If you refuse and try to keep her from me, I will offer up a greater victim, one quite fitting for Pyrrhus to sacrifice – you! Too long now has my hand refrained from spilling a king's blood; Priam calls for his counterpart!

AGAMEMNON: Priam lies dead, slain by the sword – ah, your greatest achievement in war, Pyrrhus. I would not deny that you killed your father's suppliant!

PYRRHUS: You and I both know that my father's suppliants were also his enemies. Yet Priam pleaded his case in person. You, on the other hand, were paralysed with great fear, too cowardly to approach him, and so you entrusted your entreaties to Ajax and the Ithacan while you remained locked in your tent, shaking in fear of the enemy.[16]

AGAMEMNON: I'm sure your father felt no pang of fear at the time: he was lying idle while Greek soldiers were slaughtered and Greek ships were burned, forgetful of war and weapons, strumming sweet-sounding songs on the strings of his lyre!

PYRRHUS: Don't forget that at the time mighty Hector thought little of your weapons but feared Achilles' songs, and that amid such great terror there was only peace in the Thessalian camp.

AGAMEMNON: Of course, in that same Thessalian camp there was again deep peace – for Hector's father![17]

PYRRHUS: It is the mark of a lofty king to grant life to a king.

AGAMEMNON: So why did *you* rob a king of his life with your own hand?

PYRRHUS: Often one grants death instead of life out of pity.

AGAMEMNON: And now? Is pity making you demand a virgin for the tomb?

PYRRHUS: Now you think it's a crime to sacrifice virgins?[18]

AGAMEMNON: A king must put his country above his children.

PYRRHUS: No law compels us to spare captives or stops us from punishing them.

AGAMEMNON: Some things decency forbids, even if laws do not.

PYRRHUS: Conquerors can do as they please.

AGAMEMNON: Those wielding great power should indulge themselves least.

PYRRHUS: [*pointing to the Greek soldiers present*] Are you spouting off such nonsense in front of these men here, men that you crushed beneath ten years of your despotism until I freed them from the yoke?

AGAMEMNON: Is this the insolence Scyros breeds?

PYRRHUS: At least it's free of brothers' crimes!

AGAMEMNON: Such a puny island, hemmed in by waves –

PYRRHUS: – of the sea which is related to me.[19]

AGAMEMNON: All this from you, who were conceived in secret fornication with a young woman, born of Achilles before he'd become a man![20]

PYRRHUS: Yes, born of that Achilles who has a share of the whole cosmos through his lineage, with branches spread out over the gods' three realms: the sea through Thetis, the underworld through Aeacus, the heavens through Jupiter.

AGAMEMNON: You mean the Achilles who was felled by *Paris'* hand?

PYRRHUS: This man no god would dare to fight in person![21]

AGAMEMNON: [*yielding*] I could have put a stop to your speech and chastised your brazenness by punishing you. But my sword knows how to spare even captives. No more. Let Calchas, prophet of the gods, be called forth. If the Fates demand Polyxena's blood, I will comply. [*To* CALCHAS *as he enters*] You – you once released the Greek fleet from its mooring and

removed the obstacles to war. Yours is the power to unseal
the will of heaven with the prophetic arts, to you the omens
of what is to come are revealed in symbols hidden in entrails,
in heaven's thundering, and in comets drawing their long, fiery
trails across the sky. Though your prophecies always come at
a great cost to me, tell us what the god bids us to do, Calchas.
Guide us with your counsel.

CALCHAS: A path do the Fates grant the Greeks, but at a price
they paid before:[22] a virgin must be sacrificed upon the Thessalian general's tomb. Dressed must she be in the style that
Thessalian girls are wont to wear when joined in holy matrimony. Pyrrhus must give the bride away to his father. Only
thus will she be sacrificed in a manner acceptable to the gods.

Yet this is not the only reason our ships remain in port. No,
blood yet more noble than your blood, Polyxena, is destined
to be shed. He whom the Fates demand must fall from the
tower's heights – the grandson of Priam, the scion of Hector,
must meet his doom. Only then will the seas be filled with the
sails of a thousand ships.

[AGAMEMNON, PYRRHUS, CALCHAS *and the Greek soldiers
leave. The* CHORUS *enters*]

CHORUS II: On Death and the Flight of Time

The tale, is it true? Or does fear make us believers,
that souls go on living when bodies are buried,
when dutiful wives close the eyes of their husbands
on that day, the eternal eclipse of their being,
when suns disappear and grim urns jail their ashes?
Are we availed not by interring our spirits,
but destined to live our depressing lives longer?
Or do we die wholly, no portion of us to
survive, when those final breaths flee from our bodies
and, mingling with mist, vanish into thin air,
when torches are lit underneath our cold bodies?
All that is seen by the rising and setting sun
and washed by the waves of cerulean Ocean,
as tidewaters roll in and roll out – all

this time will devour as quickly as Pegasus gallops.
As swiftly as the twelve constellations whirl round,
as swiftly as the lord of the stars ushers onward
the march of the seasons, and Hecate hastens
her horses around her tight-angled orbit –
so swiftly we speed towards our doom, and we cease
to exist once we reach those dread waters upon which
the gods swear their oaths. Just as smoke from a raging
fire disperses, a fluttering wisp of a moment,
and clouds that were threatening but seconds ago
are scattered by Boreas' whipping, chill gale-winds –
so too are the spirits that guide us disbanded.
Oblivion is death, after death there is nothing,
the finishing line of our fleeting, short lives.
The greedy can lay aside their hopes!
The anxious can lay aside their fears!
For ravenous time will reduce us to nothing.
Impartial is death, to our bodies destructive,
yet souls are not spared. The last threshold, Taenarum,
the realm of the merciless king, and the hellhound,
grim Cerberus, guard of the pitiless portal –
all fairytales, nothing but meaningless fictions,
vain stories akin to a troubling nightmare.
Where will you reside after death, you inquire?
               Where unborn things reside.

ACT III

[*Enter* ANDROMACHE, ASTYANAX *and the* OLD MAN]

ANDROMACHE: Phrygian sisters, you sorrowful throng, why do you tear at your hair? Why do you pound bruises into your breasts? Why do tears stream down your cheeks? Minor is the suffering we have endured if what we suffer now requires tears. For you Troy's fall occurred just last night. For me, it fell long ago, when savage Achilles whipped his team to a gallop and dragged my husband's lifeless corpse behind his speeding chariot. How deep were the axle's groans, how terrible was the chariot's shaking as it dragged Hector's massive body behind it! Ever since then have I been buried beneath the ruins of grief, enduring all that has happened without feeling, numbed and dazed from my suffering. I would have already stolen myself from the Greeks' clutches and followed my husband to the grave, if it were not for this son of mine. [*Gesturing towards* ASTYANAX] He is the reason I've fought that impulse to take my own life. He drives me, even after all I've been through, to keep praying to the gods and to prolong my suffering. He's deprived me of the greatest advantage the downtrodden enjoy: having nothing left to fear. Though I have no chance of a return to prosperity, there still remains an avenue for further pain, this child of mine. The most pitiful thing of all is to fear without hope.

OLD MAN: What fresh fear has turned your affliction into terror?

ANDROMACHE: Out of great evil some greater evil stirs. Troy's doom has not yet come to a close. It is still falling.

OLD MAN: What further disaster could god visit upon us, should he wish it?

ANDROMACHE: The gates of infernal Styx have been unlocked. The dark caverns of hell lie open. Even our fallen enemies issue forth from the depths of Dis to ensure that we, broken and ruined, always have something to fear. Is the path back to the world of the living available only to Greeks? Surely death is impartial! The fear that distresses and torments the Phrygian women is shared by all. But the terror that torments my mind is all my own; how awful was the nightmare I had! What a harrowing night!

OLD MAN: Tell us what you saw. Reveal your fearful visions.

ANDROMACHE: Night, the restorer of strength, had almost passed through two thirds of its course, and the seven stars of the luminous Wagon had turned towards morning when at last Sleep, a stranger in my suffering, came to me and crept over my tired eyes ever so briefly – if you can call the stupor of a distraught mind sleep. Suddenly Hector was there, standing before my eyes, not the man who carried the battle to the Greeks themselves, hurling torches made from Ida's forests on to the Greek ships, nor the man who raged through the Greek ranks, slaughtering many and stripping true spoils off a counterfeit Achilles.[23] His countenance did not radiate its usual fiery brilliance. No, he had a tired look, gloomy, weighed down with weeping no less than we, and his hair, unkempt and overgrown, shrouded his face.[24] Still, the sight of him brought me joy.

But he shook his head and said, 'Drive away sleep, faithful wife, and save our son. He must hide; this is his one salvation. Put aside your tears – are you weeping over Troy's fall? If only it had fallen completely! Quickly now, hide our little child, the delicate shoot of our family, out of sight – anywhere you can!'

The icy chill of dread came over me and shook me from sleep. Frightened, I shifted my eyes now this way, now that; with no thought of my son, I looked around for my Hector, but his ghost vanished as I tried to clasp him, cheating my embraces.

[To ASTYANAX] O son, true offspring of a great father, the Phrygians' only hope, the last heir of a ruined house and an ancient bloodline, you are too noble, too like your father! How you resemble my Hector – his face, his gait, his bearing, the way he held his mighty hands, his lofty shoulders, his fierce-looking brow, the way he tossed his long, flowing locks. O son, you were born too late for the Phrygians, too early for your mother! Will that time, will that blessed day ever come when you, the protector and champion of our native land, rebuild the citadel of a resurgent Troy, lead back its citizens scattered around the world in exile, and restore the Phrygians and their country to their rightful name?

What kind of hopes are these? I should remember my own fate; I fear that I pray for too much. No, let us live – that is all captives can hope for.

What place can I stow you, dear son? How I fear for you! Where will I hide you? Our glorious citadel, fortified by military might and the walls built by the gods, a shining beacon for all nations, a great bastion keeping envious eyes in check? But that is nothing but a deep ash-heap now. Everything's been razed to the ground, and in this great wasteland of a city there is not even enough left to hide an infant! What place will I choose for my ruse? There is my dear husband's magnificent tomb, sacred, respected by the enemy, built to an enormous size and at great expense by his father, a king lavish in his grief. Yes, it will be best to entrust you to your father – but a cold sweat drenches my whole body: I tremble at the thought of that deathly place, troubled at what it bodes for you.

OLD MAN: Those in trouble must seize whatever protection is available. The untroubled have time to choose.

ANDROMACHE: I'm deathly afraid someone will betray his hiding place.

OLD MAN: Send away all witnesses to your ruse.

ANDROMACHE: [*motions the* CHORUS *away*] And if the enemy searches for him?

OLD MAN: Say he perished during the destruction of the city. This one thing has kept many from death: the belief that they had already perished.

ANDROMACHE: There's scarcely any hope at all left. His great name is pulling him down like a heavy weight around his neck. What good will hiding do him when he's bound to fall into the enemy's clutches someday?

OLD MAN: Conquerors tend to be brutal only at first.

ANDROMACHE: [*to* ASTYANAX] What place, what isolated place removed from the eyes of men will return you to me safely? Who will relieve our fears? Who will protect us? [*To Hector's tomb*] You, Hector, who have always watched over your family. Watch over us now, too. Safeguard your loyal wife's secret. Receive this boy into your faithful ashes, so that he may live.

Son, enter the tomb, your protection – why do you shrink back? Do you reject hiding as disgraceful? I recognize your true nature: you're ashamed to show fear! O son, shed that great defiance, that courage of old, and instead play the role that Fortune has assigned us. Just look at us! What a tattered band we are: a tomb, a boy and a captive woman. We must give in to our plight. So go, be bold and enter the sacred resting place of your buried father. If the Fates choose to help us in our misery, it will save you. If the Fates deny you life, it will be your tomb.

[ASTYANAX *enters the tomb; the* OLD MAN *locks the door*]

OLD MAN: The doorway is barred. Your son is safely within the vault. So that your fear does not betray his whereabouts, leave this place, take yourself far from your son.

ANDROMACHE: I'd be less worried if I were nearby, but if you think it's best, I will retire to some other place. [*Starts to leave*]

[*Enter* ULYSSES]

OLD MAN: Wait! Hold your speech, contain your grief. The leader of the Cephallenians approaches, leaving a trail of wickedness in his wake.

ANDROMACHE: Earth, gape open! Husband, cleave a passage-way down to the caverns of the underworld and conceal our son, whom I entrusted to you, there, in the deep bosom of Styx! Ulysses is here, with hesitation in his steps and on his face. No doubt he weaves some cunning ploy in his heart.

ULYSSES: [*approaching* ANDROMACHE] I have been delegated by fate to perform a hard task, and I make a request at the

outset: do not think that what I am about to say originated
with me. It is the declaration of every Greek who is prevented
from returning to his long-desired home because of Hector's
offspring. The Fates demand this child's life. The Greeks will
always feel uneasy about this uncertain peace, always looking
over their shoulders in fear, never allowed to put their weapons
down – that is, so long as the Phrygians, even in their current
humble state, can look to your son for courage, Andromache.
This is the divine utterance of the seer Calchas. And even if
the seer Calchas had said nothing, Hector himself used to say
as much, and I dread even his offspring.[25] After all, the seed
of noble stock always develops to match its pedigree. Just so
a small calf trailing in the rear of a great herd, the first signs
of horn not yet cutting through its brow, will suddenly rear
up its neck, hold its head up high, and take charge, giving
orders to its father's herd. So, too, a tender shoot that survives
when a tree trunk is cut down will itself soon rise to match
its mother's heights, restoring shadows to the earth and its
leafy branches to heaven. So, too, the embers of a once-roar-
ing fire incautiously left to die on their own will inevitably
find their former strength.

Resentment is an unjust evaluator of events, it is true, but
if you ponder it over in your heart for a moment, you will
pardon us if, after ten winters and just as many harvests, our
soldiers, now old men, fear new wars, renewed bloodshed and
Troy because it was never put to rest once and for all. It is no
small thing that worries the Greeks, this Hector-to-be. Free
them from fear. This is all that keeps us from setting sail on
the deep sea, the one reason why our fleet remains in harbour.
Please do not think me cruel because I, on the order of Fate,
come for Hector's son. I would have even gone and fetched
Orestes. Suffer now what the conqueror once suffered before.[26]

ANDROMACHE: Son, if only you were now in your mother's arms!
If only I knew what calamity took you from me, what destiny
now holds in store for you, or even where – not even if my
whole breast had been pierced by enemy weapons and my hands
bound by chafing chains, not even if raging flames hemmed me
in on every side would I have neglected my motherly devotion

to you! Son, what place, what lot holds you now? Are you roaming over the countryside, wandering in some remote field? Was your body consumed in the fiery conflagration of your city? Did some cruel captor shed your blood for sport? Did some monstrous beast maul your tiny body and leave you as fodder for the birds of Ida to feast on?

ULYSSES: Put an end to this charade! You won't easily deceive Ulysses. I've untangled mothers' deceptions before, even when those mothers were goddesses.[27] Away with this fruitless scheme! Now, where is your son?

ANDROMACHE: Where is Hector? The rest of the Phrygians? Priam? You are looking for but one. I'm looking for it all.

ULYSSES: If you refuse to tell me, I'll force you to confess. It is a foolish brand of devotion to conceal what you must straight-way reveal.

ANDROMACHE: A woman who can, ought, and wants to die has nothing left to lose.

ULYSSES: Those proud boasts will vanish once you're staring at death.

ANDROMACHE: Ulysses, if you intend to use fear to coerce Andromache, then threaten her with life. I *pray* for death.

ULYSSES: Flogging, fire, dungeon, torture – these will cause you pain, pain which will drive the truth out of you against your will and root out the secrets buried deep inside your breast. Compulsion always trumps devotion.

ANDROMACHE: Bring on your flames, your beatings, your count-less techniques of causing unbearable pain. Bring on hunger and raging thirst, send from every side various instruments of torment. Sear iron into my flesh, lock me in the foul air of a dark dungeon – bring on all the inhuman forms of torture conquerors inflict when angry and frightened. A determined mother doesn't know the meaning of fear.

ULYSSES: That same love which drives you to be so stubborn is what prompts the Greeks to take these measures – we're think-ing of our children! After ten years, after seemingly endless warfare, I would fear the threats that Calchas prophesies less if I were worried only for myself. But you are preparing wars for my son Telemachus!

ANDROMACHE: I have no wish to bring joy to the Greeks,
Ulysses, yet I have no choice. It's time – oh the pain! – to
reveal the grief and sorrow I've been holding inside. Rejoice,
sons of Atreus! Ulysses, go report the happy news to the
Greeks as you are accustomed to do: Hector's offspring has
met his end.

ULYSSES: What guarantee can you offer the Greeks that this is
true?

ANDROMACHE: Ulysses, if I am lying, if Astyanax still looks
upon the light of day, may I be denied death, the greatest threat
a conqueror can impose, and my greatest wish. May the Fates
not unravel my life swiftly and gently or give me burial in my
own land, and may the native earth lie heavily upon my
husband Hector, if what I say isn't true. Astyanax resides
among the dead. He has been interred in a tomb and has
received the burial that the lifeless are owed.[28]

ULYSSES: I will happily report back to the Greeks that the will
of destiny has been fulfilled, that Hector's line has been snuffed
out, and that there is nothing left to fear.

[ULYSSES *begins to walk off, but stops short of exiting
and speaks an aside*] What are you doing, Ulysses? The
Greeks will believe you, naturally, but who are you putting
your trust in? A mother? But surely no mother would fabric-
ate such a story without dreading that the omen would
come true, that the child would die a dreadful death – people
fear omens even if they have nothing else to fear. And she
bound herself by a sacred oath! Yet if she swore falsely, what
worse plight could she fear? Come now, Ulysses, summon
up your guile, your tricks, your cunning. Summon up the
full power of Ulysses.

[*Observing* ANDROMACHE] The truth never wholly
vanishes. Look carefully at his mother. Look how she grieves,
cries, groans. But she also paces back and forth anxiously,
perking up her ears, listening intently for voices. This woman
here fears more than she grieves. It is time to employ your
cunning. [*To* ANDROMACHE] It is proper to comfort parents
in grief, but I congratulate you, poor woman, for the loss
of your boy. After all, a grim death lay in store for him. He

was to be flung headfirst from the last standing tower in Troy.

ANDROMACHE: [*aside*] My spirit has left my shaking and trembling limbs. My blood has grown sluggish, gripped as it is by the icy chill of fear.

ULYSSES: [*aside*] She shudders. This is the angle from which I must probe the woman. Fear has betrayed the mother; I must now redouble her fears. [*To his men*] Go, go quickly, men! Root out that child, our enemy, the last threat to the Greek name! He has been deceitfully hidden by his mother. Wherever he lurks, expose him and bring him into the open! [*A pause; to one soldier, pretending* ASTYANAX *has been found*] Excellent! We've got him. Come on, be quick! Drag him here – [*to* ANDROMACHE] Why do you look back in fear? I thought he had already perished!

ANDROMACHE: I wish I were afraid. It's just that . . . that fear has been my constant companion, seemingly forever now. It takes time for the mind to unlearn old habits.

ULYSSES: Well then, because your son perished before we performed the purification rites for the walls and cannot fulfil the seer's command, saved as he was by a better fate, there is only one way that the ships about to set sail for home can be purified: we must scatter Hector's ashes in the sea to placate it and level his whole tomb to the ground. So Calchas decreed, so it will be. Now, because that boy has escaped the death he was meant to suffer, we are forced to lay our hands upon Hector's sacred resting place.

ANDROMACHE: [*aside*] What am I to do? Twin terrors tear at my soul – on this side my son, on that the ashes of my dear husband. Which will prevail? I swear by the cruel gods and you, divine ghost of my husband, my only true god, that nothing else pleases me in my son except that he reminds me of you. Let him live, so that he may revive your handsome features.

But can I allow your ashes to be dug out of the tomb and sunk into the deep? Can I let your remains be scattered all over the vast seas?

No, let this boy meet his doom!

How can you, as a mother, stand and watch your son handed over to a monstrous death, flung from the lofty tower wall?

I can and will endure it, I will, so long as my Hector is not violated after death, so long as his ashes are not scattered into the sea by our conqueror's hands.

Yet my boy will feel his punishment, while Hector – well, death protects him from pain. Why are you wavering? Decide. Decide which you will surrender to punishment. You ungrateful woman, do you really waver? Your Hector is in there! No, you have got it wrong: Hector is in both places. But this Hector here is alive and conscious, and is perhaps destined to be his slain father's avenger. It is not possible to spare both. What on earth are you going to do? Of the two, Andromache, save the one the Greeks fear.

ULYSSES: I will fulfil the god's command. I swear I will demolish his tomb utterly.

ANDROMACHE: The one you Greeks ransomed?[29]

ULYSSES: I will not stop until his grave is completely destroyed.

ANDROMACHE: I call upon the heavenly gods and Achilles to observe their promises: Pyrrhus, protect your father's gift to us!

ULYSSES: This tomb will soon be levelled to the ground.

ANDROMACHE: Even Greeks never dared to commit such an outrage! You violated temples, even those of the gods who helped you. But even in your madness you never touched a tomb. I will oppose you, an unarmed woman against her armed foe. Anger will give me strength. Like a fierce Amazon laying waste to Greek squadrons, like a Maenad who, inspired and possessed by the god, terrorizes forests, striding with the god's steps and dealing out wounds without realizing it – just so will I rush into the fray and defend my husband's tomb, even if I should fall and join my husband's ashes.

ULYSSES: [to his men] Why have you stopped? Are you touched by this woman's pitiful protests, her meaningless raging? Carry out your orders, now!

ANDROMACHE: [putting herself in the way] You'll have to strike me down first and cut me down with your swords. [ULYSSES *pushes* ANDROMACHE *aside*] No! Don't push me away! Hector, break through the barriers of death, heave open the earth! Even as a ghost you are enough to crush Ulysses! [*Hallucinating*] See, he's brandishing weapons and hurling firebrands! Greeks, do you see Hector? Or do I alone see him?

ULYSSES: I *will* demolish the whole thing to the ground.

ANDROMACHE: [*to herself*] What are you doing? Are you not a mother? Will you allow both your son and husband to be crushed under the collapse of one tomb? Perhaps you can prevail upon the Greeks with entreaties – the enormous weight of the tomb is about to shatter your hidden boy's body. Poor child! Let him perish anywhere else, lest father smother son and son crush father. [*She falls before* ULYSSES] I fall at your knees, Ulysses, and beseech you. I have never begged before. This right hand has never touched the feet of another, but now it touches yours: pity a mother, look favourably on these prayers I make as a devoted mother. Do not react violently. The more highly the gods in heaven exalt you, the more gently you should step on the downtrodden. Fortune takes notice when you act mercifully to a person in need. In return I pray that you once again behold the bed of your blameless wife and that Laertes draws out his years until he embraces you on your return.[30] I pray that your young son welcomes you home and that he, exceeding all your hopes and desires, lives a blessed life, surpassing his grandfather in years and his father in cunning. Please, pity a mother! This son of mine is the only comfort I have left in my suffering.

ULYSSES: Produce your son, then we'll talk.

ANDROMACHE: [*turning to song, opening Hector's tomb and calling* ASTYANAX *forth from it*]
Come forth from your concealment, son,
your desperate mother's sad, sad ruse.
Look, look, Ulysses, here is what
strikes terror in your thousand ships!
Extend your hands, plead for your life,
kneel at your master's feet and beg:

if Fortune bids that we be beggars,
in begging, then, there is no shame.
Forget your royal ancestors,
old Priam's empire, renowned
throughout the world, forget your father
and play the captive. Son, if yet
you do not know your fate, kneel down
and imitate your mother's tears.

Troy witnessed once before a boy's
tears, when the king, small Priam, soothed
the threats of savage Hercules,
a terrifying man, before
whose might all monstrous beasts succumbed,
who shattered terribly the gates
of hell and forged a dark path back.
Tears, tiny tears subdued that man;
moved by his little foe's appeals,
he said, 'Assume the kingdom's reins,
sit high upon your father's throne,
but wield the sceptre with more honour.'[31]
Such was that captor's conduct. Learn
compassion from great Hercules –
or are his arms all that you prize?[32]
Behold, a suppliant now lies
before your feet, no meaner than
young Priam, begging for his life.
Kingship of Troy? Let Fortune take
that gift wherever she desires.

ULYSSES: A distraught mother's grief does move me, but I am
far more moved by the thought of Greek mothers and the
great sorrows that your boy will bring them if he grows to
manhood.

ANDROMACHE: The ruins of a city reduced to ash, these ruins
about us – do you think this boy will conjure them back to
life? Look at these hands! How could they raise up Troy? Troy
has lost all hope, all hope indeed, if these are the hopes on
which it rests. We Trojans are ruined! We couldn't possibly

cause fear in anyone. You say he gets courage from his father? The one Achilles dragged around the city? Even Hector himself would have lost courage after Troy's fall. The weight of this great disaster would have crushed him. If you want revenge, force this boy to bow his noble neck beneath the ignoble yoke of servitude. Force him to be a slave; there is no punishment worse than this. Would anyone refuse a king this mercy?

ULYSSES: Calchas refuses you this, not Ulysses.

ANDROMACHE: You contriver of deception, you architect of wickedness! No one ever fell through your prowess in war, but even Greeks have perished through the devious cunning of your malicious mind![33] Are you really using the seer and the blameless gods to disguise your nefarious plans? This is a deed of your own doing. You night-time soldier, brave when it comes to slaying children, do you only now find the courage to act unaided and in the light of day?[34]

ULYSSES: The Greeks know Ulysses' prowess in war. The Phrygians know it all too well. There's no time to while away the day with pointless words: the fleet is weighing anchor!

ANDROMACHE: Grant us the luxury of a few moments, so that I can perform a mother's duty, offer my son a final farewell, and with a final embrace try to fill the insatiable void in my anguished heart.

ULYSSES: I wish that I could show you mercy, but I at least can grant you this, a short delay. Wallow in tears to your heart's content. Crying relieves suffering.

ANDROMACHE: [to ASTYANAX] You sweet child, bond of love, glory of a ruined house, the final death at Troy and great source of terror for the Greeks: I once prayed – fool that I was – for you to equal your father's reputation in war and your grandfather's age in years. But a god has frustrated these prayers of mine. You will never wield Troy's sceptre in the royal halls as lord or dispense laws to your people. You will never conquer foreign nations and force them to bow to you, or cut down Greeks as they flee from you, or drag Pyrrhus behind your chariot. You will never wield tiny weapons in your tender hands and boldly pursue wild animals scattered throughout the wide glades, or lead the speeding cavalry squadrons in their manoeuvres, you their noble captain, during the sacred ritual of the Trojan Games.[35] You will never join in the ancient cult-dances in our Phrygian temples, swiftly leaping about the altars on nimble foot as the curved horn calls out its frenzied measures. The manner of your death is more bitter than your death itself! The walls are about to witness a death that will produce more tears than the slaying of mighty Hector!

ULYSSES: You must break off your motherly weeping now. Great sorrow does not come to an end on its own.

ANDROMACHE: Ulysses, I seek only a brief moment for my tears. Allow me to close with my own hand these tiny eyes of my child while he still lives. [To ASTYANAX] You will die a small child, yet one already greatly feared. Your Troy awaits you. Go forth, my son, into freedom. Go join your fellow Trojans who are already free.

ASTYANAX: No, mother, I beg you!

ANDROMACHE Why do you cling to my breast? Why cling to your mother's arms for protection, powerless as they are? A tender calf might nestle in close to its mother's side when it hears a lion's roar, but that pitiless lion will just push aside the mother and attack his lesser prey with his enormous jaws, mauling it and carrying it off. In the same way will the enemy wrench you from my embraces. Take these kisses, these tears, this lock of hair torn from my head. Fill yourself with my love and take all of this to your father quickly. But also take to him a few words, your mother's complaint. Ask him, 'If the ghosts below care at all about the loved ones they have left behind, if love is not extinguished by the fire that consumes the body, how, cruel Hector, how can you allow your Andromache to serve a Greek man? How can you just lie there, indifferent and detached? Achilles came back!' Here, again, take these locks of hair, take these tears, all that remain after my husband's piteous funeral. Take these kisses, son, and deliver them to your father. But leave your shirt to comfort your mother; it's touched my husband's tomb, his beloved ghost. I will press it against my face to search for any trace of ash that might still remain.

ULYSSES: There will never be any end to this weeping. Remove
   this boy who keeps the Greek ships from sailing.
      [ULYSSES *and his men leave with* ASTYANAX]

CHORUS III: The Diaspora of Trojan Women

   Captive women, what lands will we call home?
   Thessaly's high mountains and shade-rich Tempe?
   Iolcus, lording over the boundless sea, or
   small Gyrtone in Tricca's barren landscape,
   or Mothone teeming with fleeting streams, or
   Phthia, breeder of stalwart fighting men and
   hardy herds, or Trachis, that rugged city
   cloaked beneath the shade of lush Oeta's forests,
   land that sent the perilous bow to ruin
      Troy for a second time?
   Or Olenus, nearly deserted ghost town,
   or that city detested by the virgin
   goddess, Pleuron, or Troezen's curving shoreline?
   Or Mount Pelion, lofty realm of Prothous,
   final stepping stone to the gates of heaven,[36]
   where once Chiron used to reside, his giant
   body filling his cavernous mountain home
   as he trained his already savage student
   to strum songs on the lyre-strings – even then
   he was whetting Achilles' fearsome fury,
      singing of war and strife.
   Or Carystus, where marbled stones abound?
   Chalcis, land encroaching upon unsettled
   seas, the furious tides of narrow Euripus?
   Or Calydnae, easily reached in any
   wind, or Gonoessa, that windswept city?
   Enispe, which dreads the north wind's bite, or
   sprawling Crete, the isle of one hundred cities?
   Peparethus, looming over Attic shores,
   or Eleusis, joyed by its secret Mysteries?
   Is my lot true Ajax's abode, Salamis, or
   Calydon, renowned for its savage beast,[37]

or the cities washed by the Titaressus
as it crawls to the sea with sluggish waters?
Bessa, Scarphe or Pylos, land of old men,
Pharis, Pisae, Jupiter's land or Elis,
    famed for Olympic crowns?

Let that baleful tempest conduct our wretched
band wherever it will, to any Greek land –
only keep us far from the land of Sparta,
evil bringer of doom for Greeks and Trojans;
keep us far from Argos, from savage Pelops'
realm, Mycenae, from tiny Neritos, dwarfed
by Zacynthus, and Ithaca's treacherous rocks.
    [*Enter* HECUBA, POLYXENA]
Hecuba, what fate will be yours? What master
comes to carry you off? What lands will witness
a queen's slavery and her longed-for death?

ACT IV

[HELEN *enters, coming from the Greek fleet*]

HELEN: [*aside*] Every doomed, unhappy marriage that brings
with it weeping, slaughter, bloodshed and woeful groans
deserves to have Helen preside over it. I am compelled to harm
Trojans even after they have been vanquished. The Greeks
have ordered me – *me* of all people – to announce a sham
wedding with Pyrrhus, to outfit the girl in Greek dress, and
to give her the appearance of a Greek bride. By my guile, by
my deception Paris' sister will be ensnared and cut down in
sacrifice. May she never know the truth! Thus, I think, it will
be easier for her to bear. Dying without fear of death is the
finest of all deaths. [*To herself*] Why do you hesitate to carry
out your orders? After all, responsibility for a crime committed under compulsion belongs to the one who ordered it.

[*To Polyxena*] High-born maiden of the house of Dardanus,
a more compassionate god has begun to look more kindly
upon your afflicted people and is ready to dower you with a
blessed marriage. Such a union neither Troy nor Priam could
have hoped to give you, even in their former prosperous state.
The most glorious man of the Greek race, the man who holds
in his possession a far-reaching kingdom, the wide fields of
Thessaly, asks for your hand in the holy sacrament of marriage.
Great Tethys, the countless sea-nymphs, and Thetis who calms
the swollen seas, will all call you family. When you are given
to Pyrrhus in marriage, your new in-laws Peleus and Nereus
will call you daughter.[38] So remove those clothes of mourning
and put on this festive bridal attire instead. Unlearn your
captive ways. Your hair is so unkempt and bristly! Let me

arrange it into braids[39] – I'm a practised hand at this. You never know, perhaps this calamity will install you on an even loftier throne! Many women have benefited from being captured, you know.

ANDROMACHE: The conquered Trojans had suffered every kind of misfortune but one, Helen – until now. You are asking us to celebrate while our demolished city smoulders all around us. What a time for a wedding! Who'd dare to say no to *you*? Who wouldn't leap at the chance to enter into a marriage recommended by *Helen*? You of all people! You bearer of plague, you bringer of doom and disaster to both peoples, don't you see these tombs of great leaders? Don't you see the exposed, unburied remains of men littered all over the battle-field? This carnage *your* marriage caused. For *you* the blood of Asia and Europe flowed, and all the while you sat idly by, watching your husbands fight it out, undecided for whom you should pray. So go on, arrange this wedding. We've already got torches and ceremonial flames. Look! Troy's fires will illuminate this unprecedented wedding! Women of Troy, celebrate Pyrrhus' marriage, celebrate it as you should: unleash your wails, beat your breasts in mourning!

HELEN: I know that people in great pain are wholly irrational and inflexible, and that they sometimes even direct their anger towards their fellow sufferers. Still, I have a compelling case, even before a hostile judge. I have suffered worse than you. So, Andromache mourns for Hector, Hecuba for Priam? Only Helen has to mourn in secrecy for her man, Paris. You argue that servitude is harsh, hateful and heavy to bear? True. I myself have long borne the yoke of slavery; I've been a captive for ten years! Troy has been levelled to the ground, her protective gods overturned? It's devastating to lose one's country, but think how much more devastating it is to *fear* one's country. You have a whole company of sufferers to comfort you in your plight. Me? Both conqueror and conquered rage against me equally. It has long remained in doubt which Trojan woman each Greek would take as his slave. Well, my master hauled me off immediately without so much as casting lots. You say I caused the war and brought such disaster to the

Trojans? Fine, believe that if you like. But don't forget that it
wasn't a *Spartan* ship that cleaved a path through *your* seas.
Now, if I was nothing more than stolen goods hauled off on
a Trojan ship, if I was awarded as a prize to the judge by the
goddess he judged most beautiful, then it is Paris who should
be begging for your pardon, not me. At any rate, you can be
sure that my case will be decided by an angry judge. My fate
lies in the hands of Menelaus. So please, Andromache, put
aside your sorrow long enough to help me prevail upon this
girl – I can hardly hold back my own tears!

ANDROMACHE: [*aside*] How awful is the plight that causes
Helen to cry! Wait – why *is* she crying? [*To Helen*] Tell us,
what deception, what wickedness is the Ithacan now weaving
for us? Is the girl to be hurled from Ida's peaks? Thrown from
the rocky ledge of our once-towering citadel? Hurled into the
sea from these very cliffs, the sheer sea wall overhanging
Sigeum's shallows? Speak, reveal the secret you hide beneath
that false front of yours. Everything we have suffered so far
is easier to bear than imagining Pyrrhus as Priam's and Hecuba's son-in-law. Tell us! Divulge what punishment awaits the
girl. Do not add deceit to our disasters. The women you see
here are prepared to meet death.

HELEN: How I wish that the gods' mouthpiece had ordered me
to end with a sword-stroke my life, lingering too long as it is
in this hateful light, or to fall before Achilles' tomb beneath
the blow of Pyrrhus' furious hand and accompany you in your
doom, my poor Polyxena. Achilles orders that you be awarded
to him, sacrificed before his ashes, so that he may be a lawfully
wedded husband in the Field of Elysium.

ANDROMACHE: [*pointing to* POLYXENA] Do you see how
joyfully this girl's glorious spirit received news of her death?
Now she reaches for her royal wedding dress. *Now* she allows
her hair to be touched. Her earlier fate, marrying Pyrrhus, she
considered death, but she regards this death a marriage! [*Turning to* HECUBA, *who staggers and collapses*] Oh! Her poor
mother is dazed by the grim news, her mind reels, sending her
to the ground. Rise, poor woman, lift up your heart, brace
your failing courage! How fragile is the bond that keeps this

frail woman alive, how little it would take to make Hecuba
blessed and happy! She breathes. Life has returned. Death is
the first to flee the miserable.

HECUBA: Does Achilles live on to torment the Phrygians? Does
he still fight on? How weak was Paris' blow![40] His very ashes,
his very tomb thirst for our blood. Not long ago I was blessed
in children, surrounded by my brood, tiring out from kissing
all of them and dividing my motherly attention amongst my
flourishing flock. Now this girl is all that remains, my hope,
my companion, my comfort and calm amidst my troubles. She
is the whole of Hecuba's offspring, hers the one voice to call
me mother. O life, O harsh, luckless life, go on, slip away!
Save me from witnessing at least this one death!

ANDROMACHE:[41] Oh! Tears drench her cheeks, suddenly falling
like rain from her eyes overcome with sorrow! [To POLYXENA]
Child, be happy and rejoice: Cassandra and Andromache
would want this marriage of yours very much! [To HECUBA]
It is we, Hecuba, yes we, who need mourning. For the fleet
will soon set sail and bear us all over the Greek world. This
girl will be covered by the beloved earth of her native land.

HELEN: You'll envy her all the more when you learn your own
fate.

ANDROMACHE: What part of my punishment do I not yet know?

HELEN: The urn has poured out the lots, awarding captives to
masters.

ANDROMACHE: To whom am I given as slave? Tell me, whom
will I call my master?

HELEN: The youth from Scyros, Pyrrhus, took you with the first
lot.

ANDROMACHE: Cassandra, how blessed you are! Your madness
and Phoebus exempted you from the lot!

HELEN: She was awarded to the king of kings, Agamemnon.

HECUBA: Does someone want Hecuba to be called his own?

HELEN: The Ithacan Ulysses obtained you, a short-lived prize,
against his will.

HECUBA: What an unjust allotment, awarding queens to kings!
What distributor of lots is so sadistic, so harsh, so cruel as to
do this? What god distributed these captive women so

perversely? What heartless judge, oppressor of the oppressed,
does not know how to choose masters justly, and with a pitiless hand distributes unjust destinies to the vanquished? Who
would unite Hector's mother with the possessor of Achilles'
armour?[42] I am called to serve Ulysses! Now I feel conquered,
a true captive overwhelmed by disaster. I'm ashamed not of
slavery, but of my master. That, that barren island, surrounded
by the cruel sea, does not have enough room for my tomb.
Lead on, Ulysses, lead on. I won't resist. I follow my master
willingly. But know that I carry my destiny with me. You will
find no tranquil waters on your journey, only raging seas
swollen by the winds' wrath. I bring with me wars and flames
– every disaster Priam and I suffered. And while that retribution inexorably approaches, in the meantime this will serve
as your punishment: I commandeered your lot and robbed
you of a real prize.

[Enter PYRRHUS *with Greek soldiers*]

But here comes Pyrrhus with hurried steps and an intense
look upon his face. Pyrrhus, don't hesitate! Come here, unseal
my chest with your sword and unite the in-laws of your father
Achilles. Go on, you butcher of the old. My blood, too, should
be just right for you.[43] [PYRRHUS *ignores* HECUBA *and goes
straight for* POLYXENA] He seizes her and drags her off! Go
ahead, defile the heavenly gods with your foul slaughter, defile
the spirits of the dead! This is my prayer for all of you, that
you encounter dreadful seas to match this dreadful sacrifice,
that the whole Greek fleet, all one thousand ships of it, meets
the same fate that I pray *my* ship meets when I set sail.[44]

[PYRRHUS *and the Greek soldiers leave with* POLYXENA]

CHORUS IV: Suffering Loves Company

It is sweet, the sight of a mourning throng,
sweet, the echoing sounds of grief when grieving.
Sorrow stings and bereavement bites less deeply
when surrounded by crowds of fellow mourners.
Spiteful, ever spiteful is Grief, cruel creature,
cheered that many others endure the same,

that it is not Destiny's only plaything.
Misery, when suffered by all and sundry,
   none would reject or spurn.

No one would believe himself poor (even if true),
if successful folk were removed, and the wealthy
who are swimming in gold; subtract those owning
great plantations ploughed by a hundred oxen,
and the battered spirits of paupers will soar:
one's misfortune is measured next to others'.
It is sweet, when disaster swirls about you,
that no countenance wears a happy smile.

Shipwrecked men, if sailing alone on vessels
built for one, complain and bemoan their fortune
as they clutch the sands of their hoped-for haven.
They endure misfortune and storms more calmly
if they see that a thousand hulls are swallowed
by the sea alongside their own, the beaches
strewn with wreckage driven ashore by ceaseless
breakers filled with the rage of Corus' gales.

Phrixus, Helle's brother, bemoaned her fall,
when that ram with a radiant fleece of gold,
leader of his flock, bore away upon his
back both brother and sister over the deep.
Rearing up, the ram cast the poor girl into the sea.
Yet Deucalion and his wife, fair Pyrrha,
swallowed their complaints when they saw the seas
and saw nothing else but the seas around them,
the last humans left on the barren earth.

We assembled here will disband, our tears
scattered far and wide as the fleet disperses,
when the trumpet announces time to set sail,
and strong sailors, with racing oar-strokes and wind,
head for high seas, and the shoreline fades from view.
Wretched women, what thoughts will come to you

when land starts to dwindle and sea-waves swell,
when Mount Ida vanishes in the distance?
Then a boy to mother and mother to son
will point out the spot where great Troy lies ruined,
saying, 'Troy is there, where the smoke snakes skyward,
where that foul-looking cloud of ash looms large.'
This is how the Trojans will spot their country.

ACT V

[*Enter* MESSENGER]

MESSENGER: What grievous deaths! How brutal, pitiful, harrowing! Has Mars seen anything so inhuman, so grim in ten years of murderous warfare? What report would you have me give first through my own tears and groans? Whose tears should I cause first – yours, Andromache, or yours, old woman?

HECUBA: Whatever sad tale you weep over, you can be sure I weep over it too. Each woman has her own disaster weighing on her. I am weighed down by the disasters of all my people. I feel everything that perishes. Everyone who suffers adds to Hecuba's suffering.

MESSENGER: The girl has been sacrificed, the boy hurled from the walls. Both bore their deaths bravely as befits their lofty station.

ANDROMACHE: Relate the whole sequence of the slaughter, recount the twin acts of wickedness: do not leave any detail out. Those in great pain delight in examining every aspect of their suffering. Speak, describe everything.

MESSENGER: There is a tower, the only one to survive mighty Troy's fall, the customary haunt of Priam. There he used to sit, presiding over the war, directing his forces from that lofty bastion. On this tower the elderly king used to hold his grandson in his comforting arms. From here, when Hector routed the Greeks, gripped with great fear, and turned them on their heels with steel and fire, he would show the boy his father's exploits. To this once famous tower and glory of the walls, now but a menacing spire, the whole mass of Greeks swarmed, both leaders and the rank and file, leaving their ships behind

to assemble in this one place. Some climbed an outlying hill
that offered them a clear view, others sought the top of a high
outcropping, a great crowd of people poised eagerly on their
tiptoes. Some climbed pines, some laurels, some beech trees
– the whole forest shivered from the mass of people clinging
to its treetops. Others scrambled up to the top of a sheer
mountain cliff, or risked adding their weight to scorched
rooftops or an unstable, projecting stone along the teetering
wall, while still others – oh the horror! – took a seat upon
Hector's burial mound to watch – a shameful theatre for a
shameful spectacle.

Through these tightly packed crowds the Ithacan marched
with imposing strides, towing Priam's little grandson behind
him by this right hand. But the boy matched him stride for
stride and directed his steps straight to the lofty walls. When
he had taken his position, poised on the very edge of that
lofty tower, he cast fierce looks this way and that, undaunted,
fearless. Just as the tiny, tender offspring of a fearsome beast,
unable yet to savage his enemies with his teeth, will nonetheless rear up threateningly and snap its feeble jaws,
showing its readiness to fight, so too did that boy react
fiercely, gallantly, though in his enemy's clutches. He moved
to tears the rank and file, the leaders, even Ulysses himself;
out of the whole crowd the only one who did not weep was
the one for whom everyone was weeping. Then, as Ulysses
uttered the ritual prayers of the doom-dealing prophet and
summoned the pitiless gods to the sacrifice, the boy leapt of
his own will and plunged into the very heart of Priam's
kingdom.

ANDROMACHE: Has any Colchian or nomadic Scythian ever
perpetrated such an act? Have any of those lawless nations
lapped by the waters of the Caspian Sea ever dared such a
crime? Never were the altars of savage Busiris stained by a
young boy's blood; never did Diomedes give his herd of horses
tiny limbs to feed on! Who will bury your body, my son, who
will place you in your tomb?

MESSENGER: What body? Nothing could have survived that
steep fall! His bones were shattered, dashed to pieces by the

heavy impact. That glorious body, that face, those noble features, so like his father's, were crushed as his weight came crashing down to the earth below. His neck snapped on impact with the rock, his head cracked open and his whole brain gushed out. He lies there, a shapeless mass of flesh.

ANDROMACHE: How he resembles his father in this way, too!

MESSENGER: After the boy fell headfirst from the lofty walls, the whole crowd of Greeks lamented the abominable act that they themselves had perpetrated. Yet that same crowd then returned to Achilles' tomb to witness yet another atrocity.

The far side of his tomb mound is gently washed by the shallow Rhoetean waters. But the landward side is encircled by open ground, which rises gently until the whole central area is enclosed by a sandy knoll, forming a kind of natural theatre. A buzzing, packed crowd filled the whole shore: some believed that Polyxena's death would release the fleet from its mooring, while others were jubilant to see the enemy's stock be destroyed, root and branch, once and for all. The majority of the fickle crowd, however, was revolted by the atrocity – but watched all the same. Even the Trojans crowded around the funeral of their own and, full of dread, came to watch as the final act of Troy's fall played out.

Suddenly a procession of torches appeared, just as in a wedding. It was led by the matron of honour, Helen, daughter of Tyndareus, her head lowered in sadness. 'May Hermione enjoy a wedding such as this,'[45] one Trojan prayed. 'May this be how that filthy Helen is returned to her husband,' prayed another. Shock and fright gripped them, gripped them all, both Trojans and Greeks alike. The girl herself bowed her head out of modesty, but even though her eyes were cast down they were not downcast: they sparkled brilliantly and in these her final moments an unusual beauty radiated from her, just as the light of the Sun is more enchanting just before it sets beneath the horizon, when the stars rise to resume their courses and the approaching night presses hard on the dying day.

The whole crowd stood in shock. Some were moved by her glorious beauty, some by her delicate age, and others by the fickle nature of the universe. But everyone was moved by her bravery in the face of death. She walked in front, Pyrrhus behind. Everyone's hearts pounded; they looked on in both awe and pity. As soon as she had taken her place on the top of the mound and the young man had taken his stand on the top of his father's tomb, that formidable woman did not draw back, but turned to face the blow, glaring fiercely at her slayer. Such bravery struck the minds of all onlookers and caused a remarkable occurrence: Pyrrhus was slow to kill! When he did drive the sword deep into her body, burying the blade with his right hand, blood erupted from the yawning wound as death took her. Yet even in death she did not put aside her defiance: she fell in such as way as to make the earth heavy for Achilles, forward and with violent impact. Both nations wept. The Trojans grieved silently out of fear. The conquerors wailed loudly.

Such was the order of the sacrifice. The blood flowed copiously from the girl, but it did not stand or pool on the surface. No, the tomb swallowed it all at once, savagely drinking deep every drop.

HECUBA: Go, Greeks, go: head for your homes in safety now. Have your fleet unfurl its sails without worry and cut through the seas on which you have longed to travel. The girl and boy have fallen. The war is concluded.

Where will I take my tears? Where will I spit out this life-breath that keeps an old woman alive? Should I weep for my daughter or my grandson? For my husband or my country? For everything or me? O death, how I long for you! Do you only come to infants and girls, violent and vicious when you come early? Is it I alone that you fear, that you shun? I sought you out the whole night through, amidst the swords, the arrows, the firebrands – why do you flee me when I desperately crave you so? Neither the enemy nor the city's collapse nor its fires consumed my limbs – even though I stood right next to Priam!

MESSENGER: All you captive women, return to the sea at once, with no delay in your steps. The ships are already unfurling the sails. The fleet is departing!

All leave

PHAEDRA

Preface to *Phaedra*

To understand *Phaedra* fully one must know the long and some-what complicated relationship between Athens and Crete in myth. Because Seneca presents Phaedra's unnatural passion as inherited from her family, we must go back one generation and begin with her mother, Pasiphae, the wife of King Minos of Crete. Although she herself had done nothing wrong, Pasiphae was stricken with the unnatural desire to mate with a wild bull for two reasons. First, because Pasiphae's father, the all-seeing Sun, had informed Vulcan that his wife Venus was having an affair with Mars, Venus had cursed all of the Sun's offspring with bad sexual relationships. Second, her husband Minos had offended Neptune by failing to sacrifice the splendid bull the god had sent to him, as he had promised to do. This bull became the object of Pasiphae's lust, but at a loss how she might fulfil her desire, she enlisted the help of the exiled Athenian inventor Daedalus, who constructed a hollow artificial cow so that Pasiphae could mate with the bull. When Minos saw the product of his wife's monstrous coupling, the half-man, half-bull Minotaur ('Minos' Bull'), he compelled Daedalus to build the maze-like labyrinth, in which the monstrous Minotaur could safely be imprisoned.

When the young Theseus arrived in Athens and was reunited with his father Aegeus, he found the city subject to the author-ity of King Minos, who, as punishment for his son's death there, was forcing the Athenians to offer up fourteen young men and women each year to be sacrificed to the Minotaur. Theseus volun-tarily went as one of these sacrificial victims and killed the Minotaur, thus freeing Athens from Crete's control. But he could not have accomplished this mission without the assistance of

Minos' and Pasiphae's daughter Ariadne, who gave to him a ball
of string so that he could retrace his steps out of the winding
labyrinth. Although he promised Ariadne that he would take
her back home to Athens and marry her, Theseus cruelly abandoned her on the island of Naxos.

After Theseus succeeded his father as king of Athens, he sailed
with Hercules against the Amazons and while on this campaign
he slept with the queen Antiope, fathering a son, Hippolytus.
For some reason Theseus killed Antiope; we are not told why
in the play, but other sources inform us that when Theseus was
getting married to Phaedra (Minos' daughter and so Ariadne's
sister!), Antiope burst in fully armed with the other Amazons
and was killed by Theseus in the ensuing fight. However that
may be, Theseus had two sons by Phaedra, who were raised
alongside the now illegitimate Hippolytus.

Some years later, Theseus decided to assist his friend Pirithous
in his foolhardy attempt to abduct Proserpina, the queen of the
underworld, and make her his wife. This mission ended in disaster. Both Pirithous and Theseus were captured and held prisoner.
When our play begins, four years have passed since Theseus left
on this ill-starred expedition. In the intervening time Phaedra
(doomed no less than her mother Pasiphae to have an unnatural
passion) has fallen desperately in love with her strapping stepson
Hippolytus, now a young man. He, in turn, as a devotee of the
virgin goddess Artemis and the son of the man-hating Amazons,
rejects the very idea of sex with any woman, much less with his
stepmother.

Thus, at the beginning of our play we have all the ingredients
needed for a drama employing the motif of Potiphar's wife: a
married woman's attempted seduction of a younger man, his
rejection of her, the woman's accusation of rape in anger for
being scorned, her husband's blind faith in the accusation and,
finally, the demise of the innocent young man at his hands. This
is the basic outline of both Seneca's *Phaedra* and its predecessor
Euripides' *Hippolytus*, but the two could not be more different
in the portrayal of the main characters and the dramatic movement. Euripides' play begins with a prologue delivered by
Aphrodite, who proclaims that Hippolytus must die for his

rejection of her divinity and that Phaedra, though innocent, must perish in order for Aphrodite to achieve her revenge. Seneca's play not only eliminates all divine influence, but also reverses the guilt of the two main characters: Phaedra rather than Hippolytus is viewed as reprehensible. At the very end of the play Theseus gives Hippolytus a royal burial by cremation, but orders dirt to be heaped upon Phaedra's corpse, praying that 'the earth weigh heavily upon her wicked soul'.

Euripides wrote two plays on the subject and Sophocles one, but only the second Euripidean play has survived. The first, which apparently caused quite a negative reaction from the audience for something 'inappropriate and deserving censure', is lost, except for a few fragments and comments by later authors. Some have assumed that Seneca's play, because it differs substantially from the surviving Euripidean version, must have been based on Euripides' first attempt. On this reading, Phaedra's personal confession of her lust for Hippolytus in Seneca's play reflects the 'inappropriate' material in the first Euripidean play (in Euripides' surviving play the Nurse reveals Phaedra's desire). However, the argument that Seneca's play can be used to reconstruct Euripides' lost play is entirely circular and should be discarded. Seneca is also indebted to Ovid's treatment of the myth in *Heroides* 4 (Phaedra's letter to Hippolytus).

Some manuscripts give the title *Hippolytus* instead of *Phaedra*, and this may, in fact, have been the ancient title. Seneca's play – and not Euripides' – served as the primary model for Racine's famous play *Phèdre* (1677).

Characters

HIPPOLYTUS, *son of Theseus and the Amazon Antiope*
PHAEDRA, *wife of Theseus, daughter of King Minos*
NURSE *of Phaedra*
THESEUS, *king of Athens*
MESSENGER
CHORUS *of Hippolytus' huntsmen*
CHORUS *of Athenian women*

ACT I

[HIPPOLYTUS *appears with a band of huntsmen preparing
for the hunt*]

HIPPOLYTUS:

Go, surround the shady woods,
the lofty peaks of Cecrops' land!
Spread out and nimbly search the plains
that lie beneath Parnethus' crags,[1]
where rushing river waters lash
the lands along the vales of Thria,
and climb the summits always white
beneath the icy northern snows!
You, this way, here, where alder trees
form canopies along sprawling meadows,
where springtime grasses grow, caressed
to life by Zephyr's dewy breeze,
where Ilissus' trickling waters crawl
through thin-soiled fields and sluggishly
skim barren sands with its scanty stream.
You, to the left, where Marathon
unveils its glades and woodland pastures,
where dams attended by their broods
forage at night in search of food.
You, off to rough Acharnae, where
south-facing slopes catch the warm winds.
Send one to sweet Hymettus' heights,
one to Aphidnae's lowland plains.
That spot has been ignored too long,
where Sunium stands towering

over curving shores. Whoever's moved
by woodland glory, Phyle calls you:
a beast roams there, a farmer's bane,
a boar renowned for many wounds.

You, let the silent tracking dogs
follow the trail without restraint,
but leash the fierce Molossian hounds;
let the aggressive Cretans strain
their necks on sturdy chains till raw;
be sure to keep those Spartans close,
on a tighter leash – that breed so thirsts
for blood, relentless and unyielding.
A time will come when rocky vales
will ring with baying hounds; for now
their snouts must stay pressed to the ground
to track their prey and find their haunts,
while light is dim, and footprints still
remain impressed in the dewy earth.
You, hurry! Shoulder the heavy nets;
you, take the fine-gauged snares in arm.
Hem in the beasts with lines adorned
with ruddy feathers – a ruse of fear.[2]
You, wield the slender javelin;
you, use both hands to thrust with force
the heavy shaft with its wide steel blade.
You, lie in wait and drive the prey
onward with shouts; you, when it's caught,
take your curved knife and dress the guts.

Come to your comrade, virile goddess,[3]
for you control the wilderness,
and you pursue with unerring shafts
the beasts that lap the icy Aras
or romp on frozen Danube's streams;
it is your right hand that presses hard
African lions and deer in Crete.[4]
To you striped tigers show their chests,

to you shaggy bison show their backs,
and wide-horned oxen do the same.
Whatever pastures in desolate lands,
or in Arabia's rich forests,[5]
or among poor Saharan tribes,
or Russian steppes where nomads roam;
whatever lurks on the wild peaks
of the Pyrenees or in Georgian glades,
it is your bow that they fear, Diana.
The hunter that goes into the woods
with your goodwill finds prey held fast
inside his nets. No creature's feet
will break his snares; his cart will groan
from heaps of game; his hounds will sport
bloody red snouts from many kills;
his rustic troop will trundle home
triumphantly in a long parade.

O goddess, smile on me! The dogs
have raised their noisy howls. I'm called
into the woods. Along this path
I go, a shortcut to speed my trip.

    [HIPPOLYTUS *exits. Enter* PHAEDRA *and her* NURSE]

PHAEDRA: O mighty Crete, mistress of the vast seas, along your
every coast countless ships command the seas! Your power
stretches across all the waters that Nereus allows prows to
cleave, all the way to Syria's banks – so why do you allow me,
a woman handed over as hostage to a hateful house, married
off to the enemy, to live out my life in tears and misery? My
husband has gone off and left me here, exhibiting the sort of
commitment for which he is known. Right now he's bravely
making his way through the deep shadows and the infernal
waters from which there is no return, marching under orders of
a bold suitor.[6] The mission? To remove the king of the underworld's wife from her throne by force and haul her away! He
presses on, the ally of his friend's mad love, and neither fear nor
shame deters him. He's gone to the deepest quarter of hell to
search for illicit, adulterous affairs – he, the father of Hippolytus!

But a still greater pain weighs on me in my sorrow. No sleep, no deep slumber at night gives me respite from my anguish: my malady only finds nourishment and grows stronger, blazing inside me like the searing heat that pours forth from Etna's vents.[7] Pallas' loom goes unused and the wool, still unspun, just falls from these distracted hands of mine. I have no mind to visit temples with votive offerings or join the choruses of Athenian women around the altars and hurl torches that bear witness to the sacred mysteries,[8] or to supplicate with prayers and pious rituals the goddess who watches over the land awarded to her.[9] No, I yearn to drive game from their lairs, to chase them, to hurl rigid javelins from my tender hand.

Phaedra, what does this mean, this mad love for the woods? Ah, I recognize the evil inherited from my wretched mother.[10] Adultery in the woods is a brand of love my family knows too well. Mother, I pity you! Overwhelmed with an unspeakable passion, you boldly loved the savage leader of a feral herd. Wild-eyed and untamed was that lover of yours, the stud of a wild herd – but at least he loved something. What god, what Daedalus could possibly assist the flames of *my* wretched love? Even if that master Athenian inventor, that famed architect who imprisoned that monstrous creature, our family's curse, in a hidden house of darkness, were to return home, he could not offer any assistance to *my* plight. Venus loathes the descendants of the Sun, her hated enemy; *I* am the victim of her revenge, revenge taken for the chains that bound her in the embrace of her lover Mars.[11] All of Phoebus' offspring she afflicts with unspeakable indecency. Love never touches Minos' daughters lightly – it always involves some wickedness.[12]

NURSE: Wife of Theseus, illustrious descendant of Jupiter, drive those horrible thoughts from your chaste heart at once! Extinguish those flames. Do not surrender to this dreadful desire. Whoever puts up a fight and drives love away at the start leaves the battlefield safe and triumphant. But whoever nourishes this evil, sweet though it may be, by blowing on the flames, well, it's too late to refuse to bear the yoke once you've put it on! I'm fully aware that royal pride, puffed-up, unbending and unaccustomed to hearing the truth, kicks back when urged to follow a proper course of action. But I will bear whatever fate brings. I'm old, almost free, and this gives me courage.

It's best to have upright desires in the first place and never to slip from the path, but the next best thing is discretion, knowing where to draw the line when you err. How far will you go, my poor girl? Why add to the disgrace of your house? Will you outdo your mother? Moral failings are worse than monsters. You can ascribe the latter to fate, but the former to character.

But if you think that your actions are safe and you will escape unpunished because your husband does not look upon the land of the living, you're wrong. Suppose Theseus is buried, held fast in the depths of hell, and must endure the underworld forever – what about that man who holds the wide seas beneath his fist and commands a hundred cities, your father? Will he fail to uncover such an awful offence? A concerned parent is perceptive.

Still, suppose that we could keep such a transgression from getting out with a little ingenuity and cunning. What about that god who pours forth his light on to the earth, your mother's father? What about the one who shakes the earth by whirling Etna's thunderbolts from his flashing hands, the father of the gods? Do you really think it's possible to go undiscovered when surrounded by grandfathers who see everything?[13]

But let's assume that the gods' will is on your side and allows your sinful coupling to remain hidden and that your adulterous affair is kept secret by a strict bond of trust – something that is never found in great scandals. Still, what about that ever-present punishment, your conscience, full of dread, full of guilt, never trusting itself? A woman might get away with a crime, but she will never come away with a clear conscience.

So smother the flames of your sinful love, I beg you, and curb this wickedness, one that no barbaric tribe has ever committed, not the plain-wandering Getae, not the inhospitable Taurians, not the nomadic Scythians. Banish this awful idea from your chaste mind. Learn from your mother: fear unnatural sex. Are you planning to confound the beds of father *and* son, to receive a muddled offspring into your unholy womb? Go ahead, pervert nature with this unspeakable passion! Why not produce more monsters? Why let your brother's halls remain empty?[14] Will the world hear of freakish prodigies, will the laws of nature be broken *every* time a Cretan woman loves?

PHAEDRA: I know what you're saying is right, dear Nurse, but my desire compels me to follow the worse course of action. My mind spirals out of control – and I know it, too. But every time it tries to come back, striving after sensible judgement, it's no use, no use at all. It's just like when a boatman tries to row his laden vessel up a river against the current: his hard work falls for naught; his boat is overcome and swept downstream.

What good is logic? Desire has won and now rules me. My whole mind is dominated by a powerful god, winged Love. So wilful, he lords over all the land and even burns lord Jupiter with his unquenchable flames. Mars, bringer of war, felt those torch-fires. So, too, the divine blacksmith Vulcan, the maker of the three-pronged thunderbolts – yes, the one who works the ever-raging forges along Etna's crags burns with the tiniest of flames. Phoebus too, the archer-lord, has been stung by this boy's unerring arrows, his aim more accurate than the god's. This boy flits about no less oppressive to heaven than to earth![15]

NURSE: Love, a god? Lust invented *that* notion, foul vice-hound that it is. In order to have free rein it fabricated a divinity as a pretext for its uncontrollable desire. So Venus, the mistress of Eryx, sends forth her son to wander over all the earth? He flutters through the sky discharging wanton shafts from his tender hand and wields such incredible power – the tiniest of the gods? Of course he does. No, those foolish ideas have been adopted by a mind gone mad – *that* is what invented the notion of a divine Venus and her boy's bow.

Believe me, people who overindulge themselves amidst too

much prosperity and live extravagantly are always looking for something new and unusual. That's exactly when that dreaded companion of great fortune, Excess, rears its ugly head. The usual dinners don't suit these people, nor do the usual kinds of fabrics or inexpensive goblets. Ask yourself: why does this pest enter humble abodes so rarely, preferring luxurious houses instead? Why does virtuous love dwell in small homes, why does the ordinary crowd have reasonable desires, and why are those of modest means self-restrained, while the rich and powerful always seek more than is decent? Those that have too much always want what they can't have. Act how a queen with royal power should act. Fear and respect the authority of your returning husband!

PHAEDRA: *Love* holds the greatest authority over me – that's what I believe. I'm not worried about my husband's return. Never again does a man see the sky's dome once he has descended to the world below and visited the silent abodes swathed in perpetual night.

NURSE: Put no trust in Dis. Though he may have walled in his kingdom and the Stygian hound guards his dreaded gates, Theseus alone discovers impossible exits.[16]

PHAEDRA: Perhaps he will look charitably upon my love.

NURSE: He was cruel even to a chaste wife, the barbarian Antiope, who felt his savage hand. But suppose your husband can be bent from his anger – who is going to bend Hippolytus' intractable spirit? He hates and avoids the whole race of women. He stubbornly dedicates his youth to a life of chastity and rejects the very idea of marriage: you would recognize his Amazonian lineage.

PHAEDRA: Though he may haunt the ridges of snowy hills or move along rugged crags on nimble foot, I will pursue him through lofty forests and mountainous terrain.

NURSE: Do you expect him to stop and let himself be cajoled by you? To throw off his pure ways for a little impure sex? Will he put aside his loathing for you, when it is perhaps his loathing of you that causes him to torment all women? He will hardly respond to entreaties[17] – he's wild!

PHAEDRA: Love, as we've learned, can tame the wild.

NURSE: He'll flee.

PHAEDRA: If he should flee over the very seas, I will follow.

NURSE: Remember your father.

PHAEDRA: I remember my mother, too.

NURSE: He flees all that is woman.

PHAEDRA: So I won't have to fear a rival!

NURSE: Your husband will be here –

PHAEDRA: – you mean Pirithous' companion?

NURSE: And your father –

PHAEDRA: Ariadne's mild-mannered father?[18]

NURSE: By my white hairs and old age I beg you, by my trouble-worn heart and these dear breasts I beseech you: put an end to your mad desire and help yourself! Part of healing is *wanting* to be healed.

PHAEDRA: Not every ounce of shame is gone; my intentions are still honourable. I'll comply with your wishes, Nurse. Love that cannot be controlled must be conquered. I will not let my reputation be tainted. There is one plan, one way out of my dilemma: I will follow in my husband's footsteps and avert this wickedness with my death.

NURSE: Dear child, control your impulses, your reckless thoughts. Restrain your spirit. I think you deserve to live, because you believe that you should die.

PHAEDRA: I'm resolved to die. It's only a matter of how. Will I end my life with a noose? Fall on a sword? Or hurl myself from the heights of the Acropolis?

NURSE: [*moving towards* PHAEDRA] Do you think that I, old though I am, will let you go headlong into death? Stop this madness at once!

PHAEDRA: No amount of reasoning can stop someone from dying when the one resolved on death ought to die. So then, let me arm my hand to defend my chastity!

NURSE: My lady, you who are the sole source of comfort in these tired years of mine, if your mind is obsessed with such reckless thoughts, then forget your reputation. Reputation hardly resembles the truth, anyway: better repute goes to the less deserving, worse repute to those who deserve better. Let us test his dour, defiant spirit. I'll take it upon myself to

approach that wild young man and change his cruel way of
thinking.

[PHAEDRA *and the* NURSE *go into the palace*]

CHORUS I: The Power of Love

Venus, goddess born of the heartless salt-sea,
you whom twin-natured Cupid calls his mother:
your unruly boy, armed with flames and arrows,
reckless, naughty, he of the mischievous grin,
O how true his shafts when he aims his bowstring!
Though the wound is small, but a tiny pinprick,
deep the poison runs and devours our marrow.
Peace and quiet mean naught to him: worldwide he
zips and darts, releasing a flood of arrows:
all the lands saluting the rising Sun-god,
all that lie at the world's most western fringes,
all that swelter beneath the sign of Cancer,
all that stand beneath the frigid Arctic
Bear, where nomads range over frozen rivers –
all have felt his fires. He stokes the raging
passions in young men, and in tired greybeards
kindles those desires once thought gone for good;
he smites virgins' breasts with unfamiliar feelings.

Even gods take his orders, leaving heaven,
coming down to earth in their sham disguises.
Phoebus played the cowherd for Thessaly's king,
driving cattle to pasture; putting down his
lyre, he called his bulls with unequal pan pipes.[19]
Jupiter, great sky-god, cloud-gatherer, how
often he assumed a disguise beneath him!
As a bird, he fluttered his snowy wings,
singing more sweetly than swans do at death.[20]
As a fierce-eyed and frisky bull, he knelt down,
offering bold maidens his back to ride on –
one he whisked away through his brother's sea-waves,
unfamiliar places, his hooves now pliant

oars; he breasted the waves and tamed the salt-sea,
fearful for the cargo he was carrying.[21]
You, Moon-goddess, bright in the darkness burned;[22]
you neglected night and gave to your brother
your resplendent chariot-team to pilot.
Sun-gods do not know how to steer the night-time
team of two, to run in a narrow circuit:
nights ran long and the sun arose at noon-time,
and the axles groaned from a heavier god.
Hercules, the son of Alcmena, dropped his
bow and arrows and fearsome lion skin,
letting fingers be graced with emerald rings, his
bristling hair be untangled, combed and coiffed,
ankles graced with gem-studded golden bangles,
both feet covered with saffron-coloured slippers,
and his hands, which had just now borne a club,
were now spinning thread on whirling spindles.[23]

As Persia watched, and Lydia, too,
land rich in golden sands, he flung
that savage lion's skin to earth
and placed on his massive back, which once
supported heaven's mansions, a shawl,
a delicate weave in Tyrian scarlet.

That fire is heaven-sent, accursed,
unquenchable – trust those it's burned!
On earth and in the salty seas,
in heaven's dome, where silver stars
go speeding by in streaks of fire,
that cruel and heartless boy holds sway.
His arrows reach the sea-blue band
of Nereids on ocean's floor –
that flame the sea itself can't quench.
This fire winged creatures feel.
A bull that's goaded on by Love
fights wars for the entire herd.
When timid stags fear for their mates,

they challenge foes to fight, their rage
made clear with mighty bellowing.
So, too, the boar sharpens his tusks
for gashing, frothing at the mouth,
and African lions shake their manes
when struck by Love. It's Love that makes
tanned Indians fear tigers' stripes –
forests resound with mighty roars.
Leviathans in the swollen seas
and elephants know Love: Love
has conquered all, nothing is safe:
when Love commands, Hate disappears,
and age-old feuds give way to flames.
    Let us put it simply:
cruel stepmothers succumb to Love.

ACT II

[NURSE *enters from the palace*]

CHORUS: Good Nurse, what news do you bring? [*Urgently*] What is the queen's condition? Have the flames that ravage her subsided yet?

NURSE: There's no hope. Such a consuming illness cannot be assuaged; there's no stopping those raging flames. She's scorched by a silent fever, but her passion, however much she tries to conceal it, is betrayed on her face. Her eyes reveal her passion. But she cannot bring those tired eyes to face the light. Nothing satisfies her fitful mood for long. She tosses and turns, restless, in anguish. Now her legs give out, and she slumps to the earth as if dying, barely able to keep her lolling head erect. Now she surrenders herself to rest, but, knowing nothing of sleep, she draws out long nights in sorrow. She has us prop up her body, then lower it back down, and bids us to let her hair down only to make us do it up again! Her mood constantly changes, fitful and frustrated.

She has no mind for food, no concern for her health. She wanders aimlessly, stumbling about, completely exhausted. She has none of her usual energy. Her once radiant face lacks its rosy blush. Those eyes, those bright eyes that once bore the traces of her grandfather's torch, signs of her ancestry, have grown dim. Tears trail down her noble face, her eyes well up constantly with floods, just like the snows on Taurus' peaks that melt when pelted by the showers of spring.

Look, the balcony doors are opening! The queen lies upon a couch of gold, scorning her usual attire – see, she is not in her right mind!

PHAEDRA: [*from the upper balcony; she does not notice the*
CHORUS *or the* NURSE] Slaves, take away these robes dyed
in purple and gold. I'll have nothing to do with those expen-
sive Tyrian reds or the fine threads harvested from
tree-branches by the distant Chinese. Just tie a thin belt to
hitch up my clothes and keep them out of the way. Let no
necklace grace my neck, nor let snow-white pearls, the gifts
from the Indian Sea, weigh down my ears. Let my tresses
hang down without any eastern perfumes – let my locks fall
as they will over my neck and shoulders as I toss my head,
and let the wind play with my hair as I race through the
woods. With my left hand I will manage the quiver; in my
right I will wield a Thessalian spear. Just like those women
from the Tanais or the Maeotis who left behind the expanses
along the frigid Pontus to drive their throngs thundering on
Attic soil, their hair tied back into a ponytail, their flanks
protected by a crescent shield – *that* is how I will go into the
woods. [*The balcony doors close*]
CHORUS: [*to the* NURSE] Lay aside your grief: wallowing does
not help those in distress. Go appease the virgin goddess of
the countryside.
   [*The* CHORUS *exits*]

   SCENE 2: In the countryside, the haunt of HIPPOLYTUS,
   where the NURSE prays to Diana near her altar.

NURSE: Queen of sacred woods, you who haunt the mountains
in solitude, who alone are worshipped as goddess on solitary
mountains, turn these grim, threatening omens to the good!
O goddess, great power of the forests and groves, bright heavenly sphere, glory of night, you whose revolving torch-fire
illuminates the world, three-formed Hecate, come to me and
smile on my undertaking! Tame grim Hippolytus' unyielding
spirit, make him listen favourably, soften his wild heart. Let
him learn love, to receive and return the flames of passion.
Change his thoughts; make that grim, spiteful, fierce man yield
to the sovereignty of Venus. Turn your powers here: so may

you glide through cloudless skies radiant-faced and with gleaming horns; so may Thessalian incantations never draw you down as you guide your chariot across the night sky; so may no shepherd win glory from you.[24]

Come, I invoke you! Fulfil my prayers, goddess: I see that very man now making ritual sacrifice, sombre, none of his comrades at his side. Why do I hesitate? Fate is offering an opportunity. It is time to bring my skills to bear. Do I tremble? It is a hard thing to execute bold crimes entrusted to you, but fear of kings forces one to disregard what is right and to drive all propriety from one's mind. Morality is a poor minister of royal power. [*Approaches* HIPPOLYTUS]

HIPPOLYTUS: Faithful nurse, why do you bring your weary, aged steps here? Why that troubled brow, that sad face? Surely my father is in good health, and Phaedra too, along with her twin children!

NURSE: Have no fear, the kingdom is in a prosperous state, flourishing and blessed with good fortune. But you, you should indulge yourself more in this prosperity. I'm worried sick about you, deeply concerned because you're being self-destructive, inflicting great suffering on yourself. We look with pity upon the miserable, provided that the Fates are responsible. But when a man willingly punishes himself and his torment is self-inflicted, well, he deserves to lose the good fortune he does not know how to enjoy! Come, remember that you're young! Relax that hard attitude; carry a torch in some nocturnal revel, let Bacchus free your heart of its heavy cares. Enjoy your youth – it will quickly pass you by. Now your heart is free and easy, now Venus is pleasing – while you're young! Let your spirit soar! Why do you lie in a bed of loneliness, without a mate?

Unfetter your youth from this gloom. Hurry up, get in the race now, give yourself free rein. Do not let the best days of your life slip away! God has mapped out for us different tasks as he leads us through life in stages: happiness befits the young, a sour face the old. Why hold yourself back? Why stifle your true nature? The field that gives the farmer great profit is the one that, when sprouting, is allowed to abound in lush shoots, and the lofty tree that towers over the grove is the one never pruned or cut back by a stingy hand. Noble men more easily reach their full potential and status if their minds are nourished by a vigorous freedom.

So are you going to live out your early years a grizzled, gloomy, backwoods loner who knows nothing of life, forsaking Venus? Do you think the only duty imposed on men is to endure hardships, to chase horses and tame them, to wage wars with brutality and bloodshed?

That supreme father of the universe, when he saw that Fate's hands were so predatory, made sure to compensate for our losses by continually spawning new offspring. Come, let us imagine a world without Venus, who restores and replenishes depleted species. What's left? Decay, squalor, rot. The sea will stand empty without a single fish, no birds in the air, no beast in the forest. Only the winds will pass through the skies. Consider how many kinds of death claw at and erode humanity: shipwreck, swords, treachery. Even if you remove unnatural deaths, you would have us head to dark Styx on our own! If every youth refused to mate, advocating a celibate life, what you see now is all there will ever be: a single generation running all at once to its ruin.

So follow nature, our guide to life. Visit the city, join the human race!

HIPPOLYTUS: No life is more free, more pure, more faithful to the righteous ways of our ancestors than one devoted to the woods far removed from city walls. Whoever dedicates himself to a life of simple innocence along mountain ridges never feels the fires of maddening greed and cares nothing for reputation, for the mob, that undoing of good men, for noxious envy, or for the brittle backing of the crowd. He does not play slave to kings, nor in the hopes of kingship does he pursue meaningless honours or momentary riches. He is free of desire, free of fear, unaffected by the sinister sting of Spite's ignoble bite. He knows nothing of the crimes sown among peoples and cities. He doesn't dread every noise because of a guilty conscience. He doesn't make up lies. He doesn't feel the need to live beneath roofs supported by a thousand columns as a show of wealth or gild his roof-beams with lavish gold to prove his superiority. His altars aren't drenched with great bloodshed to show his piety – no hundred head of snow-white bulls lower their heads, sprinkled with sacred grains, to the knife.

But he owns the vast wilderness. He is free to go as he pleases beneath the open sky, a threat to no one and with no one threatening him. He knows how to contrive wily snares only for wild beasts. He knows the meaning of hard work, and when exhausted he refreshes himself in the snow-fed waters of the Ilissus. Now he hunts along the banks of the swift-flowing Alpheus, now through the thick-forested groves casting long shadows over the limpid streams of icy Lerna to avoid the sun's heat. Here warbling birds twitter and trees rustle gently in the wind, alders, ashes, oaks and ancient beech trees. He finds pleasure lying upon the banks of a meandering river, dozing off sweetly on bare turf, whether beside a spring gushing forth waters or next to a brook babbling gently as its stream races through a meadow of spring flowers. Fruit shaken from trees satisfies his hunger, berries plucked from low-lying bushes offer him a ready meal. Royal luxury? It's the furthest thing from his mind. Kings drink from gold cups, true, but they fear every sip. How delightful it is to lap spring waters from one's own hand! A sounder sleep descends upon the man who, carefree and easy, stretches out his body on a hard bed. He doesn't seek to hide his perversions in some dark, secret lair or squirrel himself away in some labyrinthine house in fear. He seeks out the open sky and chooses to live under the watchful eye of heaven.

Isn't this how the men of the golden age lived, in the company of gods? No blinding lust for gold gripped them, no sacred stone in the field marked boundaries between clans. No trusting ships cut their way through the open waters – each people knew only their own sea. Cities had not yet ringed their edges with mighty earthen walls dotted with numerous towers. No soldiers outfitted their hands with savage weapons, no catapults smashed down barricaded gates with heavy stones. The land had not yet submitted to serve humankind, to take orders – oxen had not yet been yoked! No, the soil of its own accord teemed with bounty, nourishing whole nations. They lacked nothing: forests provided natural wealth, shadowy caves natural homes.

But this harmonious accord was shattered: there arose double-crossing greed, uncontrollable anger, lust that sets minds afire, and bloody thirst for power. The strong preyed on the weak. Might made right. Then for the first time they made war, first with their bare hands, then using rocks or rough-hewn branches as impromptu weapons. There was no light cornel-spear tipped with a slender blade of iron, no sharp long-sword at one's side, no crested helmet conspicuous from afar. Rage made their weapons.

But Mars, bringer of war, invented new techniques, a thousand ways to kill. He caused all the lands to be stained with massive bloodshed, the seas to blush red with deep crimson. Then crimes raced inexorably through every household. No wickedness went unprecedented: brother was slain by brother, father by son, husband butchered by wife, children murdered by wicked mothers. I'll say nothing about stepmothers. It turns out that nothing is more humane than wild animals!

But the leaders of wickedness are women. These architects of crimes lay siege to our mind, and it is because of these creatures' adulterous ways that so many cities lie smouldering in ashes, so many nations feel the sting of war, so many nations lie crushed beneath the ruins of their once mighty kingdoms. I'll mention only Aegeus' wife Medea: all by herself she proves women to be a vile bunch.

NURSE: Why blame them all for the wickedness of a few?

HIPPOLYTUS: I loathe them all. I shun them, spurn them, scorn them. I don't know if it's rational, just my nature, or some terrible madness, but I want nothing to do with them. Sooner will you join water to fire, sooner will the dangerous waters of the Syrtes offer friendly passage to ships, sooner will Tethys lift up the bright day from the distant western seas, sooner will wolves nuzzle up against deer than you'll convince me to think kindly of any woman.

NURSE: Many times has Love broken stubborn men and harnessed them, transforming hate into love. Just look at your mother's kingdom – those Amazon women, defiant as they are, feel Venus' yoke. You're proof of that, the sole living male child of their race.

HIPPOLYTUS: This one comfort I derive from the death of my mother: now I can hate all women. [*Walks away*]

NURSE: [*aside*] He rejects my pleas just as a hard, unyielding crag resists and repels the incoming waves. [*Enter* PHAEDRA] But what's this? Phaedra rushes in, heedless, unable to wait. How will this turn out? What will her madness come to? Oh! She falls to the ground, lifeless, her face all but the colour of death! [*Runs to* PHAEDRA, *who is caught by* HIPPOLYTUS] Lift up your head, say something! Look, darling, you are in the arms of your Hippolytus!

PHAEDRA: Who revives me to my anguish, who restores waves of suffering in my soul? How good it was to have lost myself! [*Moving away, hiding her head*]

HIPPOLYTUS: Why do you recoil from the sweet gift of light restored to you?

PHAEDRA: [*aside*] Come, Phaedra, be bold, make an attempt, carry out your charge! Speak fearlessly: a timid request begs for refusal. A great part of my crime is already done. It's too late for shame now. I have set unspeakable things in motion; if I follow through with them, perhaps I can conceal my transgression with a legitimate marriage. Sometimes success makes a crime honourable. Come, Phaedra, begin! [*To* HIPPOLYTUS] Lend me your ears, I beg you, in secret. Please send any companions away.

HIPPOLYTUS: There's no one here; see, no witnesses in sight.

PHAEDRA: [*aside*] I want to speak, but my mouth allows no passage for my words. A great power sends them forth, but a greater one checks them. Bear witness to my words, all you heavenly gods! I do not want these desires!

HIPPOLYTUS: Are you unable to say what is on your mind?

PHAEDRA: Trivial concerns speak; weighty ones cannot.

HIPPOLYTUS: Entrust your concerns to my ears, mother.

PHAEDRA: Mother? That name's too lofty, too strong. A humbler one fits my disposition. Call me sister, Hippolytus. Or slave. Yes, slave's better: I'll submit completely. If you ordered me to traverse the deep snows of Pindus' icy heights, I would not shy away; if you commanded me to run through fire, through enemy lines, I would not hesitate to offer my chest to drawn swords. Accept the sovereignty I bestow on you; take me as your slave. It is not a woman's task to watch over a kingdom of many cities, but you, you are strong, in the prime of your life, in the flower of your youth. Be bold, take your rightful place on your father's throne and rule your people. Receive me, your suppliant and slave, into your protective arms and watch over me. Take pity on a widow!

HIPPOLYTUS: May the highest god prevent that from coming to pass! My father will be here shortly, safe and sound.

PHAEDRA: The lord of the unrelenting realm, of silent Styx, blocks all passage back to the upper world once it is left behind. Do you think he will release the abductor of his own wife? Unless, of course, Pluto's judgments are sympathetic to love.

HIPPOLYTUS: The heavenly gods will be just and return him to us. But so long as god keeps our prayers in uncertainty, I will look after my dear brothers with the caring they deserve, and I will do everything in my power to make sure you do not feel widowed: I will take my father's place.

PHAEDRA: [aside] O hope, all too trusting, bane of lovers! O deceitful Love! Have I said enough? I must go on and beg him with entreaties. [To HIPPOLYTUS] Take pity, hear out the desires I've longed to utter. I want to speak, but to do so makes me ill.

HIPPOLYTUS: What matter troubles you so?

PHAEDRA: One you would hardly believe could happen to a stepmother.

HIPPOLYTUS: Your words are a tangled labyrinth of uncertainty. Speak plainly.

PHAEDRA: My heart is inflamed, kindled to madness by the heat of passion. A raging wildfire courses through my deepest marrow, through my veins, just like a swift-moving flame races through dry timber along a tree-line.

HIPPOLYTUS: The love with which you burn – no doubt it's the pure love you feel for Theseus.

PHAEDRA: Hippolytus, it's like this: I love Theseus' looks – well, those looks of his earlier years, when he was just a young man, with the first signs of a beard gracing his fair cheeks, when he faced the Cnossian monster's dark dwelling and escaped the twisting labyrinth by gathering up the long trail of thread. God, how magnificent he was then! His temples were wreathed in headbands and ribbons, his tender cheeks tinged with the tawny blush of innocence. Powerful muscles resided in those lithe arms. He resembled your Phoebe, or my Phoebus – or better yet, he resembled *you*. Oh yes, that's exactly how he looked when he charmed his enemy, and he held his head high, proud, just like you! But you – you've got a ruggedness about you. You radiate toughness, a good-looking toughness. Yes, you've got your whole father in you, and yet a tiny part of your stern mother contributes her own grace in equal measure: a Greek face with austere Scythian features! If *you* had stepped foot on to Cretan shores alongside your father, my sister would have spun those threads not for him, but for you. [*Aside*] O sister, in whatever quarter of starry heaven you shine, I invoke you – our cause is the same: two sisters captivated by a single family – you by the father, I by the son. [*Throwing herself at* HIPPOLYTUS' *feet*] Behold, at your feet lies the child of a royal house, now a humble suppliant begging for mercy. No stain has ever tarnished my honour. It has always been unblemished, but now I've changed for you alone. This day will bring an end to my pain, or else my life. Pity your lover!

HIPPOLYTUS: Great ruler of the gods, do you hear? Do you see such wickedness but refuse to act? When, when will you hurl your thunderbolt with ruthless force, if now the sky remains serene? Demolish the bright dome of heaven! Bring it all crashing down! Plunge the day into dark clouds! Drive the stars back crosswise along their course! Can you, glorious celestial body, radiant Sun-god, can you stand to watch the wickedness of your own brood? Bury the light! Flee into the shadows! O mighty ruler of gods and men, why does your right hand remain empty? Why does the whole world not blaze beneath your three-forked lightning-torch? Release your bolt against me! Impale me! Drive your swift fires through my chest and consume me! I am guilty. I have earned death – I have brought on my stepmother's desire!

[*To* PHAEDRA] How could this happen? Do I look like the adulterous type? Was I the only ripe fruit around for you to poison with your crime? Is this the reward for my sober living? You surpass the whole female race in wickedness! What nerve you have! Your sin is greater than that of your monster-bearing mother; you are worse than the one who bore you. She defiled only herself with debauchery, but even so, her offspring with its double form revealed the crime kept hidden for so long – a mother's wickedness betrayed by her hybrid baby's bestial features.

That is the belly that bore you.

Three and four times blessed are you who have been destroyed, devastated and delivered to death by deceit and hatred! Father, I envy you. This foul creature is worse than your Colchian stepmother,[25] a worse plague indeed!

PHAEDRA: Even I recognize my family's destined fate: we pursue what we should avoid. But I'm not in control of my actions. I would pursue you even through fire, through the raging seas, over rocky crags, through rivers swollen into springtime torrents. Wherever you take your steps, that is where I am sure to go, swept away, no say in the matter. So once again I throw myself at your feet, at your mercy. Do not reject me!

HIPPOLYTUS: Remove your impure hands from my pure flesh! What's this? You rush to my embraces still? A drawn sword will exact the punishment you deserve. [*Seizing* PHAEDRA *and hauling her to* DIANA's *altar*] Behold, goddess, I have bent back her impure head, gripping her hair in my left hand. O goddess, queen of the bow, never has blood more justly been spilled on your altars!

PHAEDRA: Hippolytus, now you are fulfilling my prayers: you are healing a sick woman. This is even more than I dreamed of – I will die in your arms but with my virtue still intact.

HIPPOLYTUS: [*pushing* PHAEDRA *away*] Away with you! Go and live – you won't obtain *anything* you want from me. And this sword, defiled as it is now, I cast away from my chaste

side. God, what river could cleanse me of this stain? The Tanais
or the Maeotis rushing over me with all the waters of the
Black Sea? Not even mighty father Neptune with the whole
of Ocean could wash away all this filth! O woods! O creatures
of the wild! [*Exit* HIPPOLYTUS, PHAEDRA *collapses*]
NURSE: [*to herself*] Her secret's out in the open! Come,
Nurse, do not delay or falter now: we must deflect the blame
and set out to prove *him* guilty of incestuous love. One wrong
must be concealed by another. It's safest to attack when
afraid – whether we propositioned him or suffered wickedness at his hands, who's to know? Her desire was revealed
in secret!

   Athenians, come quickly! Faithful band of servants, bring
help! Hippolytus means to steal our lady's chastity, intimid-
ating her, menacing her with death. Quick, he's threatening
our pure lady with a sword. [*Enter* CHORUS *of* HIPPOLYTUS'
huntsmen] Look, he's running off, and in the panic of flight
he dropped his sword. We have proof of the crime.

   But first, revive our disconsolate mistress. Wait, leave her
tousled hair, her torn locks just as they are – they are the
evidence of his heinous crime. Take her back to the city. Regain
your composure, my lady. Why do you tear at your cheeks
and turn away from us? Remember, it's your will, not what
happens, that makes you impure.

CHORUS II: Ode to Hippolytus' Beauty

Like a raging gale-wind Hippolytus fled,
swifter than the northerly squalls of Corus,
swifter than a shooting star's course in heaven
when the winds dislodge it and send it streaking,
                              a long trail of fire.
Legend, spellbound captive of ancient lore, may
tell of olden beauties, but none compares to
you, Hippolytus, who outshine all others
as Moon outshines the lesser celestial bodies,
when her crescent horns come together, joining
her two blazing points, and her orb becomes full:

thus when Phoebe the whole night through displays her
ruddy countenance from her speeding chariot,
lesser lights grow pale and their flames disappear.
Thus shines Eveningstar, the dark night's great herald,
calling shadows forward, arising from
the waves cleansed, but when shadows are dispelled,
                        he shines as Morningstar.

You, father Liber, from thyrsus-bearing India,
a young man forever with unshorn long tresses,
controlling your tigers with vine-covered spear-point,
concealing your horn-sprouting head with a turban[26] –
Hippolytus' rough, bushy hair you won't conquer.
Trust not too much in your beautiful features;
remember the famous account of that hero
whom Phaedra's young sister preferred over Bacchus.[27]
   Beauty, you double-edged boon for mortals,
   brief is your gift and of short duration.
   How swiftly you flee on those scurrying feet!
No quicker are meadows that bloom in the springtime
despoiled by the blistering heat of the summer,
when long August days start to swelter at noontime
and unequal nights race along shorter courses.
No quicker do lilies grow pale and start wilting
or roses that grace human temples start fading,
than radiant blush on fair cheeks starts abating,
the victim of time. Every day, every moment
comes ravaging bodily splendour and beauty.
A fleeting possession is beauty. Be prudent,
rely not at all in this blessing so brittle:
enjoy it and revel in it while you may!
Time silently wears you away, and the moment
that passes you by is pursued by a worse one.

So why do you live in the wilderness? Beauty's
no safer in solitude! Hide in the forest:
when Titan, the Sun-god, sits high up in heaven,
the Naiads, an amorous band, will surround you –

their habit is drowning young beauties in fountains;[28]
while napping outside they will ambush your sleep,
   lustful forest nymphs,
      and mountain-roaming Pans.
If Moon should espy you from star-spangled heaven,
divinity younger than ancient Arcadia,[29]
her bright, shining team would she fail to manoeuvre.
Just lately she blushed, though no thick, murky cloudbank
was blocking her luminous orb from our sight;
alarmed as we were at her power's disruption,
convinced that Thessalian spells had bewitched her,
great clanging we raised to offset them.[30] But *you* were
the obstacle, *you* were the cause of delay, while
you-gazing the Night-goddess stopped her swift orbit.

Expose your fair face much less often to winter,
and keep it away from the sun in the summer:
its gleam would shine whiter than Parian marble!
How pleasing to eyes is your manly appearance,
intensity, gravity stamped on your forehead!
Your radiant neck would compete with lord Phoebus';
his long-flowing locks, never bound up or gathered,
adorn and embrace him with cascading tresses;
the rugged look flatters your face, with hair cropped
and unkempt. If you wished, you'd surpass the relentless
and war-loving gods with your brawn and your might,
exceeding them, too, with your muscular body:
though young, you have equalled great Hercules' brawn,
your shoulders are broader than Mars', the war-bringer.
If riding hoofed stallions were to be your desire,
the Spartan steed Cyllarus you would manoeuvre
more deftly than Castor, the master horse-rider.
Now fit your two fingertips snug in the spear-thong,
and hurl that light javelin, use all your muscle:
not even the Cretans, the archery experts,
could equal your distance with slender, light arrows.
If you should decide to shower the sky
with innumerable shafts like the Parthian host,

each shaft would rain down with its avian prey,
embedded in bird-flesh, still warm, without fail.
Rare is the man whose great beauty goes unpunished.
Examine the ages. But you, may the god pass
you by without harm, and instead of your beauty
see a deformed and grizzled image of old age.

What would that maniacal woman not dare? She's plotting
to wreck his blameless reputation with unspeakable accusa-
tions. Just look at her villainy: to be more credible she rends
her hair, defiles her once beautiful head, and wets her cheeks.
Every womanly wile is brought to bear for her deception.
    [THESEUS *enters from the wings*]
But who is this, carrying himself in kingly fashion, holding
his proud head high, grace upon his countenance? How much
he resembles Pittheus' youthful grandson, Theseus! But his
face is ashen, pale, and ghostly, his hair and beard bristly,
unkempt, and filthy. O glorious sight! It is he! Theseus has
returned to the land of the living!

ACT III

THESEUS: At last have I escaped the region of eternal night, that vast prison dome burying the shades of the dead in darkness. Scarcely can my eyes endure the light I've yearned to see. Eleusis has reaped its fourth harvest, the gift of Triptolemus, and four times has Libra made day and night equal since my agonizing ordeal began. Uncertain of my lot, I was held in limbo, between the evils of life and death. One part of life lingered in my lifeless existence: I could feel my agony. Alcaeus' grandson Hercules brought an end to my torment; when he forcibly hauled the hellhound out of Tartarus, he also led me back to the land of the living. But my strength is spent. I lack my former vigour. My weak legs shake to keep me upright. Oh, what toil it was to journey from the deepest quarter of hell to the distant skies above, to run from death, to match the giant steps of Hercules!

But what is the doleful din that strikes my ears? Someone tell me, now! Mourning, tears, grief: no more fitting reception, I suppose, for a visitor from hell.

NURSE: [*enters from palace*] Phaedra's resolved to kill herself and refuses to budge from her intention – she rejects our tearful pleas and is bent on death!

THESEUS: Why? Why die now that her husband's returned?

NURSE: That's just it, your return – that's why she is resolved to hasten her death.

THESEUS: Something dreadful lurks beneath these tangled words. Speak plainly: what pain weighs on her mind so?

NURSE: She will not tell anyone. She buries her secret in sorrowful silence, determined to carry with her the curse that is the

cause of her death. Now go, Theseus, go see her, I beg you –
waste no time!

THESEUS: Unbolt the doors of the royal palace! [*The slaves open
the palace doors;* PHAEDRA *is revealed, holding* HIPPOLYTUS'
sword] O bed-mate of mine, is this how you welcome your
husband home? Is this how you greet the face of the man for
whom you have waited for so long? Why don't you divorce
your hand from that sword and allay my fears; tell me what's
driving you from this life.

PHAEDRA: By your mighty sceptre, great-hearted Theseus, and
by the promise of our children, by your safe return and my
soon-to-be ashes, I beg you: let me die.

THESEUS: What propels you to death?

PHAEDRA: If the reason for my death is revealed, its profit is
lost.

THESEUS: No one, save me, will hear what you have to say.

PHAEDRA: It's the ears of her husband that a chaste wife fears.

THESEUS: Put your trust in me: I'll keep your secret locked safely
in my heart.

PHAEDRA: If you want another to keep a secret, keep it to yourself.

THESEUS: I will not allow you to die.

PHAEDRA: You cannot keep those who want to die from dying.

THESEUS: What transgression must be atoned for by death?

PHAEDRA: That I live.

THESEUS: Do my tears mean nothing to you?

PHAEDRA: The best death is dying while still deserving your
family's tears.

THESEUS: [*aside*] She refuses to confess. But whips and chains
will force her old nurse to reveal what she will not. [*To his
attendants*] Bind the old woman in chains! Let blows to her
back extract the secrets from her mind.

PHAEDRA: No, stop! I'll tell you. [*Starts to weep*]

THESEUS: Why avert your sad eyes from me? Why draw your
dress across your face to hide those sudden tears drenching
your cheeks?

PHAEDRA: Creator of the heavenly gods, I call upon you to be
my witness, and you, shining beam of heavenly light, from

whose seed our whole family descends: I tried to resist his advances with pleas, I swear, but he threatened me with this sword. Though my mind never submitted, my body nonetheless suffered the violence of rape. My blood will wash away this stain on my honour.

THESEUS: Who – tell me! – who brought ruin on our good name?

PHAEDRA: The one you'd least expect.

THESEUS: I want to hear his *name*.

PHAEDRA: His identity? Just look at the sword the rapist abandoned in the panic of flight, when he heard the footsteps of his fellow citizens.

THESEUS: Dear god, what wickedness do I see? What horror do I witness? The hilt gleaming in royal ivory, engraved with my family's emblems, the glory of the Athenian race.

Where is he *now*?

PHAEDRA: These servants here saw him running off, alarm and fear in his swift steps.

[PHAEDRA *lingers while* THESEUS *appeals to heaven, then enters the palace*]

THESEUS: O sacred Devotion! O ruler of heaven, and you, too, who sway the second kingdom with sea-swells, where did that, that bane from a monstrous family arise? Did Greek lands nurture him? Or the Scythian Taurians? Or Colchians along the Phasis? Breeding always reflects one's ancestors, inferior blood a sign of a second-rate pedigree. This is without doubt the madness of that warrior nation, to reject the bonds of Venus and remain chaste for so long, only later to prostitute their bodies to everyone in town. What a revolting race, unbroken by the laws of a better land! Even his beloved wild animals shun forbidden acts of Venus; an instinctual sense of right and wrong upholds the laws of procreation!

So much for that swindler's sham disguise, his feigned austerity, his gruff style of dress evoking the old-fashioned way of life, his grim, gloomy outlook on life, that serious disposition! O deceitful life, how you harbour hidden feelings and cloak loathsome souls with beautiful faces! Innocence

veils a dirty mind, a gentle demeanour conceals brazenness,
a virtuous exterior shrouds wickedness. Liars outwardly
champion the truth; the decadent pretend to be austere. All
that time you lived as a simple bumpkin, wild, innocent,
undefiled – were you saving yourself to destroy *me*? Did
you yearn to inaugurate your manhood in *my* bed, with such
a horrific act? Oh how I thank the heavenly powers above
that your mother Antiope fell by my hand, that when I was
heading down into the caverns of hell, I did not leave her
for you.

So go ahead, run, flee across the distant lands of unknown
peoples. Though you may inhabit some far-removed land in
the farthest reaches of the world, separated from me by
Ocean's great expanse, though you may dwell on the opposite
side of the world, or lie hidden in some far-off corner of the
world, past the bristling regions beneath the lofty pole, past
the blizzards and white snows, past the menacing roar and
icy sting of the north wind – you *will* pay for your crimes. I
will stalk you wherever you hide. I will stop at nothing. I will
traverse distant lands, isolated, hidden, hostile, impassable
lands. No obstacle will deter me – you know the place from
which I've just returned.

And if my weapons cannot reach you, I'll send my prayers
after you: my sea-dwelling father granted me three wishes
that he must grant, a gift made inviolable by calling on Styx
to witness. Hear me, lord of the sea! Carry out your promise,
grim though it may be: I wish that Hippolytus no longer
looks upon the light of day, that he, despite his youth, goes
to join the spirits of the dead who are hostile to his father.
Father, perform now this loathsome service for your son! In
no way would I now exhaust the final gift of your godly
power if I were not in desperate straits. Even while I was in
the clutches of the Tartarean abyss, the harrowing realm of
Dis, and faced the menacing threats of the infernal king, I
refrained from using this last wish. Now fulfil your promise
to me!

Father, why do you not act? Why does the sea lie silent still?

Whip up the winds, roil the dark clouds, drape the world in
night, rob the world of stars and heaven! Flood the seas! Rouse
the watery host! Summon waves from Ocean himself for your
mighty tidal wave!

CHORUS III: Gods Care Not for Justice

Great Nature, mother of the gods!
You, lord of fire-spangled Olympus,
who swiftly spin the whirling sky,
the scattered stars, and roving orbs,
so lightly twirling heaven's dome:
why do you take such care to guide
the ceaseless cosmic ebb and flow,
so that the hoary winter frost
denudes the trees of summer's leaves,
then shade returns to woods anew,
then Leo, summer's scorching sign,
bakes Ceres' crops with searing heat,
to give each season its proper turn?
So why do you, who guide the whole,
who safeguard cosmic balance, keeping
massive celestial orbs on track,
care not for humans, always distant,
not bothering to help the good
and punish evil, wicked men?
How randomly does Fortune rule
human affairs! She flings her gifts,
eyes closed and favouring the wicked.
The pure are overcome by lust;
in palaces deceit is king,
cities rejoice in giving vile
men power. The same men we love
we soon will loathe, then love again.
What undeserved prizes greet
a life of purity and virtue;
grim poverty weighs down the chaste,
adultery's repaid with crowns –

Innocence, how worthless!
 Honour, how useless!
 [MESSENGER *enters from the same wing by which Hippol-*
 ytus left]
Look, a messenger approaches! I wonder what his haste
means, why his sorrowful eyes drench his face with mournful
streams of tears.

ACT IV

MESSENGER: How sad, how harsh is my lot! O heavy task! Why must I be the messenger of such an unspeakable tragedy?

THESEUS: Have no fear; take courage and tell me the bitter details of the disaster. My heart is not unused to hardship.

MESSENGER: My tongue refuses to give voice to my sorrow, my grief.

THESEUS: Speak! What calamity convulses our already shaken house?

MESSENGER: It's Hippolytus – oh, the pain! – he's met a pitiful death!

THESEUS: Long now has my son been dead to me. Now that rapist has met his end. Tell me every detail of his death.

MESSENGER: After he fled the city in panicked steps, rapidly covering ground with hurried strides, he at once yoked his chariot to his mighty steeds and fitted the bit tightly to their obedient mouths. Then, after muttering much to himself and cursing his country's land, he cried out his father's name several times, then sharply lashed his horses to action and gave them free rein. Suddenly, the mighty sea rumbled from its depths and swelled to the stars. No wind was whipping up the salt-sea. No quarter of the peaceful sky thundered. The calm sea was disturbed by an upheaval all its own. Never have I seen the sea like this, not even when south winds whip up Sicilian waters, not when north-westerlies drive the Ionian sea into a swollen rage, buffeting sea-crags with a mighty pounding, scourging Leucas' heights with hoary sea-surf. The sea, in all its enormity, swelled up into a colossal mound, but that terrifying mass was not meant to be the ruin of ships: no, it took aim at the land. The surge advanced slowly, ponderously; the wave was carrying something monstrous in its pregnant womb. Was Earth about to reveal some new land to the stars above? Was another Cycladic island rising to the surface?

The crags of Epidaurus, famed for divine Asclepius' power, disappeared behind the sea-wall – the god had willed it so. Soon Sciron's rocks, land notorious for a brigand's crimes, fell from view, then Corinth, that narrow slip of land between two seas. While we were watching all of this in shock, the whole sea began to roar and the cliffs rumbled on all sides. Sea-spray erupted from the wave's summit; again and again waterspouts spewed forth, just like when an immense whale unleashes from its mouth the sea it gulps down as it glides through the deep waters of Ocean. The whole mass of water then rose into a giant bristling arc and broke, releasing its load on to the shore, a bane beyond our fears. The sea rushed on to the lands behind the monstrosity it bore – my lips tremble even to tell it.

What an awesome appearance, what a massive body! It was a bull, a towering bull – its neck was sea-blue, a tuft of hair sprouted high from its green brow, and its bristling ears stood erect. In its eyes there were streaks of different colours as befit a mighty leader of a wild flock, and one born under the sea: one part flashed fire, another sparkled brightly with cobalt tones. Rippling muscles bulged along its sleek neck, its nostrils flared wide as it snorted. Green mossy patches clung to its dewlap and chest, red seaweed was strewn along its broad flanks. Down past its back its body converged into a monstrous shape – a massive sea-creature with an immense, scaly tail – just like those leviathans in the distant seas who swallow and destroy swift-moving ships.

The earth shook. Panicked herds fled throughout the fields in every direction, but the cowherds had no mind to pursue their cattle. Wild animals scattered from their pastures into the woods, yet pale hunters froze, shaking under the icy grip of terror. Only Hippolytus was immune to fear: he gripped the reins tight to control his horses, spurring his panicking team on with encouraging shouts with his familiar voice.

There is a road that runs towards Argos along the high cliffs, hugging the sea that stretches beneath it. Here that massive creature began working itself up into a frenzy and rehearsed its rage. Once it had found its full fury, whipping its head back and forth, it charged like a speeding arrow. Its galloping hooves hardly touched the earth and, faster than you could say it, the creature, wild-eyed and menacing, stood in front of the chariot and shaking team. Yet your son did not blanch in the face of that monster. No, he rose up to his full height and returned a fierce, threatening look. He thundered mightily: 'Ha! you will not break me; your menace is futile – defeating bulls is a task I learned from my father!'

At once the horses swerved, disobeying the reins, and careered off the path, carried wherever fear and fright drove them. Heedless and wild, they raced over the rocky crags. Yet your son was as deft as a helmsman who keeps his craft aright on the turbulent sea, not allowing his ship to go broadside, skilfully thwarting the waves. No less deftly did he steer his careering chariot, now pulling tight on the reins, now spurring his horses on with repeated blows to their backs. But his persistent companion followed, relentlessly, now racing along-side the chariot, now wheeling around to block its path. It brought terror from every direction. Eventually there was nowhere left to turn. That monstrous, horned sea-creature made a full frontal charge. Your son's stallions, gripped with panic, paid no heed to his commands and fought to free them-selves from the yoke. Rearing up on their hind legs, they discarded their burden.

As Hippolytus tumbled face first from the car, his body got tangled up in the reins, a treacherous snare. The more he struggled, the more tightly the web of rope gripped him fast. His steeds felt what had happened: with the chariot lighter, and no master at the reins, they raced wherever fear took them. Such was the chariot-team of the Sun, when they raced through the sky with an unfamiliar rider, a burden they did not recognize; resentful that the day had been entrusted to an impostor, they jettisoned wayward Phaethon from heaven's vault.

He left a long swath of blood over the land as his head struck and bounced off boulders. Briars tore out locks of hair and his beautiful features were ravaged by harsh rock; his doomed beauty vanished beneath many a wound. His dying limbs were mangled as the racing wheels rolled over and over them. Finally he was snagged, caught on a tree-stump that had been burned into a sharp stake. The point drove right through his groin. With the wound his pair of steeds lurched to a stop, but only for a moment. As they tore free they also tore their master. Every thicket, every bristly briar patch with its sharp thorns cut into the flesh of the man, now half-dead, and every patch of brushwood stole part of his body.

His servants, a mournful train, wandered through the countryside, through the places where Hippolytus had been dragged to his death and ripped apart, following the long bloody trail that marked his path. His faithful hounds, baying sorrowfully, tracked down his missing limbs. But for all his mourners' painstaking toil, they were not able to reassemble his mangled body. [*Enter attendants with* HIPPOLYTUS' *body*] Is this all that is left of his glorious beauty? The man who was just now the illustrious partner of his father's power, the heir to the throne, who shone like a glorious star in heaven – his remains are being collected from all over and assembled here for his funeral pyre, for the last rites of the dead.

THESEUS: O Nature, you are too powerful! How strong is the blood-bond you forge between father and son! How we honour you, even against our will! I wanted that guilty man dead, but now that he is gone, I weep.

MESSENGER: One cannot reasonably lament what one wanted.

THESEUS: You've reached the pinnacle of misfortune, I think, when circumstances force you to wish for something repulsive.

MESSENGER: But if you still hate him, why are your cheeks
   drenched with tears?
THESEUS: I weep not because he died, but because I destroyed
   him.
      [MESSENGER *enters the palace.* THESEUS *remains onstage*]

CHORUS IV: Great Men Must Face Great Trials

How mighty the waves that toss the mighty!
Yet Fortune stings lesser men less.
God smites the humble with humble force.
A private life is a life of peace;
in lowly homes men live to see
their hairs grow grey in security.
   But rooftops that reach towards heaven's high gates
   catch Eurus' gales and the gales of Notus;
      they feel the winter rage of Boreas
      and stormy Corus' squalls.
How rarely felt are lightning strikes
along the watery valley floors!
Yet the massive peaks of Caucasus,
the groves of mother Cybele,
shudder beneath the forceful bolts
of thundering Jove: in fear for heaven's
well-being, Jove assails what's close.
But a pauper's home with lowly roof
will never feel those mighty blasts.
For flashing lightning aims for kings.

Time flits about on fickle wings,
and fleeting Fortune offers no
one guarantees: behold, the man
who slipped from death's tenacious grip
and reached the shining skies above
bewails a mournful homecoming,
one far more tearful than hell itself.

Pallas, hallowed goddess of Attic soil!
Though your Theseus escaped the Stygian swamps
and now gazes on heaven and shining skies,
you owe no death-debt to your greedy uncle:
your account with the king of hell stands balanced.[31]

ACT V

CHORUS: Whose cry resounds in the lofty palace walls! [*Enter* PHAEDRA, *who runs to* HIPPOLYTUS' *body*] Oh! Phaedra's hysterical, brandishing a sword! What does she mean to do?

THESEUS: What madness, what grief stokes you to such hysteria? Why that sword, that howling? Why do you lament over that hateful corpse, beating your chest in grief?

PHAEDRA: Me, assail *me*, you pitiless lord of the deep sea! Send all your monsters in the dark sea against *me*, whatever distant Tethys harbours in her deep bosom, whatever Ocean embraces and hides beneath the shifting waves of his far-off streams! O Theseus, always cruel, you never return home without ruining your kin! Both your son and father paid for your home-comings with death; you always wreck your family, whether it be out of love or loathing for your wives.[32]

Hippolytus, what awful sight do I see? Your face, ruined! Did I do this to you? Or did some savage Sinis or Procrustes litter the ground with your limbs? Were you torn to pieces by some Cretan bull-monster, one that makes Daedalus' prison resound with mighty bellowing, a ferocious, two-bodied, horned-face beast? O where has your beauty gone? What happened to those eyes that once shone like stars for me? Is there any breath left in you? Hold on just a little longer, hear what I have to say. I will utter nothing shameful: with this hand will I atone for my sins against you; I will plunge this sword into my wicked breast and, with one blow, release Phaedra from life and from guilt.

Let me make peace with your ghost: here, accept this token taken from my head, a lock of hair cut from my brow which

I have torn in grief. Though we could not be joined together
in life, at least we can be in death. Die, Phaedra. If faithful,
for your husband; if unfaithful, for your love. How can I go
to my husband's bedroom, defiled as it is by such a great sin?
This one wicked act I did not dare to do, to enjoy my husband's
bed as if I were blameless and my honour had been vindicated.
O Death, sole remedy for a cursed love! O Death, greatest
glory for a ruined reputation, we are fleeing to your safe
harbour. Open up your gentle embraces!

Listen to me, citizens of Athens, and you, a father more
deadly than a deadly stepmother: I made up a false story, I lied
about his wicked act – one that I myself contemplated and
obsessed over in my fevered mind. You punished your son for
nothing, father, and now that faithful boy lies dead, the victim
of a faithless accusation, a virtuous, innocent victim. [PHAEDRA
plunges the sword into her body. To HIPPOLYTUS] There, you
have your old reputation back. My wicked chest has been
unsealed by this righteous blade, my flowing blood a funeral
offering for a blameless man. [*To* THESEUS] What you, a father,
should do when your son has been stolen from you, learn from
a stepmother: bury yourself in the depths of Acheron.

THESEUS: [*raising his hands to the heavens*]³³

Gaping jaws of grim Avernus,
    caverns of Taenarum,
Lethe's stream, you salve of sorrows,
    lifeless lakes in hell!
Seize this godless head and bury
    me in endless torment!
Come, leviathans of Ocean,
    creatures of the sea,
all that Proteus veils from view
    in his distant waters:
sink me in the deep abyss, the man
    who enjoys such outrage.
You, too, father, always ready
    to fulfil my anger:
I do not deserve a quick death,
    I who filled the fields

with the pieces of my mangled
    son – a new form of death;
while I sought my retribution
    for a trumped-up crime,
I, that rigid discipliner,
    wrought a crime myself.
I've filled heaven, hell, the salt-seas
    with my wicked actions.
I have nowhere left to turn now;
    I'm known in all three realms.

Is this what I returned for? Is this why a pathway to heaven lay open for me, so that I could witness two deaths, two funerals? So that I, widowed and bereaved, could set fire to the funeral pyres of my son and spouse with a single torch? Hercules, Alcaeus' mighty descendant, you who restored the cheerless light to me, send back your gift to Dis! Restore me to my rightful place among the dead, to the death which you stole from me!

In vain I call upon the death I left behind – my selfish curse against my son makes it so. No, Theseus, you crude architect of death, contriver of new, barbaric deaths, you must impose just punishment on yourself. Perhaps you should tie yourself to two pine-trunks bent down to the ground, which, when released, will tear you in two, or hurl yourself over Sciron's rocks? I've seen even more dreadful punishments, those that Phlegethon commands guilty souls to endure while imprisoned within the circle of its fiery waters. I know full well what place, what punishment awaits me in hell.

Guilty souls, make way! Let old Sisyphus' rock, his eternal labour, be transferred to these shoulders, right here, and weigh down *my* arms until they are spent. Let the river washing Tantalus' chin mock *my* lips instead. Let the savage bird fly past Tityus and come to devour *my* flesh and let *my* liver continually grow back for more punishment. You, too, Ixion, father of my dear friend Pirithous, be still: let *my* limbs be spun like a tornado on that ever-whirling wheel. Earth, gape open! Receive me, dark void, I beg you! This is a more virtuous journey to the dead than I took before: I accompany my son. Have no fear, you king of the dead, our journey is not for sex.[34] Receive me into that eternal abode, one from which I will never depart. [A pause]

The gods are unmoved by my prayers. Yet, if I were to ask them to do something criminal, how ready they are to act!

CHORUS: Come, Theseus, you will have the rest of time for your tearful laments. But now you must offer your son a proper funeral. Quickly lay his mangled body, so foully torn, to rest.

THESEUS: Bring the remnants of my dear son's corpse here. Give me that heap, that tangle of limbs and flesh. [Attendants bring the body to THESEUS]

Hippolytus? Is that you? I now realize my crime: it was I who destroyed you. And I was guilty not just once, nor did I limit the guilt just to myself: no, I, a father venturing on a reckless act, implicated my own father in the crime. [Gesturing to the body] Behold, this is my reward for using my father's gift. O death of a child, bane that brings sorrow to these broken years! Kneel down Theseus, you pitiful soul, embrace his body and clutch close to your sad heart all that remains of your son.

Go on, father, arrange the broken limbs of a mangled body, put the misplaced parts where they belong: here is where his powerful right arm should be; here should be placed his left hand, so skilled at controlling the reins. This looks like his left side. How much is still missing, how much will not feel the warm tears I shed!

Be strong, my hands, finish your sad task however much you tremble. Eyes, be dry. Hold back your sobs while a father catalogues his son's limbs and refashions his body. What is this misshapen and unsightly piece, torn on every side from many a wound? I do not know what part of you it is, but it is certainly you. Put it here – it's not the right place, but at least an empty one. Alas, is this your face, once beaming with star-fire, eyes radiating vitality? Is this what your beauty has become? How ill-starred your fate, how cruel the gods' blessing! Is this how a son returns to his father in answer to his prayers? [Pouring oil on the body] Here, accept this last gift from your father, these funeral rites, you who will be buried many times. For now, let fire consume these remains.

Open up the doors of the palace, polluted by murderous death. Let all of Attica, land of Mopsopus, resound with shrill lamentation. You, ready the fires for the pyre, a funeral for kings; you, range over the lands and look for the scattered remains of his body. As for the woman, dig a grave and cover her body with soil – may the earth weigh heavily upon her wicked soul.

All leave

OEDIPUS

Preface to *Oedipus*

When Laius, king of Thebes, and his wife, Jocasta, were about to have children, he received an oracle from Apollo at Delphi that he would be killed by his son. Ignoring the warning – or being too drunk to care – Laius slept with his wife and fathered a son. Fearful of the oracle coming true, Laius bored holes through the child's ankles, bound his feet together with pins and a leather thong, and handed him over to a shepherd to be exposed on Mount Cithaeron. In accordance with the oracle, the child did not die. Either the Theban shepherd could not go through with the cruel deed and gave the child to a Corinthian counterpart (the tradition followed in our play) or he was found exposed by a Corinthian shepherd while pasturing his flocks on Cithaeron. In either case, the shepherd delivered Laius' son to the queen of Corinth, Merope, who was cursed with childlessness. She passed the boy off as her own, and Oedipus (Greek 'Swollen Foot'), named after the physical defect caused by the pins, lived his life under the assumption that he was the royal son of King Polybus and Merope.

When he grew into a young man, Oedipus was insulted by his friends, who claimed that he was not the true son of the king. Wanting to find out the truth, he travelled to the famed oracle at Delphi, asked the god Apollo about his parentage and received the ominous message: 'Do not travel to your country; for you will kill your father and have sex with your mother.' Believing that Polybus and Merope were his biological parents, Oedipus did not return to Corinth, but travelled instead towards Thebes. Along the way, at a place where three roads meet, Oedipus ran into his biological father Laius, who was travelling to Delphi a

second time because of ominous portents. A scuffle ensued over
the right of way; the haughty king pushed aside young Oedipus,
who retaliated with a blow from his staff, killing the older man
and thus fulfilling the first part of the oracle. When he reached
Thebes, the city was being haunted by the monstrous Sphinx,
part-woman, part-bird, part-lion, who proposed inscrutable
riddles and killed all those who could not answer them. Oedipus
solved the riddle of the Sphinx and freed the city from its bane.
In return for this good turn, Thebes rewarded Oedipus with the
vacated kingship and married him to the widowed queen Jocasta,
his own mother, fulfilling the second part of the oracle.

Seneca's play is set ten years after his arrival at Thebes. The
city is stricken with a virulent plague caused by Oedipus' presence. This is the central religious concept of *miasma* ('pollution'),
which not only afflicts the guilty person but also infects everything else in that person's presence. Thus, the Theban plague
does not strike Oedipus alone, but afflicts the livestock, crops,
climate and other people as well.

When Oedipus appears at the beginning of the play, he intuit-
ively understands that he is the cause of the plague, not because
he has done something wrong, but because he believes he will.
Declared father-killer and mother-lover by Apollo, he knows
that he is doomed to kill his father and to have sexual relations
with his mother – it is only a matter of when. This knowledge
makes Oedipus extremely nervous and paranoid, as is revealed
in his opening speech. He is thus nothing like the confident
protagonist of Sophocles' play (*Oedipus the King*), who, with
great self-assurance, proclaims that he is resolved to discover
the cause of the plague and bring it to an end. Seneca's Oedipus,
on the other hand, is paralysed by guilt, fear and worry, and
anxiously wonders why the plague has spared him and him alone
of all those in the city. He is right when he states that Fate is
preparing something particularly vicious for him – the realiza-
tion of his past crimes.

Seneca's play essentially follows the basic outline of Sophocles'
more famous play, which Aristotle praises in his *Poetics* for its
excellence. The characters enter in the same order (Oedipus,
Creon, Tiresias) and the plot development is roughly the same,

at least in terms of Oedipus' self-discovery. There is, however, a great deal different about Seneca's play in addition to the characterization of Oedipus. There is no confrontation between Oedipus and Tiresias, who in Sophocles' play directly accuses Oedipus of being the killer and is in turn accused by him of being in a conspiracy with Creon. Instead, Tiresias conducts an extensive extispicy ('examination of entrails', Act II) to uncover the killer's identity; it is, like the Delphic oracle's response, ambiguous. This uncertainty leads to another scene that has no parallel in Sophocles' version, Creon's eye-witness account of Tiresias' necromantic ritual ('raising the dead'), in which the seer compels Laius to rise from the underworld and name the killer – Oedipus. Both the extispicy and the necromantic ritual are practices entirely within the Roman imperial cultural context. The play ends in typical Senecan fashion and, again, differently from Sophocles' version. Oedipus' self-blinding is narrated in gory (and gripping) detail and Jocasta kills herself onstage with a sword in the presence of her blind husband-son Oedipus.

Aeschylus and Euripides also wrote a version of *Oedipus*, both preserved in only a few fragments; one of these from Euripides' play indicates that Oedipus is intriguingly blinded not by himself, but by Laius' attendants. Seneca's play was (heavily) adapted by Ted Hughes and performed at the Old Vic Theatre in 1968 – heralding the resurgence of interest in Seneca's plays.

Characters

OEDIPUS, *king of Thebes*
JOCASTA, *his wife and mother*
CREON, *Jocasta's brother*
TIRESIAS, *Theban seer*
MANTO, *his daughter*
OLD MAN *from Corinth*
PHORBAS, *shepherd of Thebes' royal flocks*
MESSENGER
CHORUS *of Theban citizens*
ATTENDANTS *of Oedipus* (Mute)

ACT I

SCENE: Before the royal palace in Thebes. An altar sits in front. The time is early dawn.

[OEDIPUS *and* JOCASTA *enter from the central door.*]

OEDIPUS: Ah, dawn already breaks. Night has been driven off, and the Sun-god rises once again, reluctantly, his rays dim behind mottled clouds. As he raises his grim light, a torch of mourning, he will see the homes devastated by the ravenous plague. Day will reveal the heaps of dead that night has wrought.

Does anyone find joy in being king? Power, you deceitful blessing! How seductive an exterior you have, but what troubles you conceal! Just as high mountain peaks are constantly battered by whipping winds, just as rocky crags that separate mighty seas are pounded by waves, even when the sea is calm, so too are those perched on the lofty pinnacle of power always exposed to Fortune's blows. What foresight I had to flee my father Polybus' kingdom! As an exile I wandered about carefree, without a worry in the world, until I stumbled – I swear on the gods in heaven! – I *stumbled* into the power I now possess.

I fear unspeakable things, that I will kill my father with my own hands. This is the prophecy of the Delphic god whose temples are graced with laurel. Yet a still greater crime he declares I will perform. What sin could be greater than slaying one's father? O wretched family ties! I am ashamed to utter my fate. The bed of my mother, an unholy union beneath an incestuous marriage torch – this is what Phoebus threatens me with! This is the fear that drove me from my father's kingdom; this is why I left my father's home for exile. I have so little faith in myself that I had to ensure that Nature's laws could not be broken. When dread seeps into the very depths of your soul, you fear even what you do not think could possibly happen. I tremble at everything, and I cannot trust even myself.

Right now – I'm certain of it – the Fates are preparing to unleash some disaster on me. Why else would that pestilence now wreaking havoc upon Cadmus' city and leaving countless heaps of dead in its wake, spare me and me alone? For what fell punishment am I being reserved? Even as I walk through a decaying city, through piles of bodies, through never-ending funerals demanding ever fresh tears, I remain unscathed – I, who was condemned by Phoebus!

Did you really expect that a kingdom awarded to such a criminal as you could remain healthy? I have made the skies poisonous! No gentle breezes or soft-blowing Zephyrs with their cooling caresses soothe the raging fever in men's breasts. No, the Sun-god, as he presses hard upon the Nemean Lion's back, only increases the scorching fires of the Dogstar.[1] River-beds have lost their streams, the grasses their colour. Dirce's waters are dry. The Ismenus is but a trickle, barely wetting exposed rocks with its meagre stream. Phoebus' sister, the Moon-goddess, glides through the heavens beneath a cloak of gloom, casting an unholy pall on the world below, leaving it colourless and grim. No stars shine in clear night skies. A black fog lies heavily upon the earth, and a hellish shroud obscures the gods' citadels and mansions in heaven. Our crops, though mature, yield nothing. Ceres denies us her bounty; though the fields are full of tall rows of grain, the crop is barren and withers on arid stalks.

No group has been spared, no age or sex exempt – all are swept away to their doom together. The young are sent to death hand in hand with the old, fathers with their sons. A single torch cremates both husband and wife. Our funerals lack weeping and lamentation. The unrelenting carnage wrought by this pestilence has reached the point that our eyes have grown dry. This is what happens when you reach the bitter end – even your tears perish.

An ailing father carries one son to his final fire, while his

wife, a distraught mother, hauls another, only to hurry back
to bring a third to the same pyre. In the midst of grief new
grief arises. Grieving mourners fall dead as they attend a
friend's funeral. Then people start burning their dead on other
peoples' pyres. Fire is stolen. People at wit's end feel no shame.
There are no tombs for the dead. It is enough just to cremate
them, yet how few of them become ash! We have no land left
for tombs, no forests to provide timber for funeral pyres. The
stricken are helped neither by prayers nor by medicine. Doctors
die. The disease drags down all that come to help.

I prostrate myself before this altar and lift my hands in
prayer. I beg you, gods: bring my fate to fruition now! I want
to meet my doom before my country's utter collapse. Do not
make me my kingdom's final fatality! Gods, how cruel you
are! Fate, how harsh! Death stands right there before my eyes,
mocking me, shunning me alone of all those that populate
this city! Quit this kingdom, which your death-dealing hand
has infected. Leave behind the tears, the deaths, the stale,
poisonous air, which you, a cursed refugee, have brought with
you. Do not delay! Flee quickly – even if it means returning
to your parents.

JOCASTA: My dear husband, why make things worse by
complaining? Your troubles are already heavy enough! If you
ask me, it is the mark of a king to tackle adversity head-on.
The more precarious the situation, the more the weight of the
kingdom is teetering on the edge of collapse, the more firmly
and resolutely you must stand there and hold it up. Turning
tail before Fortune's threats is hardly the manly thing to do.

OEDIPUS: No one can condemn or accuse *me* of cowardice. My
bravery is proven. I have never felt the icy grip of fear. If
swords were drawn against me, if an army of Mars' bristling
soldiers were charging at me, I would boldly go forth into
battle – even if it meant grappling with savage Giants.

I did not shrink from the Sphinx, that weaver of inscrutable
riddles. I stood unflinching before the bloody maw of that
monstrous poetess, that priestess of doom. I stood bravely on
the ground made white by the scattered bones of her victims.
When she appeared on her rocky perch above me, already

slavering over her would-be prey, flapping her wings, lashing
her tail like a vicious lion, summoning up all of her menace,
what did I do? I demanded the riddle. She screeched dreadfully
above me, gnashed her jaws and impatiently tore at the rocks
with her talons in anticipation of my flesh. But I unravelled
her knotted words, her tangled trick. *I* solved the grim riddle
of that pitiless, winged monster.[2]

Fool, why do you now, at this late hour, pray for death?
You could have died right then and there! And what was the
reward for your good deed, your dispatching of the Sphinx?
What was your payment? Rule of the city![3] Now, now I see
it clearly: that monster, that cunning monster is now renewing
her war against me – from the grave! That is the plague bringing Thebes to its ruin! There is but one means of salvation:
perhaps Phoebus can show us some way to deliverance.

[JOCASTA *leaves.* OEDIPUS *remains onstage. The* CHORUS
enters from the wings]

CHORUS I: The Ravages of the Plague

You are perishing, noble line of Cadmus,
with the rest of the city; wretched Thebes,
you see fields bereft of their fallen farmers.
One by one, lord Bacchus, your army dies off,
your companions in furthest India,
boldly riding their steeds on eastern plains,
boldly planting your standards at the world's edge,
men who saw Arabia, rich in groves of
cinnamon, who looked on the Parthians' backs
as they shot formidable arrows, feigning
flight, deceptive tactics as they retreat,
men who marched to India's ruby seas,
where lord Phoebus rises, unveiling his light,
tanning unclothed Indians with nearby flames.

Our unconquered line passes to extinction,
sinking down beneath Fate's relentless pull.
One parade to Death ends, another begins:

sad-faced throngs, as far as the eye can see,
rush to join the dead, but the grim procession
lurches to a halt; seven gaping gates
are too few for the throngs that head to their graves.
Heaps of dead are littered about, a foul sight,
corpses slumped on corpses and joined in death.
The first outbreak attacked the livestock. Sluggish
sheep could barely nibble on verdant grasses.
When the priest stood ready to cut the bull's neck,
hand raised high and poised to deal the death-blow,
it collapsed, lethargic, its gleaming, gilded
horns now drooping; under the force of heavy
steel the neck was severed and gaped wide open,
but the blade was not stained with blood, but oozing,
fetid pus, a dark and diseased secretion.
Listless racehorses crumpled on the track,
pitching jockeys headlong as they buckled.

In the pastures abandoned flocks lie dying,
and bulls waste away as their herds die off;
cowherds fail to tend their diminished stock,
dying as they are amid wasting cattle.
Predatory wolves do not frighten deer,
angry lions' roars are now hushed and silent,
shaggy bears have lost their ferociousness,
lurking serpents no longer have their venom –
as their poison dries, they shrivel and die.
 Forests have lost their foliage
 and cast no shadows on the hills.
 Farmland lies fallow, brown and barren;
 no grapes weigh down great-clustered vines
 and bring them drooping to the ground.
 Everything suffers from our blight.
 Hell's sisters, hoisting baleful torches,
 have broken through the gates of darkness;
 the fire-river Phlegethon
 sends Stygian waters from its banks
 and mixes them with Theban streams.

Black Death now opens wide his greedy
jaws and unfurls his wings out full.
The ferryman,[4] who transports souls
across the turbid waves on a roomy
vessel, a wizened, tough old man,
but with a young man's vim and vigour,
can scarcely move his weary arms,
exhausted as they are from constant
poling, worn out by endless trips.

And now, they say, the hellhound has
escaped his iron chains and haunts
our lands. Groans issue from the earth.
Ghosts, giant ghosts, larger than life,
wander about our woods and forests.
Twice, they say, trees in Cadmus' grove
shivered and shook the snow right off.
Twice Dirce's streams ran red with blood.
Twice in the dead of night dogs howled
around the walls Amphion built.

Ghastly, these symptoms, this new death.
Dying, more grim than death itself!
Our limbs are limp with lethargy,
our sickly faces flushed in red,
lesions erupting on our skin.
Then searing heat attacks our heads,
swelling our cheeks with excess blood;
our eyes grow rigid, ears start ringing,
and from our nostrils pitch-black blood
comes oozing out of ruptured veins.
A constant coughing shakes our chests,
a crackling wheeze, the rattle of death:
accursed fire devours our limbs.

Some press their bodies on cold stones
to soothe the heat, a sad embrace,
while some – no longer quarantined

now that their guards have been removed
and buried – flee to find cool springs
and gulp down water to slake their thirst.
Great ailing crowds lie prostrate at
the altars, begging for death's release;
this plea alone the gods grant freely.
They visit temples – not to placate
god's will with prayers, but to glut
the gods themselves with dying bodies.

But who is this who seeks the royal palace with hurried steps?
Can it be true? Is it that man of noble blood and noble deeds
Creon? Or does my fevered mind deceive me? It is! It is he,
the man we have all prayed would come!

    [CREON *enters from one of the wings*]

ACT II

OEDIPUS: [*aside*] I shudder to think where Fate is leading me.
My breast trembles, buffeted by the tides of two emotions:
when happiness and hardship are tangled in uncertainty, the
anxious mind yearns to know the truth but fears it all the
same. [*To* CREON] Brother of my wife, if you have some news,
some relief for our troubles, out with it quickly. Tell us at once!

CREON: Ambiguous was the oracle's response, a tangled web of
words.

OEDIPUS: Offering ambiguous help is like giving none at all.

CREON: It is the Delphic god's way to conceal secrets in contorted
words.[5]

OEDIPUS: Tell me, however ambiguous. Oedipus alone has the
gift of teasing out knotty riddles. [6]

CREON: The god commands us to atone for king Laius' murder,
to avenge his death by exiling the murderer. Not before this
will we see the shining orb race brightly through heaven, nor
will the skies we breathe be healthy and pure.

OEDIPUS: Who murdered our illustrious king? Tell us the man
Phoebus named, so that he may receive his just deserts.

CREON:[7]

    May I be allowed, I pray,
        to tell of dreadful things –
    how my limbs are numb with fright
        and blood is chilled with fear!
    I had entered Phoebus' shrine
        to ask for needed aid,
    and had lifted up my hands
        to say a solemn prayer

when Parnassus' snowy summits
 thundered violently,
and Phoebus' laurel shook its leaves
 above me threateningly.
Suddenly, Castalia's sacred
 springs went wholly still.
She, Apollo's seer, began
 to shake her bristling locks,
madly, for the god possessed her.
 Just outside the cave
an inhuman sound burst forth,
 a mighty, deafening din:
'Mild will the skies return to Cadmus' Thebes,[8]
once that fell refugee that you took in,
king-murderer and bearer of this blight,
marked out by Phoebus in his infancy,
should leave Ismenian Dirce's land. Yes, killer,
short-lived will your rewards for murder be:
you will wage war against yourself, and leave
your sons a legacy of war, you who
foully returned unto your mother's womb.'

OEDIPUS: I am fully prepared to follow the god's commands,
but our fallen king deserved this long ago, lest others should
hope to violate the sanctity of royal power through treachery
and get away with it. A king must doggedly defend the security of kings. After all, subjects care not a whit about their lord
once he is dead, no matter how much they feared him while
alive.

CREON: Our concern for our fallen king was trumped by a
greater fear.

OEDIPUS: What fear could keep you from your duty?

CREON: The dire threats of that accursed riddler.

OEDIPUS: Then we must now punish the crime, as the gods
command.

 I call upon all gods who look favourably on kings and their
kingdoms. First, I call upon you Jupiter, whose hands conduct
the whirling heavens; and you Sun-god, greatest glory in the
clear blue skies, who pass through the twelve constellations

in your ever-changing course and usher in slow-moving seasons on swift chariot; and you Moon-goddess, night-wandering Phoebe, who dutifully come to meet your blazing brother; and you Neptune, lord of the winds, who drive your dark-blue chariot over the deep seas; and you Dis, who allot final resting places in the land of darkness – all of you hear me and grant my wishes! May the man who brutally murdered Laius find no peaceful residence or friendly home. May no land kindly receive him in exile. May he grieve over a shameful marriage and children born from incest, and may he brutally murder his own father too with his bare hands. May he perform all the wicked deeds that I avoided. No severer sentence could I render.

There will be no room for mercy. I swear this by the kingdom which I now rule here in my new-found land, and the one I left behind. I swear this by the gods that protect my household, and by you, father Neptune, who embrace with gentle waves the shores on both sides of my realm. I call upon you, too, to be witness to my words, Apollo, you who inspire the Delphic priestess's fated oracles. I swear that no favour or influence will save this man from me, so help me gods. If I do not stand by these words, may my father Polybus not enjoy a carefree old age and spend his final days as lord on his lofty throne in peace, and may my mother Merope come to know the bed of someone other than Polybus.

Someone tell me: where did this fell deed take place? Was Laius slain in open warfare, or was he ambushed?

CREON: Upon his journey to the lush woodland of holy Castalia, he came upon a path that was overgrown with brush, making the road tight and narrow. Here, three roads branch out into the open countryside: one carves a path through Phocis, the land cherished by Bacchus, where the gentle slopes of twin-peaked Parnassus leave the lowlands and ascend towards heaven. A second road runs towards Sisyphus' lands wedged between two seas.[9] The third path winds its way into the fields of Olenus, following a deep valley and skirting a meandering stream, finally cutting across the ice-cold shallows of the River Evenus. It was here, at the crossroads, that Laius, his guard let down in a time of peace, was suddenly ambushed by a band of brigands. Swords drawn, they attacked and left no witnesses to their crime.

[TIRESIAS *and* MANTO *enter with attendants and sacrificial animals*]

But here comes Tiresias, and at a good time, too, aroused by Phoebus' oracle, shuffling along as quickly as his aged, shaking legs will allow, led in his blindness by his faithful companion Manto.

OEDIPUS: Holy prophet, god-loved, Apollo's interpreter, decipher the oracle. Tell us: whom do the gods demand for punishment?

TIRESIAS: My king, that my tongue is slow to speak, that it needs time, should not surprise your benevolence. For from one without sight much truth lies hidden. Nevertheless, I go where my country calls, where Phoebus calls. We must dig to unearth the god's will. I no longer have the vital strength of my youth, else I would receive the god into this very breast of mine.

[*To his attendants*] Drive to the altar a white-backed bull and a heifer that has never felt the curved yoke upon its neck. Manto, dear child, you must guide your father who lacks the gift of sight and describe the omens made manifest in this ritual of divination.

MANTO: A fattened victim now stands before the sacred altar.

TIRESIAS: Now pray to the gods with solemn words, summon them to our offerings. Heap up eastern incense on the altar, a gift to the gods.

MANTO: I have placed an abundance of incense upon the sacred altar-fires of the heavenly gods.

TIRESIAS: And the flame? Has our generous offering caught fire?

MANTO: It suddenly flashed bright, but just as suddenly died down.

TIRESIAS: Did the fire dart straight up? Was it a vivid and bright tongue of fire lifting skyward, unfurling wispy flames and disappearing into the air? Or did it creep about the sides, directionless, smouldering with billowing smoke?

MANTO: The shifting flame kept changing its appearance, just as when Iris, the bringer of summer rains, weaves together her tapestry of colours, a great arc coursing through the vault of heaven heralding impending showers. You could hardly tell which colours were present and which were absent. The flame first shimmered blue mixed with bronze streaks, then it turned blood red. In the end it vanished into darkness.

Wait! The fire's separating into two halves, the embers of a single sacrificial fire divided, at odds.[10] Father, I shudder at what I see. The sacrificial wine poured on to the fire has turned to blood, and a dense cloud of smoke has descended around the king's head, settling even more thickly around his very eyes, blocking out the gloomy light with a dense cloud. What does this mean, father? Tell us!

TIRESIAS: I wish I could say, but I'm torn in confusion. It's bewildering. It defies interpretation. Some evil lurks here, yes, some grave evil, but it lies deeply hidden. The gods' wrath is usually made known by clear signs. But this – what is it that they want yet do not want revealed? Why do they keep the cause of their bitter wrath hidden? Something, I know not what, shames the gods.

Here, child, bring the cattle quickly. Sprinkle the sacred salted grains upon their heads. What is their reaction? Do they endure the ritual and being handled by the attendants with serene expressions?[11]

MANTO: At first the bull stood there majestically, holding its head high, but when it was positioned to face the rising sun, it grew deathly afraid of the light. Now it averts its gaze in terror and shrinks from the sun's rays.

TIRESIAS: Is one blow enough to bring them to the ground?

MANTO: The heifer rammed herself into the bared blade and from that one wound fell. But the bull has been struck twice, and still he thrashes this way and that. Though wounded and weary, the beast still clings to life, reluctant to yield up his life without a fight.

TIRESIAS: Does the blood gush out of narrow gashes, or does it ooze out slowly, pooling in the deep wounds?

MANTO: A copious stream of blood flows from the heifer, through the open wound in her breast. But the bull's deep gashes are stained only by a few drops – a great mass of blood has run back internally and comes out through his mouth and eyes.

TIRESIAS: These ill-omened signs kindle great terror inside my breast. Now describe to me the marks on the organs which will leave no doubt.[12]

MANTO: Father, what does this mean? The organs do not quiver gently as usual, but cause my whole hands to shake! A strange liquid spurts from the veins – is this blood? The heart is diseased and withered, hidden deep within the cavity. The veins are discoloured, a sickly black. Most of the entrails are missing. The liver is putrid, foaming and bubbling with black bile, and there – what a horrible omen, portending doom for sole power – twin protruding lobes of equal mass![13] But each is cleft and covered by a sheer membrane that allows no secrets to lurk undetected. The hostile side extends upwards along the healthy tissue, with seven veins fanning out over it. But the course of all of these is cut off by a slanting fissure, allowing none of them to return.[14] The position of the organs is altered, nothing sits in its right place – everything's been pushed back. The lungs lie in the right part of the chest, shrivelled and clotted with blood – hardly enough for a breath. The heart is not on the left, nor does the caul stretch its fatty folds over the intestines in a soft lining. The natural order is confounded. The belly is a confused mess. Wait, something is causing great stiffness in the entrails – let me investigate. Great gods, what's this abomination? This heifer has conceived, a virgin birth! But the foetus is not where it should be, filling its mother in a strange place.[15] It groans as it moves, its frail and stiff limbs jerking and twitching. Dark blood has turned the entrails black.

The butchered carcasses are trying to walk! The bull, nothing more than an empty shell, has risen and attacks the attendants with its horns! The entrails keep slipping from my hands. And the sound that strikes your ears – that's not the deep bellowing of the herd nor the lowing of terrified cattle you hear. It is the moaning of the altar-fires and the rumbling of the sacred hearth.

OEDIPUS: What do these terrifying sacrifices portend? Reveal the

meaning! I will fearlessly drink deep your every word. Men find
boldness in desperate times – they have nothing left to lose.

TIRESIAS: You will come to envy these misfortunes for which
you seek relief.

OEDIPUS: Provide the one answer the gods wish us to know.
Name the man who polluted his hands by murdering the king!

TIRESIAS: Neither the flight of winged creatures who carve a path
through the skies on light wings nor entrails wrested from the
bodies of living creatures will reveal the name. We must try
another path to the truth. We must conjure up the king from
the realm of eternal night, so that, released from the darkness,
he may identify the perpetrator of the murder. We must unseal
the earth and take our pleas to Dis, pitiless, unyielding god that
he is; we must extract the Theban host housed in deepest hell
and lead them here to the land of the living.

Tell me: to whom will you entrust this ritual? It is forbidden
for you to behold the dead shades since it is in your hands
that the highest power in the land rests.

OEDIPUS: You, Creon, you are man for this task. All within my
kingdom regard you as my second-in-command.

TIRESIAS: Very well. While we go and unlock the gates of hell's
abyss, let these citizens here sing songs in praise of Bacchus.

[TIRESIAS, MANTO, *and* CREON *leave through one of the
wings.* OEDIPUS *remains onstage*]

CHORUS II: In Praise of Bacchus

[1]
Great god, whose hair is bound with bobbing ivy,
whose tender hands are armed with Nysa's thyrsi,
     Bacchus, shining glory of heaven,
          hear our prayers! Noble Thebes,
          your people, lift their hands to you.
     Turn your gaze here, so like a maiden's,
          spread your grace, dispel the clouds
          with your starry countenance.
               Fend off Death's dark threats
               and Fate's greedy jaws.

Springtime flowers should grace your hair,
your soft temples veiled in a Tyrian turban
or crowned in berry-bearing ivy,
with tresses streaming freely down,
or drawn back and tied in a knot.
This is how you looked
when in fear of your angry stepmother
you were raised in a sham disguise,
    soft limbs,
    a maiden's flaxen hair,
    dresses tied by saffron sashes.
Since then you have loved
    soft looks,
    draping dresses,
    and flowing, ornamental robes.
The vast eastern lands saw you like this,
the Indians who drink from the Ganges,
the nomads who break through the icy Araxes:
    you sat upon your golden chariot
    and guided your chariot-team of lions,
    in a long dress.

[2]
Old man Silenus follows you on humble
donkey, his portly temples wreathed in vines,
while lewd recruits perform your secret rites.
    A troop of Maenads escorts you,
    pounding the earth in ecstasy
    upon Pangaeus' lofty heights
    or Thracian Pindus' mountaintop.
Now comes Agave, wicked Maenad,
with Cadmus' daughters, mothers all,
attendants of Bacchus, god of Thebes,
with sacred fawn-skins on their backs.
For you these mothers, rapturous,
inspired by your power, let down
their tresses, shook their staves in madness
and tore King Pentheus' limbs apart.

But when the sting of madness ended,
their bodies lulled, they saw the blood,
recalling nothing of their crime.

[3]
Cadmean Ino, Bacchus' aunt, now rules
the shining seas, a choir of Nereids
around her, and her son, no mean god he,
Palaemon, rules the waves, a new arrival.
   A band of pirates, Tyrrhenian outlaws,
   abducted you when you were but a lad.
   But Nereus calmed the swollen seas,
   and turned the waters into meadows.
   A plane tree extended verdant branches,
   a laurel unfolded its foliage loved by Phoebus,[16]
   and on their branches birds chirped noisily.
   Creeping ivy seized the oars,
   vines wound round the mast and sails,
   on the prow a Phrygian lion roared,
   and an Indian tigress crouched astern.
        The pirates,
       white-faced
     with fear,
   leapt overboard,
     forms changing
       as they plunged
        into the deep:
chests and bellies fused as one,
tiny flippers dangled from their sides;
with crooked backs they dived below
and carved the sea with moonlike tails.
They pursued the fleeing ship
as humpbacked dolphins.

[4]
You sailed upon the golden Pactolus,
a river racing through rich Lydia.
The Massagetes, who drink a blood-milk brew,

for you put down their Getic bows and arrows.
Ax-man Lycurgus' lands felt Bacchus' might.
  So, too, the land of the fierce Zalaces,[17]
  all the northern wanderers
  battered by Boreas' blasts,
  all the peoples living along
  Maeotis' frigid waters,
  all that sit beneath the starry gaze
  of the Great Bear and its twin, the Wagon.
Bacchus tamed the scattered Geloni,
and wrested arms from warlike women,
Amazons who dwell along the Thermodon:
  they fell prostrate before you,
  giving up at last their whistling arrows;
they became Maenads and worshipped you.
Sacred Cithaeron, bathed in blood,
witnessed the slaughter of Pentheus,
descendant of the Serpent Race,
as he was torn limb

                    from bloody

     limb.
Proetus' daughters made for the woods,
and Argos came to worship Bacchus,
despite his stepmother's presence there.[18]
Naxos, encircled by Aegeus' Sea,
gave a forsaken maiden a marriage,
making good her loss with a better mate.[19]
  From dry pumice Bacchus made wine flow:
  babbling brooks

                     carved paths

    through the grasses,
and the earth drank deep the sweet juices,
    white springs of milk,
    thyme-scented Lesbian wine.
He led his new bride into great heaven,
as Phoebus,
    hair cascading
      down his back,

sang a festive wedding song,
and twin-natured Cupid
waved the wedding torches.
Jupiter put his fiery weapon aside,
hiding his thunderbolt
as Bacchus approached.[20]

[5]
As long as shining stars in timeless heaven
speed on their paths, as long as Ocean rings
the world with waves and Moon replenishes
the fires of her orb, as long as Dawnstar
heralds the Sun's arrival in the morn
and the great Bear sinks not beneath the waves
of sea-blue Nereus, will we adore
the shining countenance of comely Bacchus!

ACT III

[CREON *enters*]

OEDIPUS: Your grim face already tells a sorrowful tale. Still, tell us whose life we must forfeit to placate the gods.

CREON: You bid me to speak; fear bids me to keep silent.

OEDIPUS: If Thebes' downfall is not enough to sway you, at least be swayed by the fact that your family's power is slipping away!

CREON: You will soon regret what you are now so eager to know.

OEDIPUS: Ignoring the situation – what a pathetic way to deal with trouble! Do you intend to withhold information that could save the state?

CREON: When the medicine is repulsive, one loathes being cured.

OEDIPUS: Tell us what you heard. [OEDIPUS *motions to his attendants to arrest* CREON] Else I'll break you with excruciating torture and teach you what force an angry king can bring to bear.

CREON: Kings come to hate the words they extract from subjects.

OEDIPUS: You will be sent to the dark land of death, your one despicable life sacrificed for us all, unless you disclose, in your own words, the secrets revealed at the ritual.

CREON: Please, do not compel me to speak. I beg you to give me this one right, the smallest request that one can make of a king.

OEDIPUS: The right to remain silent has often caused more damage to a king and his rule than free speech.

CREON: If we don't have even the right to remain silent, what rights do we have?

OEDIPUS: Remaining silent when ordered to speak – that's insubordination!

CREON: Since you force me to speak, I beg you to listen calmly. Do not grow angry at me.

OEDIPUS: Who ever has been punished for speaking under compulsion?

CREON: [*pausing to summon up courage*] Far away from the city, in a vale watered by Dirce's streams, there sits a grove, a lair of darkness beneath black holm oaks, a sinister place. Tall cypresses soar above the forest, their evergreen trunks always covered in foliage, and ancient oaks stretch out their crooked branches rotting with age. The trunks of some have been eaten away by the jaws of time; others' roots have so weakened that they now lean, propped up by other trees. There are other kinds there too: bitter-berried bay trees, graceful lindens, Paphian myrtles, alders that will one day become the oars that propel Greek ships over vast seas, and stone-pines that strain to greet the sun, exposing their smooth trunks to the west winds.

At the very centre of the grove there stands a giant tree that looms over its lesser companions and casts a heavy shadow over the whole grove as it extends its branches wide. It is a lone sentinel standing guard over the woodland sanctuary. Down beneath this tree stands a cheerless pool of water, eternally cold, never knowing Phoebus' rays, a sluggish, gurgling spring surrounded by mire and swamp.

As soon as the aged priest set foot in this place, he brooked no delay: the spot afforded darkness like night. A pit was dug and torches stolen from funeral pyres were pitched in. Tiresias wrapped himself in a drab funereal cloak and waved a branch over the pit. The old man, unkempt, grim-faced, covered in ash, stepped forth to begin the ritual. A dark, dusky robe swept the ground as he moved and his silver hair was bound by a wreath of yew, the tree of death. Black-fleeced sheep and black heifers were dragged to the pit[21] and hurled in. The fire devoured the offerings. The animals convulsed in the flames, living flesh in a deathly fire.

Then he invoked the buried ghosts, the lord who rules over the dead and the hound who guards the gates to the lakes of hell. He intoned a long magical spell, furiously chanting dark incantations meant to placate or compel the ghostly shades. He poured a libation of blood upon the fires, burned the carcasses whole and drenched the entire pit with the gore of his victims. He also poured a libation of snow-white milk and then of wine, the gift of Bacchus, with his left hand. He began his spells again; staring at the ground, he tried to conjure up the dead in a deeper, possessed voice.

Hecate's hounds howled; three times the valleys resounded mournfully. Deep convulsions shook the whole earth. 'Success!' the seer said. 'My spells were efficacious. We have been heard. The dark void has been unsealed. The hordes of Dis are granted a path up to the world above.'

The whole forest recoiled. Its foliage bristled. Solid tree trunks split open. The whole grove shook and shivered with fear. The earth sank and groaned deep within. We wondered: were the hidden depths of Acheron upset at the disturbance? Was the earth itself cracking open to provide a path for the dead? Was three-headed Cerberus thrashing about in anger and rattling its heavy chains?

Suddenly the ground split open and gaped wide into an enormous cavity. I saw with my own eyes the ashen-faced gods in the dark shadows of Hell; I saw the sluggish rivers and darkness darker than night. My blood ran cold and stopped in my veins. A dreadful army leapt forth from the chasm; the whole Serpent Race stood there with weapons drawn, that squadron of brothers born from the serpent's teeth beside Dirce's stream. Then there was a wild-eyed Fury, screeching dreadfully, blinding Madness, hair-raising Horror, and every other creature created or concealed in the land of eternal shadows: Grief tearing at its hair; Disease struggling to keep its sickly head up, Old Age, a burden to itself; anxious Fear; and even the bane that now insatiably devours the Theban people, Plague.

Our wits left us. Even Manto herself, well-versed in the rites and practices of the old man, was left stunned. But her father was undaunted, emboldened by his blindness, as he summoned up the bloodless throngs of pitiless Dis. The dead darted up like wispy clouds to that very spot and breathed deep the open air. Countless were the souls that were conjured by the seer's voice – more than the leaves that fall on the slopes of Eryx, more than the myriads of flowers growing in Hyblaea in the height of spring, more than the ceaseless parade of waves that crash along the Ionian seas, more than the flocks of birds that migrate from the Strymon river to escape the icy blasts of winter, carving a path through heaven, exchanging northern snows for the warmth of the Nile.

The quivering ghosts fearfully sought out hiding places in the grove's shadows. The first to rise from the ground was Zethus, restraining a fierce-horned bull with his right hand, and his twin brother Amphion, who held in his left hand the lyre whose melodious strains once moved stones. Next was Tantalus' daughter Niobe, along with her brood of children, together at last. Now safe in her arrogance, she walked about proudly and counted the ghosts of her children; her stern face still wore disdain. Another mother followed, even worse than Niobe, raging, god-possessed Agave, followed hard by the whole troop of Bacchants that helped her tear apart her son and king, Pentheus. And he, mutilated and bloody, dogged their steps, still raging and threatening them even in death.

At last, after his name had been invoked again and again, the one we had come for rose from the earth. Face red with shame, he sought a place far removed from the rest and hid himself out of sight. But the priest Tiresias pressed on and redoubled his efforts, repeating his infernal spells, until, finally, Laius brought himself into view of us all. Describing it makes my skin crawl: he stood there, the frightful image of death, his whole body soaked in blood, his hair dishevelled and caked in filth and gore. His mouth foamed as he spoke in a wild voice:

'Descendants of Cadmus, you savages who delight in the blood of your kin, go on, shake your thyrsi! Go on, tear apart the bodies of your children while possessed by the god![22] Less grotesque, that crime, than the one that haunts you now, the most heinous ever committed in Thebes: mother love. Thebes, you are ravaged not by the gods' wrath, but by the wickedness of one among you. Your destruction is not caused by pestilential breezes blowing in from the south, nor by some arid heat released by the rain-parched earth. No, it is a murderous king who, with blood all but still on his hands, claimed – no *seized* – the rewards of his brutal murder: your throne and his father's bed, a violation of all that is holy. He then inexorably thrust himself back unto his origins and filled his mother with an unholy seed for a second time. Yes, he did what even wild beasts would not do: he fathered his own brothers! A tangle of wickedness, an abomination more convoluted than the knotty riddles of his celebrated Sphinx!

'You who rule Thebes wielding the sceptre in your blood-stained hands, make no mistake. I, your father, your unavenged father, will hound you, along with everyone else in your kingdom. I will bring with me the Fury who presided over your marriage, and her whip-wielding sisters Vengeance and Revenge. I will destroy that incestuous house of yours and obliterate your whole line in a terrible familial war.

'Banish this man from your realm, now! Drive him into exile, wherever! Make him take his deadly presence from this land. Only then will the earth grow green again in flower-bearing springtime; only then will the life-sustaining breezes provide you fresh air to breathe; only then will the forests regain their glorious foliage; only then will Death and Destruction, Ruin, Suffering, Decay and Pain, a worthy entourage for such a man, leave as one alongside him.

'He will want to quit this land with swift steps, but I will slow his departure and hinder him on his journey. He will hobble along, uncertain of the way, tapping the grim path before him with an old blind man's staff. You, deny him the earth. I, his father, will take away the skies.'

OEDIPUS: An icy shiver shakes my bones to the core! What I feared I'd do I've been accused of already doing! But Merope, still married to Polybus, disproves that I've entered into some unholy incestuous union. And the fact that Polybus is still alive, well, that proves my hands are clean. Each of my parents rebuts a charge: my father clears me of murder, my mother of incest. How can I be guilty? Thebes mourned Laius' death long before I ever set foot in the land of Boeotia. Is the old seer a fraud or does the god hate Thebes?

[*Pausing, gazing at* CREON] Oh, now, now it's becoming clear, this clever plot – you two are conspiring against me! That account you just unravelled – it's nothing more than a seer's invention, a cover story about the gods conjured up to mask your own treachery. He's promised you the throne on which I sit!

CREON: Do you really think that I would want my sister banished from the royal palace? Even if loyalty to my kinsman – remember, I swore an oath to you – even if that did not keep me firmly fixed in my current position, consider this: the very idea of such a lofty position frightens me. It is always full of worry. I do hope that you can extricate yourself from this burden unscathed and that it does not crush you as you try to escape from under it. You will soon be in a less hazardous position, less prominent to be sure, but less hazardous nonetheless.

OEDIPUS: So you are urging me to give up the weighty responsibility of being king willingly?

CREON: Yes. I would recommend it even to those who still have options. You, well, you have no choice – you must submit to your fate.

OEDIPUS: Ah, to praise the ordinary life, to speak of easy living, rest, relaxation! That is the surest path for a man desiring power. The ambitious often feign a lack of ambition.

CREON: Do my loyalty and long service mean nothing?

OEDIPUS: Loyalty provides traitors with an opportunity to do harm.

CREON: But I have everything you enjoy as king without the burden of being king. My house is thronged with crowds of visitors, and as the days go by, not one passes when my home does not overflow with the good bounty flowing from my kinsman's power. I have fine clothes and lavish banquets, and many people owe me their lives through my influence. What could I possibly think is missing from this perfect life?

OEDIPUS: The one thing that's missing: prosperity always hungers for more.

CREON: So will I be convicted without a hearing?

OEDIPUS: Did *you* two consider the facts of my life? Did Tiresias
hear my side of the story? No. And yet I was declared guilty.
You set the precedent. I'm following your lead.

CREON: What if I am innocent?

OEDIPUS: It is in a king's nature to treat possible threats as real.

CREON: Kings overreacting to imaginary fears earn real ones.
Once a person is blamed, he is filled with hate – even if the
charge is dismissed.[23]

OEDIPUS: So, when in doubt, exterminate.

CREON: That's a recipe for earning the people's hatred.

OEDIPUS: Hatred – a king worried about that doesn't have a
clue how to rule. *Fear* keeps subjects in line.

CREON: Yet brutal kings who rule with an iron fist come to fear
those who fear them. Terror comes back to haunt the one who
causes it.

OEDIPUS: [*to his attendants*] Take this guilty man to a rocky cave,
shut him inside and watch him. I must return to the royal palace.

[OEDIPUS *enters palace;* CREON *is hauled off through one
of the wings*]

CHORUS III: Thebes' Eternal Haunting

Oedipus!
You are not the cause of our great perils;
your fate does not haunt Labdacus' descendants.
No, it is the anger of the gods that haunts us,
an ancient anger, stretching back to the time
when Castalia's grove provided shade
to a visitor from Sidon,
and Tyrian immigrants
bathed in Dirce's streams.
   Cadmus,
     son of great Agenor,
     exhausted from searching
     for his sister,
       Jupiter's mistress,
         his stolen love,
           all over the earth,

stopped in our woods, heart pounding,
and prayed to his sister's abductor.
Phoebus' oracle had bidden him
to follow a wandering heifer,[24]
one that had never suffered
      beneath the curved yoke
         of a slow-moving plough
            to till the earth.
And here he stopped,
abandoning his chase,
and gave his new land
a name from that accursed heifer:
Cow-country.[25]
Since then the earth has
not stopped producing
freakish monstrosities:
      First a serpent in a deep, deep valley,
                              gigantic,
         hissing,
slithering about the ancient trees.
It towered above the pines,
lifting its sapphire head
above the primeval oaks,
but the bulk of it
                              rested
      down below.
Then the pregnant earth gave birth[26]
      to armed men,
      brothers
who felt no love for each other.
The curved cornet blared,
the bent trumpet resounded,
clarion calls to war.
Their newly born tongues,
mouths unused to speech,
uttered their first sounds –
the rebel yells of war.
The fields were filled with battle lines,

kin worthy of their forebear Mars.
Their life-spans measured but a day,
born after Dawnstar set in morn,
dead before Eveningstar had risen.
The new arrival watched in horror
as new-born soldiers clashed in war,
a fearsome sight; he stood in fear,
awaiting their attack, until
these savage youths fell dead, and Earth,
their mother, took her children back
into her folds, a brood just born.[27]

May civil strife thus cease for good!
May Hercules' fair city, Thebes,
see wars of brethren nevermore!

Now add the doom of Cadmus' grandson:
   antlers of a spirited stag
     shaded his brow,
       unnatural branches.
His pack of hound-dogs
   chased him,
   their master,
and he, Actaeon,
   took to flight
   and dashed away
   on speeding hooves,
far from the mountain woods,
weaving
               through glens
   and rocky crags,
avoiding
              the feathers[28]
   stirred by the wind,
eluding
              the nets
   he had set himself.
At last he reached a placid spring

and in its glassy waters saw
  horns
  and feral features –
here, at the same spring
where the virgin goddess,
unforgiving defender of her modesty,
had just been bathing her maiden limbs.[29]

ACT IV

[*Enter* OEDIPUS *and* JOCASTA *from the palace with attendants*]

OEDIPUS: My mind keeps returning to troubling thoughts. I cannot shed this feeling of dread. Both heaven and hell impute Laius' death to my wicked actions, but my mind contradicts this charge. I know myself better than the gods ever could, and I am certain that I am innocent. Yet, a faint memory stirs in my mind. Once a man I encountered fell to the earth from a blow of my staff[30] and was delivered to Dis. He was a high and mighty old man who started the scuffle by forcing me, a young man at the time, off the road with his chariot. It was far from Thebes, in the land of Phocis, where three roads meet.

Dear wife, my soulmate, help me work out my confusion, I beg you. When Laius died, what span of years had passed since his birth? Was he killed in the prime of his life, full of vitality, or was he a weakly old man?

JOCASTA: He was neither young nor old, but closer to old age.

OEDIPUS: Was the king escorted by a large entourage?

JOCASTA: A great many had wandered off the road, confused by the uncertain path, but a few faithful men stayed close by the king's chariot as it toiled along the way.

OEDIPUS: Were any of these slain, joining the king in his fate?

JOCASTA: There was one, a loyal and brave man, slain in defence of the king.[31]

OEDIPUS: I have the guilty party. It all adds up: the number, the place – now tell me when.

JOCASTA: It is now the tenth harvest since . . .

> [*Enter* OLD MAN *from Corinth from the left wing, inter-rupting* JOCASTA]

OLD MAN: Hail, Oedipus! The Corinthian people call upon you to assume your rightful place upon your father's throne. Polybus has found eternal rest.

OEDIPUS: How savagely Fortune rages against me from every direction! Come, tell me how my father met his end.

OLD MAN: Deep sleep gently unwound his aged soul.

OEDIPUS: My father, dead, without bloodshed! You are my witnesses: I may now with a clear conscience raise my hands to heaven – they are untainted and no longer fear committing murder. Yet another, more fearful part of my destiny looms over me.

OLD MAN: Once you take your seat upon your father's throne, all of your fears will vanish.

OEDIPUS: My father's throne I will come for – it's my mother I dread.

OLD MAN: Why do you fear your mother, who anxiously awaits your return?

OEDIPUS: It's my devotion to her that keeps me away.

OLD MAN: Will you abandon her now that she's a widow?

OEDIPUS: There, you've hit upon my very fears.

OLD MAN: Tell me what deep-seated fear weighs upon your mind. I've kept many royal secrets locked safely away.

OEDIPUS: Sharing a bed with my mother, the Delphic god's prophecy – the very thought sends shivers through me.

OLD MAN: Put an end to these empty worries, and banish those revolting fears. Merope isn't your real mother anyway.

OEDIPUS: What? What benefit did she seek by passing me off as her own?

OLD MAN: Children keep disdainful kings faithful.[32]

OEDIPUS: Tell me, how do you know these bedroom secrets?

OLD MAN: Why, these hands of mine brought you to the mother who raised you when you were but a babe.

OEDIPUS: You . . . you brought me to my mother? Who gave me to you?

OLD MAN: A Theban shepherd, beneath the snow-covered ridges of Cithaeron.

OEDIPUS: What business had you in those woods?

OLD MAN: I was on that mountain pasturing my herds of horned cattle.

OEDIPUS: Tell me: do I have any distinctive marks on my body?

OLD MAN: Your feet – they had been pierced through with an iron pin. That's how you got your name, from that defect, from the swelling of your feet.[33]

OEDIPUS: I want to know who presented me to you.

OLD MAN: He shepherded the king's flocks. He was in charge of a group of shepherds that reported to him.

OEDIPUS: Tell me his name.

OLD MAN: I'm a tired old man. The first thing to go is the memory, which fades after long years of decay.

OEDIPUS: Would you recognize his face, his looks?

OLD MAN: Perhaps, perhaps. Often even the slightest reminder will evoke a distant memory that is buried beneath the sands of time.

OEDIPUS: [to his attendants] All of the animals have been driven to the altars for sacrifice. Their herdsmen will be with them. Slaves, go quickly, summon the man who supervises the herds. [Slaves leave]

JOCASTA:[34] Whether the answers you seek have been kept from you for some rational reason or by chance, you should let what has remained hidden for so long stay hidden. Unearthing the truth often means disaster for the one digging it up.

OEDIPUS: What disaster could be greater than what we face now?

JOCASTA: Make no mistake, what you seek with great effort must be great. The public's welfare rushes in from the right, the king's from the left; they're equally matched. Keep your hands clear. Don't stir up matters, and let Fate work itself out.

OEDIPUS: There's no reason to stir things up when times are good, but what harm is there to try and change things when the situation is desperate?

JOCASTA: Do you yearn for something more distinguished than

a royal heritage? Be careful: you may loathe the father you find.

OEDIPUS: I will find proof of my bloodline, even if I should regret it. I'm determined to know whatever the cost. [*Enter* PHORBAS; JOCASTA *shrinks backstage and enters the palace*] Ah, here comes the ancient man now, the one who had once been in charge of the royal flocks, Phorbas. [*To the* OLD MAN *from Corinth*] Do you recall the old man's name or face?

OLD MAN: He has a familiar look – I can't quite place his face, but then again it isn't completely unknown to me, either.

OEDIPUS: [*to* PHORBAS] You – when Laius held the throne, did you serve him? Did you pasture his well-fed flocks on the lowland slopes of Cithaeron?

PHORBAS: Cithaeron, lush Cithaeron, always full of green grasses; yes, it offers summertime grazing to our herds.

OLD MAN: Do you recognize me?

PHORBAS: My memory's foggy. I . . . do not know.

OEDIPUS: This man here – did you not once hand a small boy over to him? [*Pause*] Answer me! Don't you know? Why do your cheeks blush? Why are you searching for words? The truth hates delay.

PHORBAS: You're rousing memories buried beneath a great span of years.

OEDIPUS: Admit it, or torture will compel the truth from you.

PHORBAS: Yes, yes, I gave this man an infant, a useless gift. He never had the chance to enjoy life under the light of heaven!

OLD MAN: Say no such fell words! He lives, and may he long live!

OEDIPUS: What makes you say that the child you gave him does not survive?

PHORBAS: A slender iron pin was driven through both of his feet and kept his legs pinned tight. The flesh around the wound had swelled up, an inflamed and oozing mass, and the infection caused a great fever. His little body was burning up.

OEDIPUS: [*aside*] What more do you need? Your destiny's already at hand. [*To* PHORBAS] Who was the infant? Tell me.

PHORBAS: But I promised –

OEDIPUS: Someone, a torch, now! Fire will soon make you forget your promises.

PHORBAS: Is the truth to be learned through such bloody methods? Spare me, I beg you!

OEDIPUS: Do I seem cruel? Out of control? You have your revenge right at your fingertips. Just tell the truth. Who is he? Who sired him? Who gave birth to him?

PHORBAS: She gave birth to him, your wife. [PHORBAS *and the* OLD MAN *leave*]

OEDIPUS: Earth, split open! And you, lord of the dead, king of the shadows, cast me, an unholy inversion of sire and son, down into the depths of Tartarus! Citizens of Thebes, rain a shower of stones down upon this unholy head of mine, strike me down with your spears! Let fathers assail me with steel, and sons, too; let husbands and wives take up arms against me, and brothers, too. Let the ailing public take firebrands from funeral pyres and hurl them at me. Look at me! I'm on the loose, the disgrace of a whole generation, an abomination to the gods, the ruin of all that is right and holy – I, who deserved death on the day I took in my first awkward breaths.

Now summon up the courage equal to your transgressions, Oedipus. Now steel your nerves to perform some deed to match your sins. Go on, head into the palace, and quickly now. You must congratulate your mother for increasing our household with children! [OEDIPUS *leaves*]

CHORUS IV: The Golden Mean

> If the Fates allowed me
> to mould my life as I like,
> I would trim my sails
> to catch gentle Zephyrs.
> No gale-winds would pummel
> my sailyards and set them shaking.
> A steady, gentle breeze,
> a favourable wind from behind,
> would propel my ship carefree.
> Safe is the middle course;
> may my life flow gently so.

Recall the reckless lad,
who, fearing the Cretan king,[35]
took to flight, relying
on a strange new device,
artificial wings.
He headed for the stars,
trying to surpass real birds;
too much he asked of his wings
and gave his name to the sea.[36]
But shrewd old Daedalus
marked the middle course,
neither too high nor too low,
and waited for his winged son
beneath the mid-lying clouds –
just like a mother bird
who escapes an eagle's talons
and gathers in her brood
that has scattered out of fear.
Then he saw his son
in the sea, flailing his arms
hampered by his wings.
Whoever exceeds the norm
is poised to plunge to earth.

[*Enter* MESSENGER]
But what is this? The doors
are opening! Here comes
a slave of the king, beating
his head in grief and sorrow.

[*To the* MESSENGER]
Tell us, what news do you bring?

ACT V

MESSENGER: After our king realized that his fate was as foretold
to him and uncovered his unspeakable family history, he
pronounced himself guilty, condemned himself, then made for
the palace bent on violence. He raced into that hateful house,
just like a lion in the Libyan desert, raging, shaking its tawny
mane, glaring menacingly. His face was wild and full of
madness, his eyes feral, and he let out a deep roar of pain.
Covered in an icy sweat, his mouth foamed as he unleashed
a long string of threats, omens of evil. His heart-wrenching
pain, buried so deep, was now erupting.

  In his rage he was pondering some momentous act, something that would match his own fate. 'Why do I put off
punishment?' he said. 'Won't someone assail my wicked breast
with steel, or consume it with fire, or crush it with stones?
Won't some tigress or savage bird fall upon me and feast on
my flesh? Or what about you, accursed Cithaeron, witness to
so many crimes? Why don't you unleash the wild beasts from
your forests against me, or a vicious pack of dogs? Bring Agave
back! Oedipus, why do you fear death? Only death can free
the innocent from Fortune's grasp!'[37]

  After he had said this, he put his murderous, incestuous
hand upon the hilt and drew his sword. 'So this is how it will
be? Will you atone for your sins, great as they are, with a
death so swift? Is a single blow enough to redress them all?
Your death – enough for your father, perhaps. What about
your mother? Or the children sinfully brought into the light?
Or your poor country that pays for your sins by suffering such

destruction? What will you do for them? You cannot repay all of your debts! Nature changed her long-established laws for you alone, Oedipus, by inventing unheard-of forms of procreation; she must again be altered for your punishment! You must be allowed to live again and die again, to be reborn repeatedly so that you can atone for each of your sins with ever new punishments.

'Use your ingenuity, you miserable fool! If punishment cannot be repeated, it must last, yes, it must last a long, long time. You must choose a drawn-out death, find a way to roam the earth, neither joining the dead nor completely removed from the living. Die, but keep from your father's reach!

'What's the matter, Oedipus? Look, great showers of tears cascade down your face and drench your cheeks. As if crying were enough! No! My eyes must pour forth light drops no longer. They must be wrenched from their seats and follow those tears. These *married* eyes must be gouged out at once!'

As he finished speaking he flared up in rage. His menacing eyes burned with angry wildfire; the orbs seemed ready to leap out of their sockets. The man's gaze was violent, fierce, enraged, more intense as he got ready to dig. Then, bellowing and howling dreadfully, he thrust his hands towards his face. His eyes, still fierce, moved down to meet their hands, left eye to left hand, right to right, and went willingly to their wounds. He probed his eyes greedily and hooked his hands like talons around the orbs, and from their very roots he wrenched his eyeballs out, bringing both of them tumbling out together. He let his hands linger in the void, scratching the nails into the deep, hollow cavities, futile in his rage, reckless in his fury – so great was his desire to flee the light! He lifted his head up and as he surveyed the vast expanses of heaven with his vacant eyes he experienced only night. He tore off the mangled flesh still attached to the sockets and in triumph he invoked all of the gods at once: 'There! Now spare my country, I beg you! I have given the dead their due; I have endured the punishment I deserve – at last, I have found a night worthy of my marriage bed!' As he spoke, hideous streams of gore ran down his face

as his mangled head spewed blood from the torn veins.
[MESSENGER *leaves*]

CHORUS (Interlude): Fate[38] is Inescapable

Fate rules our lives. Submit to Fate!
None of your anxious worries will
alter the threads of destiny.
All that the human race endures,
all that it does, is wrought in heaven;
Lachesis spins our destinies,
life-threads immutable and fixed –
she does not brook a change of plan.
All travel down a preset path,
day one determining the last,
a string of causes, step by step;
not even god can shift the outcome.
And so it goes, each person's fate,
relentless – futile are all prayers.
So many fear itself has harmed;
while fleeing from our destinies,
we often meet them as we run.
    [*Enter* OEDIPUS]
The doors are creaking: Oedipus,
bereft of sight, marks out his path
alone, no guide to lead his steps.

OEDIPUS: All is well. It is done. I have repaid my debt, the last
    rites owed to my father. The darkness pleases me so. What
    god, at peace with me at last, has swathed my head in dark
    clouds? Who forgives my crimes? I have escaped the daylight,
    the witness to my crime. Parent-killer, you have done nothing!
    It was the light that fled from you. This, yes, this is the face
    that befits an Oedipus.
    [*Enter* JOCASTA]

CHORUS: Look! Jocasta, wild and distraught, bursts forth from
    the palace frantically, just like raging, god-struck Agave when
    she tore off her son's head – or rather, when she realized what

she had done. She baulks, uncertain whether she should address the poor man, desiring but dreading it all the same. Her anguish has overcome her shame, but the words still cannot escape her mouth.

[JOCASTA *pauses, preparing to address* OEDIPUS]

JOCASTA: What should I call you? Son? You squirm! Then you *are* my son – only a son would be ashamed. Say something, my reluctant son! Why do you turn your head, your hollow eyes away from me?

OEDIPUS: Who prevents me from enjoying the darkness? Who returns my sight? My mother's, oh!, my *mother's* voice! All of my efforts have been wasted! [*To* JOCASTA] It is forbidden for two unholy souls like ours to be together. We should be separated by the vast seas, removed from each other in distant lands. One of us should be carried away to the world that hangs beneath ours and gazes on different stars and the far-away sun![39]

JOCASTA: Fate's to blame for this. You are not at fault.

OEDIPUS: Spare me your speeches, mother, please. Spare my ears. I beg you by this mangled shell of a body, by our ill-starred bond of blood, by both the decent and wicked titles that define our relationship.

JOCASTA: [*aside*] Why do you move so slowly, Jocasta? Why do you refuse to pay the penalty for the crimes in which you were complicit? It was *your* incestuous ways that disturbed and destroyed all sense of decency governing humankind. Die, expel your unholy breath with steel. Is that enough? Even if the father of the gods who propels this world were to hurl his flashing bolts against me in violence – not even then would the punishment fit my crimes. Yes, death is certain. But how? [*To* OEDIPUS] Come, assist me, lend a mother your hand, if you are a parent-killer: this last step will complete your task. [*To herself*] No, let me seize his sword. This is the blade that laid low my husband – why don't you call him by his real title? He is your husband's father! Shall I plunge the blade into my chest or press it into my open throat down to the hilt? Oh, Jocasta, how little you know about choosing a wound!

[*Gesturing to her belly*] Hand, you must strike here, strike this spacious womb which bore both husband and sons![40] [*Kills herself*]

CHORUS: The queen is dead! Her hand died along with the wound and the great surge of blood pushed the blade out along with it.

OEDIPUS: Prophet-god, protector of the truth, I call you to task! I owed only my father's life to the Fates. Now I am twice parent-killer, more guilty than I feared. I have killed my mother, too! She was destroyed by my crime. Phoebus, you liar! I have surpassed my wicked destiny!

With nervous steps begin your treacherous journey. Carefully plant every footfall, guide yourself with your trembling right hand through this darkness. No, run hurtling away, scrambling as your steps slip out from under you. Go, you outcast, move! Wait, stop – you might stumble into your mother.

My people, you who with tired bodies weighed down by disease drag your half-dead shells about, behold, I am quitting this place. Lift up your heads! Gentler skies will come as I leave. All of you who lie gasping for air, clinging to your last breaths, rise! Draw in the life-giving air. Go, bring aid to those left to die. Look, I take with me the death-bringing blights of our land. Come, violent Death! Come, shivering Disease! Come, wasting Plague! Come, excruciating Pain, come with me! You will I gladly take as my guides.

[OEDIPUS *leaves*]

THYESTES

Preface to *Thyestes*

The horrors perpetrated by the house of Tantalus – perhaps the most dysfunctional of all Greek mythical families – begin with Tantalus himself. According to the tradition followed in *Thyestes*, Tantalus killed his son, cooked his flesh and fed him to the gods. For this crime Tantalus was punished in the underworld by being placed in a pool of water under a fruit-laden tree and stricken with dire hunger and thirst. But whenever he attempted to drink or eat, the water would recede and the fruit would spring away – the origin of our word 'tantalize'. His son Pelops – his limbs reassembled by the gods – was no less wicked. When he came to Greece to race King Oenomaus for the hand of his daughter, he bribed the king's charioteer Myrtilus, who rigged the chariot such that it fell apart in the middle of the race, giving Pelops victory. Despite this good turn, Pelops callously hurled Myrtilus into the sea. By some accounts, as Myrtilus was falling, he cursed Pelops' descendants with eternal wickedness.

In fulfilment of Myrtilus' curse, Pelops' sons Atreus and Thyestes constantly feuded and fought over the kingship of Argos, kingship which belonged to the possessor of the magical golden ram of Argos. At first Atreus possessed this ram, but Thyestes seduced his wife Aerope and with her help stole the sacred emblem of power, became king and banished Atreus from Argos. We are not told in *Thyestes* how Atreus regained power, but since he is king at the beginning of the play, he must have somehow regained the throne and exiled Thyestes, who was forced to live in the wilderness with his three sons.

This is the background of Seneca's *Thyestes*, which is focused on Atreus' further revenge against his brother. Despite the title, it is Atreus who commands our attention as he plans and executes his sinister plan. In Act II Seneca focuses on Atreus' all-consuming search for the *scelus ultimum* ('the ultimate crime'), one that will surpass the crimes of his brother and his ancestors – indeed, surpass all crimes that have ever been or ever will be. There are precedents for Atreus' crime: Tantalus himself had attempted to feed Pelops to the gods (see above), and Procne fed Tereus their own son. Atreus, however, successfully multiplies the crime, luring Thyestes back to the palace, sacrificing his *three* sons, and watching with relish as Thyestes happily devours all of their flesh. Some modern scholars have viewed Seneca's depiction of a heartless and vengeful Atreus as a thinly veiled criticism of the Emperor Nero and his murder of his brother Britannicus (see Preface to *Octavia*). Certainly, the author of *Octavia* saw Atreus as an analogue to Nero; he models the debate between Nero and Seneca directly on that between Atreus and his Adviser in our play (both Act II). But Seneca has made Atreus so compelling that it is hard to believe that criticism is what he had in mind. We are spellbound as Atreus, like a playwright deftly directing his own drama, controls his brother like a puppet and, act by act, lures him into his gruesome trap.

Thyestes, by contrast, comes across as weak, gullible, gluttonous and power-hungry – no matter how much he may protest otherwise. When invited back to share power with Atreus (Act III), he allows himself to be persuaded by his children, making the feeble claim that he is only doing it for them. When Atreus threatens to lay aside his own power after Thyestes refuses to take his share, the latter abruptly gives in and accepts the crown and regalia. When the Messenger describes (Act IV) and later we see (Act V) Thyestes at his gruesome banquet he is overjoyed, reclining on purple and gold, dressed in royal robes, his hair dripping with perfumed oils and graced with a garland, and he is gobbling down the feast before him so voraciously that food gets caught in his throat. He belches with contentment. Seneca is not portraying a Stoic wise man overcome by pure evil, as some have contended, but a deeply flawed man, irresolute, spineless, repulsive. In short, Atreus is far more appealing than Thyestes, despite his heinous crime.

Although the play ends with a triumphant Atreus and a miserable Thyestes, this will not be the end of the revenge. Following an oracle, Thyestes will father by his own daughter a son who will exact revenge against Atreus. This is Aegisthus, who will kill not only Atreus, but also his son Agamemnon (as told in Seneca's *Agamemnon*, not translated in this volume) after seducing his wife Clytemnestra. Agamemnon's son Orestes will, in turn, exact revenge against his mother and Aegisthus; only when he is brought to trial and exonerated does the cycle of crimes that began with Tantalus come to a close.

The long-lasting feud between Atreus and Thyestes was a favourite subject of Greek and Roman tragedians, but of the twenty plays that treated it only Seneca's survives complete. Sophocles' and Euripides' plays are almost wholly lost; the plays of the Roman tragedians Accius (fragmentary) and Varius (one line preserved) were well regarded in antiquity. Seneca's play itself was a model for many revenge plays of the Elizabethan and Jacobean periods, in particular Shakespeare's *Titus Andronicus* and Marston's *Antonio's Revenge*, although there is much disagreement as to the extent or degree of that influence.

Characters

GHOST OF TANTALUS, *grandfather of Atreus and Thyestes*
FURY, *punisher of familial wickedness*
ATREUS, *king of Argos, grandson of Tantalus*
ADVISER *to Atreus*
THYESTES, *brother of Atreus*
TANTALUS, *son of Thyestes*
PLISTHENES, *son of Thyestes* (Mute)
an unnamed son of Thyestes (Mute)
MESSENGER
CHORUS *of Argive men*
ATTENDANTS *of Atreus* (Mute)

ACT I

SCENE: Before the royal palace of Argos.
The time is just before dawn.

[TANTALUS' *ghost enters from a trapdoor in the stage*]
GHOST OF TANTALUS: Who, who has fetched me from my cursed seat in hell, where I was grasping for the food that flees my starving mouth? Who with malice in his heart shows to Tantalus once again these skies and the hateful mansions of the gods in heaven? Has some punishment been found that is worse than parching thirst amid pools of water? Worse than a hungry mouth always gaping for food? Am I to bear Sisyphus' slippery rock on my shoulders? Will Ixion's swiftly whirling wheel wrench my limbs? Will I suffer the punishment of Tityus, who lies stretched out in a vast cavern and feeds dark birds his mangled innards, growing back at night what they consume during the day, fresh fodder for those monstrous beasts when they return anew? To what new torture am I assigned?

O harsh judge of souls, whoever you are who dole out new punishments to the dead, invent some new form of torture, add it to your list! Devise something terrifying, something that would make the guardian of hell's grim dungeon tremble, send shivers through gloomy Acheron, and cause even me to quake in fear. For from my seed there arises a new brood that will outdo its ancestors in crime and make me look innocent. They will do what no one has dared to do before. [*The* FURY *rises from the trapdoor behind* TANTALUS] If there is any empty space left in the region reserved for the wicked, *I* will fill it. So long as Pelops' line remains, Minos will never have rest.[1]
FURY: [*cracking a whip with menace*] Go on, you damned ghost! Start tormenting your wicked family with madness! Make

your descendants fight using every sort of crime and continually draw their swords in retaliation. Let there be no limit to their hatred, nor any shame. Let blinding rage incite their minds. Let parents' madness linger and let their long cycle of crimes be passed on to their children. Allow them no time to feel resentment for an old crime – no, let a new crime always arise on its heels, and not just eye for an eye, but while an old crime is avenged let the new one grow greater.

Haughty brothers will lose their kingdoms, then be recalled from exile to rule again. The destiny of their house will swing violently back and forth between short-lived kings; the powerful will become humble, the humble powerful. Fortune will carry the kingship on a constant wave of uncertainty. When god restores to their country those exiled because of their crimes, they will return only to commit more. Everyone else will hate them as much as they hate each other. In their anger they will consider nothing off limits: brother will fear brother, father son, son father. Children will suffer wicked deaths but be born out of even greater wickedness. A hostile wife will plot against her husband. But in this wicked house adultery will be the most trivial of crimes. Righteousness, Faith, Law – all will perish.[2] Wars will be carried across the seas; every land will be irrigated by bloodshed. Lust will exult victoriously over the mighty leaders of nations. Not even heaven will be exempt from your wickedness! Why do stars still shine in heaven's vault? Why do their flames still feel obliged to offer their splendour to the world? No! Let there be deep night! Let day retreat from the sky! Embroil your household! Summon Hatred, Slaughter, Death! Fill the whole house with your contagion, fill it with the essence of *Tantalus*. Let the lofty columns and doors be festooned with lush laurel, and let a fire worthy of your advent blaze brightly. Let the Thracian crime be reenacted here – but in a greater number.[3]

Why is the uncle's hand idle? Will he ever raise it? It is time: let fires be lit, cauldrons be brought to a boil, and flesh be cut into pieces and thrown in. Let blood stain the ancestral hearth and the feast be laid out. You, Tantalus, you will come to this feast, a guest of a crime all too familiar to you.[4] I have given you a day of freedom; I release you from your hunger to attend this banquet. Break your fast, satisfy your ravenous appetite! Look on, while wine mixed with blood is drunk! [TANTALUS *backs away, turns and runs*] Have I found a meal from which even *you* would flee? Stop! Where do you think you're running off to?

GHOST OF TANTALUS: To the pools, the streams, the receding waters – even the fruit-laden tree that flees from my very lips! Please, I beg you, let me return to my dark prison cell! If you do not think that I suffer enough, then move me to a different river: let me be left in the middle of your stream, Phlegethon, surrounded by your fiery waters! Hear me, all of you who are sentenced to punishments doled out by the law of the Fates, you who lie within hollow caves and cower in fear of mountain walls threatening to collapse, you who are bound and tremble before the fierce maw of ravenous lions and the dread ranks of the Furies, and you who, already half-burned, try to hold off the onslaught of torches – hear the voice of Tantalus as he hurtles towards you! Trust me as one who knows: be thankful for the punishments you have! [*To the* FURY] When will you allow me to leave the world of the living?

FURY: After you have thrown your house into turmoil, after you have filled it with war and sword-lust, an evil to kings, and driven uncontrollable madness into their bestial hearts.

GHOST OF TANTALUS: I should *endure* punishment, not *be* one. Am I dispatched as some poisonous vapour from the earth's fissures? Or some pestilence to spread a baleful plague among my people? Will I lead my grandchildren into unspeakable evil? [*Holding up his hands*] Great parent of the gods, and mine too, however much it may shame you! Even though my tongue may be assessed a heavy penalty and tortured for speaking out, I will yet voice this warning, too:[5] descendants of Tantalus, do not defile your hands with accursed slaughter or stain the altars with the bloodshed of your mad revenge! I will stand my ground. I will thwart this crime. [*The* FURY *rises up to her full height and threatens to lash* TANTALUS] Why do you threaten me with lashes and terrorize me with writhing

snakes, rekindling that hunger residing in my deepest marrow?
It burns, how my heart burns with thirst, and the flames of
hunger flare up inside my burning belly! [*Relenting*] I'll
comply.

FURY: [*cracking her whip*] Spread this, yes *this* madness throughout your house. Let your descendants be carried away, blinded
by fury, and with hostility in their hearts thirst for each other's
blood. Ah, the whole house senses your entrance, shuddering
mightily at your wicked touch. Good, you have done more
than enough. Now go back to the caverns of hell and the
streams you know so well. Already the grieving earth revolts
beneath your feet. See how the springs disappear, driven back
underground? How the riverbeds grow dry? How few clouds
are borne along by the scorching winds? Look, all the trees
wither, their fruits gone, their branches barren. The Isthmus,
once echoing with the roar of neighbouring waters, once dividing neighbouring shoals with a slender slip of land, now
stretches wide, the distant sounds of the opposing seas now
but a murmur. Lerna's spring has retreated into the ground.
Inachus' channels lie hidden. The Alpheus no longer issues
forth its sacred waters. No part of Cithaeron's peaks is white
with fallen snow. Noble Argos fears the return of its primeval
drought.[6] Look! The Sun-god himself wonders whether he
should pull on the reins and compel the day that is destined
to perish to continue on its path!

[TANTALUS *and the* FURY *leave through the trapdoor*]

CHORUS I: The Wickedness of Tantalus' Descendants

If some god still treasures Achaean Argos
or Elean Pisa, land famed for chariots,[7]
or the realm of Corinth, that slender slip of
land dividing the sea, and its twin harbours;
if some god still loves the majestic snow-capped
peaks of mount Taygetus, made white by Boreas'
icy storms that blow in the wintertime,
only to be melted in summer months
by Etesian breezes that fill ships' sails;

if some god is moved by Alpheus' limpid,
frigid streams, renowned for Olympic races –
may he turn his benevolent powers here
and prevent a cycle of crimes from repeating!
May this generation prove worthier
than its ancestors! May this younger brood
find no joy in outdoing crimes of old!

Have the wicked offspring of parched, dry-mouthed
Tantalus, grim haters of kin, not yet slaked
their wild thirst for shedding each other's blood?
We have had enough! Let their blood-lust perish!
We are glutted with vengeance and reprisals.
Decency and respect for law have brought no end,
nor has widespread wickedness.
                                        Myrtilus,
who betrayed his king, was himself betrayed
and then murdered. Borne by the trust with which
he had borne his master, he made the sea
famous, giving it his own name: no story
is more told by sailors on Ionia's seas.

A little boy[8] ran to his father for a kiss,
only to be welcomed by savage steel.
On the hearth your son fell, untimely victim
he, carved up by your cruel hands, Tantalus,
to become a feast for the gods, your guests.
Now eternal hunger, eternal thirst
haunt you for this banquet; no punishment could
be more fitting for this barbaric feast.
Tantalus stands weary, his gullet empty;
over his condemned head hangs much to plunder,
but his prey is fleeter than Phineus' birds.
Here and there a tree droops down, branches bowed
by the heavy fruit, and it rustles, cruelly,
taunting Tantalus' gaping, starving jaws.
Hungry, craving, yearning to reach at once,
he, deceived so often before, holds off –

he averts his gaze, and his mouth he squeezes
shut and locks his hunger behind clenched teeth.

The whole grove then lowers its riches; languid
leaves now graze his head, and the fruits, so ripe,
shake and rustle above him, a callous dance
of temptation, kindling his hunger's fires.
Hunger orders him to stretch out his hands,
useless hands, but when he obeys its order
and surrenders eagerly to the trick,
the whole harvest, that fickle, faithless forest
springs away, pitched high back into the air.

Then dire thirst sets in, as severe as his hunger.
When his blood has come to a boil, and searing
torches stoke the flames, the poor creature stands there,
water lapping his chin; he tries to drink
with his lips, but the fleeting stream retreats
and deserts its channel, its banks abandoned.
Yet poor Tantalus tries to catch it: he drinks,
where great torrents once flowed, great gulps of dust.

ACT II

[ATREUS *and his* ADVISER *enter from the palace*]
ATREUS: [*reproaching himself*] You listless, spineless, gutless
fool! And – the worst reproach against a tyrant in a time of
crisis – you remain unavenged! After your brother's many
crimes, after all his treachery, after his violation of all that is
right, is your only action to sputter empty complaints? Is this
all that an angry Atreus can bring to bear? Long before now
the whole world should have been shaking beneath your
forces, your fleet combing the twin seas, the fields and cities
blazing bright in flames. Long before now swords should have
been drawn, the glint of steel everywhere! Let the whole
Argolid thunder with the hoofbeats of your cavalry. Scour
every forest, search every mountain fortress – let your enemy
have no shelter. Sound the battle call! Call forth your subjects
from Mycenae! Let the man who conceals or protects your
enemy's hateful life fall in bloodshed. Let even this mighty
palace of renowned Pelops collapse upon your head – so long
as it collapses on your brother's as well!

    Come, Atreus, do what no future generation would approve,
or ever forget. Yes, you must resort to some evil deed, grim
and bloody – the very kind your brother would wish were his
own. The only way to avenge a crime is to surpass it. But what
could be so savage as to surpass him? You know he's not lying
low; he's not one to show restraint in prosperity or resignation
in adversity. You know the man's stubborn ways. He cannot
be bent. He must be broken. Now then, before he finds his
feet and readies his dogs, he must become the prey lest he prey
on me while I sit passively by. It's either destroy or be destroyed.

The crime is sitting there for the taking – the first to pounce wins.

ADVISER: Do you not fear your subjects' disapproval?

ATREUS: Not at all. This is the greatest benefit of power: subjects must not only endure their ruler's actions, but also praise them.

ADVISER: Men forced into feigned praise by fear are the very ones fear makes into enemies. A king that seeks the glory that comes from true public support desires genuine praise more than false acclaim.

ATREUS: And yet, even the lowly enjoy genuine praise. Only the mighty enjoy *false* praise. We make them want what they do not.[9]

ADVISER: If a king pursues honest practices, the people's wants will be the same as his.

ATREUS: A king that has recourse only to honest practices is poised to fall.

ADVISER: No, it is the reign that does not observe decency, respect for the law, sanctity, piety or fidelity that is unstable.

ATREUS: Sanctity? Piety? Fidelity? Those are the common man's virtues. Kings may do as they please.

ADVISER: It's wrong to harm one's brother, even an evil one.

ATREUS: What is wrong to do to a brother is in his case justified. Tell me, what has he left unscathed by his evil actions? When has he refrained from crime? He stole my wife by adultery, my kingdom by thievery! With his treachery he attained the ancient emblem of power; with his treachery he threw my house into chaos.

In the majestic stables of Pelops there lives a splendid beast, a magical ram, the leader of a magnificent flock. Its whole body is covered by a rich fleece of gold, gold which gilds the sceptres that new Tantalid kings wield. Whoever possesses the ram is king; wherever it goes, the fortune of this mighty house follows. That hallowed beast grazes in sheltered meadows, in its own separate area enclosed by a stone wall that protects and conceals the fateful pasture. This ram my brother stole away, a venture great and bold, he the seducer of my wife, making her his accomplice in crime. This was the beginning of our feud, this, the beginning of our mutual destruction. Exiled and afraid, I drifted here and there in my own kingdom. In my own kingdom! Nothing of mine was left untouched by his treachery: my wife was seduced, confidence in my rule shaken, my house infected, and the paternity of my children cast in doubt. Nothing is certain – except that my brother is the enemy. [*To himself*] Why are you delaying? For god's sake, do something! Summon your courage! Look to Tantalus and Pelops: these are the examples you must follow. [*To* ADVISER] Come, advise me: how should I exterminate that accursed man?

ADVISER: Let him spit out his hateful life slain by the sword.

ATREUS: You speak of the outcome of punishment. I mean the punishment itself. The tyrant who merely kills is soft. In my reign death is something to be begged for.

ADVISER: Does family devotion not move you at all?

ATREUS: Devotion – if you've ever been in our house – leave now! Let the dread troop of the Furies come forth in your stead: Erinys, bringer of discord; Megaera, shaker of twin torches. The fury that blazes inside my breast is not enough; I yearn to be filled with something far more monstrous.

ADVISER: What new crime are you concocting in your madness?

ATREUS: Something that goes beyond the limits of ordinary pain. I will overlook no deed, and no deed will be enough.

ADVISER: Sword?

ATREUS: Not enough.

ADVISER: Fire?

ATREUS: Still not enough.

ADVISER: Then tell me: what weapon will such unquenchable pain employ?

ATREUS: Thyestes himself.

ADVISER: This madness goes beyond the bounds of human anger!

ATREUS: Yes, I know. Some supernatural turmoil has gripped my breast and churns deep inside. I am swept along – where, I do not know. I am not in control. The ground bellows from its depths, the clear sky thunders and the whole palace rattles as if breaking apart. Even the household gods have moved, averting their gaze. Yes, that's it! The crime that I will perform must be one which you, gods, fear.

ADVISER: What *are* you planning to do?

ATREUS: My mind swells with some irresistible superhuman force, and it goads my sluggish hands on. Scarcely do I know what it is, but it is something awesome. There it is, Atreus, seize it! For it is the kind of crime both Thyestes and Atreus ought to perform. Tereus' palace in Thrace once witnessed abominable meals – a delectably monstrous revenge to be sure, but one already taken. My pain must find some deed even greater than this. Give me strength, Procne, you parent and sister (our cause is similar), stand by me and drive my hand! Let the father in greed and glee rend his sons and devour their flesh. This is enough, yes, this is plenty. This form of punishment pleases me – for now.

    So where is he? Why is Atreus kept innocent for so long? Ah, the whole image of the carnage now plays out before my eyes: childlessness stuffed down a father's gullet! [*Hesitating*] Atreus, why are you again afraid? Why shrink before the deed? Come, you must be bold. This is the most delicious part of your wicked drama: Thyestes will play the lead.

ADVISER: By what snare will you catch your prey? How will he be drawn into our nets? He believes the enemy is lurking everywhere.

ATREUS: You cannot trap someone unless he is looking to trap you. Even now he hopes for my kingdom. In this hope he will undergo the perils of the swollen seas; in this hope he will enter the treacherous shoals of the Libyan Syrtes; in this hope he would face Jupiter even as he brandishes his thunderbolt; in this hope he would do what he reckons is the most perilous thing of all. He will look upon his brother.

ADVISER: Who will assure him that the truce is genuine? On whose word will he believe such a change of heart?

ATREUS: Shameless hope *wants* to believe. Even so, I will give a message to my children to deliver to their uncle: 'Leave behind your shelters and the nomadic life of an exile. Exchange your hardships for hegemony and rule over Argos with a share of the power.' And if Thyestes stubbornly rejects our entreaties, then I will take my appeal to his tender children, who, worn out by heavy trials, will be easily ensnared. On the one side his deep-seated lust for power, on the other grim poverty and hard toil will break the man, no matter how hardened he has become from his many trials.

ADVISER: Time has by now made his hardships light.

ATREUS: Wrong. Each day makes him more acutely aware of his plight. It's easy to bear misery for a day, onerous to do so for ever.

ADVISER: Choose someone else to carry out your grim plan. The young eagerly drink in the worst sort of instruction. What you teach them to do to their uncle they will do to you. Wicked deeds often come back to haunt the one who teaches them.

ATREUS: Even if no one teaches them the ways of deceit and crime, *power* will. Are you afraid that they may *become* evil? Our children are born that way! What *you* call cruel and harsh, what *you* believe is too severe and wicked – that very same thing is perhaps being planned in my brother's camp as well.

ADVISER: Will your children know that they're setting out the snare?

ATREUS:[10] Secrets aren't well kept in years so young. They will, perhaps, betray the plot. Silence is only learned through life's many trials.

ADVISER: So will you deceive the very ones through whom you would deceive another?

ATREUS: Yes, to absolve them from all responsibility. But why must I involve the children in my crime at all? I'll wage my feud by myself. Atreus, you coward! Are you retreating? If you spare your own children, you spare his, too. My son Agamemnon will carry out my plan, his brother Menelaus at his side, and both will be fully aware of my plan. From this crime will I seek proof of their doubtful paternity: if they refuse to conduct this war of hatred, if they call him 'uncle', he is their father. It's decided. They are to go.

But a troubled look often gives secrets away. Great designs betray men even against their wills. I will make sure they do not know how horrible a crime they are transacting. [*To the* ADVISER] As for you – keep our enterprise secret.

ADVISER: You do not have to warn me. Loyalty and fear will
    keep your secrets locked safely in my heart – but loyalty more.
        [ATREUS *and his* ADVISER *exit into palace*]

CHORUS II: The True King

At last! Our far-famed house,
the ancient line of Inachus,
has settled brothers' threats.
What madness goads you
into shedding blood by turns
and claiming the crown through crime?
You know not, palace-seekers,
where true kingship lies.
A king is not made by wealth
or the purple of Tyrian robes
or a royal crown upon one's brow
or ceilings that glitter in gold.

A king has banished fear
and dreadful vice from his heart;
he cares not for wild ambition
or the ever-shifting support
of the reckless, impulsive mob.
A king cares not for treasures
dug from western mines
or all the gold that Tagus
sweeps down in its gleaming bed
or Libyan harvests winnowed
on scorching threshing-floors.
A king is unshaken by the slashing
thunderbolt's path to earth,
by Eurus' roiling of the deep,
by the blustery Adriatic's
raging swells and savage seas,
undaunted by soldier's spears
and glinting swords unsheathed.
A true king is unassailable,

gazing down in tranquillity
at everything beneath him.
He freely meets his doom
and dies without complaint.

Let every king band together –
those who incite the nomadic
Dahae, those who rule
the shallows of the ruby shores
and the crimson sea, dyed
red with shimmering gems,
those who unbar the Caspian
Gates to stout-hearted Sarmatians.
Add those who boldly tread
on the frozen Danube's streams,
and – wherever they may reside –
the Seres famed for silk:
a good mind protects its kingdom.

No need for cavalry
or spears or the cowardly
shafts shot by the Parthian
host as it feigns retreat.
No need to bring forth engines
of war to smash down cities
by whirling boulders from afar.
A true king fears nothing;
a true king desires nothing.
This kingdom we give ourselves.

Let all who wish to stand
upon the slippery summit
of power take their chances.
As for me, may the sweet,
quiet life fulfil me;
may I enjoy the peaceful
pleasures of obscurity;
may my life flow gently on,

unseen by the public eye.
So, when my days have passed
without fuss or bother, may I die
an old and ordinary man.

Death is a burden to him
who, too well known to all,
dies without knowing himself.

ACT III

[THYESTES *enters from one of the wings, his three sons lagging slightly behind him*]

THYESTES: How I've longed for these sights! My country's rooftops, the treasures of Argos, and a miserable exile's greatest and most comforting gifts: the stretch of my native soil and ancestral gods – if gods exist. Ah, the sacred towers built by the Cyclopes, the glory that no human toil could achieve. Ah, the stadium thronging with young men. How many times I rode there in my father's chariot bearing the celebrated palm of victory! Argos will come to greet me, all its people will crowd around me – but, of course, so too will Atreus. No! Return to your refuge in the woods, to the thick mountain forests, to your rough bestial life in the wild. Do not allow the brilliant shine of power to blind your eyes with its seductive lustre! When you look at the gift, make sure you look at the giver too.

Just now, in conditions that everyone else thinks are harsh, I was resolute and happy. But now I am relapsing into fear. My mind is racked with doubt and wants to make my body go back. I try to take a step, but my foot refuses to go.

TANTALUS: [*aside*] What's this? Our father stands there in a sluggish daze, turning his head back and forth, unable to make up his mind.

THYESTES: Thyestes, why are you indecisive? Why torture yourself so long over a decision so easy to make? Will you put your trust in things most insecure, your brother and power? Why do you fear the troubles you've already surmounted, already

tamed? Why are you running away from the hardships you've
come to terms with? You are now happy being miserable –
turn back while you still can and save yourself! [*Turns around
and moves towards his sons*]

TANTALUS: [*to* THYESTES] Father, what makes you turn back
within sight of your country? Why do you close off your
pockets to such wealth? Your brother has put aside his anger.
He wants to reconcile and offers you a share of the power. He
is restoring the limbs of a mangled house and wants to return
you to your rightful standing!

THYESTES: You demand to know the reason for my fear. I don't
know myself. I see nothing to be afraid of, and yet I am
afraid. I am resolved to go, but my limbs grow slack and my
knees shake. I am torn, carried in a different direction than
I am striving to go, just as a boat propelled by oar and sail
is driven back downstream by currents that fight oar and
sail.

TANTALUS: Overcome whatever stands in your way and hinders
your judgement. Consider what great rewards await your
return. Father, you can be king.

THYESTES: Yes, since I am able to die.

TANTALUS: Being king is the ultimate –

THYESTES: – is nothing, if you desire nothing.

TANTALUS: You will leave it to your children.

THYESTES: A kingdom does not have room for two kings.

TANTALUS: Who chooses to suffer when he can be happy?

THYESTES: Trust me, people like things that are called great,
though they are really not. They irrationally fear what they
think are hardships. Listen, so long as I stood on the lofty
perch of power, dread was my constant companion, and I
feared the very sword at my side. How wonderful it is to be
in no man's way, to dine on carefree meals while lying upon
the ground! Crimes do not enter humble homes. One may lift
a cup from a meagre table without fear; it is from golden
goblets that poison is drunk. Believe me, I speak from experience: prosperity is not always better than poverty.

I don't have a palace perched on a high hilltop that towers
over and strikes fear into the cringing city beneath it. I don't

have gleaming ivory shining from high ceilings or a guard to
sit outside my bedroom to protect my slumber. We don't need
whole fleets to catch fish, nor do we force back the sea with
concrete piles and giant constructions. We do not feed our
insatiable bellies with the tribute of whole nations; no fields
beyond the distant Getae and Parthians are harvested on my
account. No one worships me with incense. My altars are not
adorned without paying respect to Jupiter. No forest sways
on my rooftop, no pools send forth steam heated by the work
of many hands, and we do not devote our days to sleep and
spend our nights awake in Bacchan revelry.

   All true. Yet no one *fears* us. We need no weapons to protect
our home. We have few possessions, but we have great peace
of mind. Truly awesome power is to be able to live without
it.

TANTALUS: But if god gives us power, we should not refuse it.
I'm not saying we should strive after it, but your brother is
asking you to rule.

THYESTES: He *asks*? Now that's something to fear. There's some
trick lurking beneath all this.

TANTALUS: Love of family often returns to those who once cast
it aside. Real love finds its former strength.

THYESTES: Love for Thyestes? My brother? Sooner will the seas
swallow the heavenly Bears,[11] sooner will the raging currents
of the seething Sicilian tides stand still, sooner will ripe grain
sprout from the Ionian sea, sooner will dark night provide
light for the earth, sooner will water make treaty and trust
with fire, life with death, wind with sea.

TANTALUS: Still, what treachery do you fear?

THYESTES: Every kind. What limit should I put on my fear? His
potential for harm is as infinite as his hatred!

TANTALUS: What could he do to you?

THYESTES: I no longer fear for myself; *you* are the reason I fear
Atreus.

TANTALUS: Are you wary of walking into a trap?

THYESTES: It's too late to be wary once the trap's been sprung.
Fine. We'll go. But as your father I want you to know one
thing. I do not lead. I am merely following you.

TANTALUS: God will look favourably on your good decision. Go forth with unwavering steps.

[*Enter* ATREUS *with* ATTENDANTS *holding robes and a crown*]

ATREUS: [*aside*] We have set out our nets, and our prey has fallen into our clutches! I see the one I'm after along with his whole litter of children, the future of his hateful line. Now my revenge is guaranteed: at long last Thyestes has fallen into my hands, yes, and with his whole brood at that! Scarcely can I control my mind, scarcely will my grief obey the reins. It is like when a sharp-smelling Umbrian hound, held by a long leash, follows its prey by pressing its nose to the ground to inspect the trail. So long as the scent of the boar is faint and its prey is far away, the hound obeys its master and rambles over the area with a silent snout. But when its prey is close, it strains with all its might against the leash and with a growl calls its sluggish master before it frees itself from its handler. When anger smells blood, it does not know how to conceal itself.

And yet it must. Just look at how terribly overgrown his hair is, how it falls over his gloomy face. How filthy his beard is! Our act must be convincing.

[*To* THYESTES] Brother, how good to see you! Return the embrace that I have longed for. Let bygones be bygones. Let us put aside our anger. From this day forward let us foster brotherly devotion and rid our minds of our accursed grudges.

THYESTES: I would refute every accusation if you were not so gracious. But I confess, Atreus, I confess: I'm guilty of every crime you suspected. The brotherly love you have shown me today makes my case indefensible. Whoever is guilty in the eyes of such a devoted brother is truly guilty. My case must rely on tears. You are the first to see me beg. By these hands of mine, which have never touched anyone's feet, I implore you: put aside your anger and rid your mind of its swollen pride. As an assurance of my good faith, brother, here, take these innocent children of mine.[12]

ATREUS: Take your hands from my knees. Seek instead my embrace. Come children, you who will protect us in our old age, you, too, put your arms around my neck. My, so many! Brother, take off those filthy clothes, spare our eyes! [*Motioning to the* ATTENDANTS] Take these royal robes, equal to my own, and joyfully accept a part of your brother's kingdom. Restoring my brother to his ancestral glory only adds to my own. Having power is owed to chance. Bestowing it shows virtue.

THYESTES: Brother, may the gods repay your gracious gifts with fitting rewards! But I fear I cannot touch the crown and my hand shrinks from grasping the sceptre – look at how filthy I am! It would be a bad omen. Just let me blend in with the rank and file.

ATREUS: This kingdom has room for two.

THYESTES: I have no doubt that what is yours, brother, is also mine.

ATREUS: Who refuses to accept fortune's gifts when they flow freely in?

THYESTES: One who knows by experience how easily they flow away.

ATREUS: So you would keep your brother from great glory?

THYESTES: Your glory is already complete. Mine? That remains to be seen. I am wholly resolved to reject all power.

ATREUS: I will relinquish my share, if you do not accept yours.

THYESTES: [*a short pause*] Then I accept. But in name alone will I wield the power that you've forced upon me. As for laws and arms, they will serve you, as will I.

ATREUS: Wear this crown upon your honourable head as a bond of your assent. I must be off. I must sacrifice the appointed victims to the gods above.

[ATREUS, THYESTES *and the children enter the palace*]

CHORUS III: The Power of Brotherly Love

Unbelievable! Our raging king, unyielding,
unrelenting, out of control – yes, Atreus
was stopped cold at the sight of his brother.
Nothing conquers true love of family:

angry feuds persist when it comes to strangers,
but those bound by true love will always love.
Learn: when Anger, aroused by great transgressions,
severs blood-bonds and sounds the call for war,
though fleet chargers clatter beneath their armour,
though the flurry of sword-strokes has begun,
a wild melee spurred on by raging Mars
in his thirst for fresh bloodshed – even then
Love will sheathe their swords, reuniting them
and restoring peace, even against their wills.

What god suddenly gave us peace amidst
such great turmoil? Just now throughout Mycenae
preparations for civil war resounded.
Mothers, pale with fear, clutched their children close;
wives felt fright for their husbands in arms
when their hands could not unsheathe unwilling
swords, blades rusted, a defect caused by peace.
One man struggled to buttress crumbling walls,
while another shored up decaying towers;
a third barred the gates with strong iron bolts
and spent anxious nights in defence of the walls,
lying terror-stricken upon the ramparts.
Worse than war is the fear of looming war.

Now the threat of furious strife has ended,
now the deep-pitched trumpets have fallen silent,
now the blares of bugles resound no more.
Once again the city enjoys deep peace.
Likewise, the relief right after a storm
when great waves from the deep come crashing in
and nor'westers batter the Bruttian Sea:
Scylla howls as her lair takes a beating,
even sailors in port cringe as Charybdis
violently disgorges the sea she swallowed,
and wild Cyclops, seated on roiling Etna's
rocky crags, is afraid that father Neptune

will unleash an enormous tidal wave
and extinguish his ever-burning forges,
and, as Ithaca quakes, poor old Laertes
thinks his realm might be swallowed by the sea.

But once the great gale-winds have spent their strength,
the sea is more gentle than tranquil pools,
and the deep, which ships were afraid to cleave,
is now speckled with countless sails unfurled
and provides smooth sailing to boats at play:
you could peacefully count the fish submerged
there, where once a furious tempest's blasts
made the shaken Cyclades fear the sea.
No condition remains long: pain and pleasure
come and go – but pleasure is more short-lived.
Brief, the moment exchanging low and lofty:
mighty kings who place crowns on others' brows,
before whom whole nations bow down in awe,
at whose whim foreign states put down their arms,
Medes and Indians living next to Phoebus,
Dahaean horsemen threatening Parthian posts –
even they wield their sceptres anxiously,
nervously, for they know how fickle fortune
and capricious time keep all things in flux.

You, on whom the lord of the earth and sea
has bestowed the power of life and death,
put aside your puffed-up and haughty airs!
Cow your subjects, terrify them with threats –
these same threats you face from your master's hand.
Every kingdom, however great, is always
poised beneath the fist of a crueller kingdom.
Every man that the dawning day sees haughty
that same man will the dying day see humbled.
Do not trust too much in prosperity,
nor despair of better days in misery!
Clotho mixes good and bad, never letting

Fortune stand still; she spins our lives at will.
No one has the gods on his side so much
that he can promise himself tomorrow.
God keeps spinning our fortunes round and round
          like a swiftly whirling top.

ACT IV

[*The* MESSENGER *enters from the palace, dazed and confused*]

MESSENGER: How I wish that some whirlwind would sweep me into the air, envelop me in dark clouds and take such a horrific crime from my sight! O family that would make even Pelops and Tantalus feel shame!

CHORUS: What news do you bring?

MESSENGER: Where, where am I? Argos? Sparta, land of devoted brothers? Corinth that commands the Isthmus lying between twin seas? Or the Danube, providing the barbaric Alani a means of escape? Hyrcania, always white with snow? The lands where nomadic Scythians roam? What place is this that witnessed such a monstrous crime?

CHORUS: Speak. Reveal the wickedness, whatever it might be.

MESSENGER: I will when my mind stops reeling, when my body releases my limbs frozen with fear. The image of the brutal deed still stands fixed before my eyes. O raging tempest, carry me far off to the place where the sun goes when it is stolen from our sight!

CHORUS: You torture us by keeping us in suspense. Tell us what causes your chilling horror. Identify the perpetrator. I do not ask *who*, but rather which *brother*.

MESSENGER: At the highest point of the city there is a wing of Pelops' palace that faces south. Its facade rises to the height of a mountain and towers over the city menacingly, as if poised to strike the people should they rebel against their ruler. Here a vast ceiling gleams, spacious enough for a crowd of visitors. Lofty columns, richly marbled, support beams gilded with gold. But past these public spaces where crowds would gather, the opulent palace recedes into various areas.

In its deepest recesses there lies a secret region where an ancient grove is hemmed in by a deep vale, the hidden heart of the kingdom. Here no tree offers lush branches or is pruned by iron. No, here sways a dark forest of yew, cypress and black ilex. Rising above them all, an oak tree looks down from on high, towering over the grove. Here Tantalus' descendants solemnly inaugurate their reigns and seek relief in times of disaster and uncertainty. Votive offerings hang fastened here: blaring trumpets, a broken chariot, spoils from the Myrtoan Sea, the vanquished wheels and the rigged axles – every crime of his family. Here hang Pelops' Phrygian turban, spoils taken from the enemy, and an embroidered robe from his triumph over barbarians.

Beneath the shadow of this tree lies a sullen fountain, trickling sluggishly and forming a black cesspool, just like the foul waters of grim Styx that bind the gods to their oaths. Legend has it that here, in the blinding darkness of night, the gods of the dead groan, the grove echoes with the sounds of rattling chains, and ghosts raise their wails. Stories that cause people to shiver are here witnessed: masses of dead from time immemorial rise from their ancient graves to wander the earth, and from the ground spring creatures unimaginable. The whole forest always seems to be in flames, and the treetops blaze though there's no fire. The grove echoes with triple-barkings,[13] and enormous phantoms cause panic within the palace. Even day does not dispel the terror. The grove has a night all its own, and even at high noon fear of the dead reigns supreme.

It is here that men come to get answers in times of uncertainty. Oracles are loosed from the inner sanctum like thunder, and the cave rumbles when the god releases his voice.

It was here that Atreus came, seething, dragging his brother's children at his heels. After he decorated the altars – who could adequately describe the scene? He drew the noble hands of those young men behind their backs and tied crimson ribbons around their mournful heads. He left nothing out: incense, Bacchus' sacred wine, the knife used to scatter the salted meal on the victims' heads. Every detail of the ritual was observed to ensure that so great a crime would not be tainted.

CHORUS: Who laid his hand upon the sword?

MESSENGER: He acted as priest himself. He chanted dark incantations, prayers of death, gnashing his teeth as he spoke. He stood before the altar. He handled, arranged and prepared the victims consecrated to death. He acted as overseer. No role in the ritual was lacking.

The grove began to shudder. The earth shook and the entire palace swayed, teetering, shifting its weight this way and that like a storm-tossed ship. On the left a falling star drawing a dark trail behind streaked down from the sky. The wines poured into the fires as a libation flowed out as blood. The royal crown slipped off two, three times, and the ivory statues in the shrines began to shed tears. These portents disturbed everyone – everyone except Atreus. He alone stood unmoved and unshaken. He even raged against the gods, striking fear into them despite their menace.

Without delay he took his position at the altar, his eyes brooding and twisted. He moved like a hungry tigress in the forests along the Ganges, pacing back and forth between two bullocks, desirous of both victims but uncertain where to sink her teeth first, turning her jaws this way and that, holding her hunger in suspense. Just so did grim Atreus stalk the victims consecrated to his impious wrath. He debated which of the two he should strike first and which he would reserve for the second sacrifice. It did not matter, but even so he lingered, taking cruel pleasure in contemplating his bloody crime.

CHORUS: So where did the blade fall first?

MESSENGER: Do not think Atreus has no regard for family. The place of honour was dedicated to his grandfather: Tantalus was his first victim.

CHORUS: How did the young man react? What look had he in the face of death?

MESSENGER: He stood there steadfast, fearless. He refused to make pointless entreaties. But Atreus, he ferociously thrust the sword down into the boy's neck and pressed it deep into the wound, bringing his hand all the way to Tantalus' throat. When he removed the blade, the cadaver just stood there as it decided which way to fall. At last it fell, forwards, onto its uncle.

Then that savage hauled Plisthenes to the altar and united him with his brother. With a single stroke he decapitated him. The trunk below the severed neck collapsed forwards, while the head rolled away, mumbling some unintelligible protest.

CHORUS: What did he do then, after he had performed his twin slaughter? Did he spare the youngest? Or did he heap crime upon crime?

MESSENGER: He was like a thick-maned lion in Armenia's forests, which, though triumphant amid much slaughter, still broods over the herd. Its jaws drip with gore, its hunger sated, but even so does not yet put aside its rage, charging at bulls here and there, threatening the calves with bared but tired teeth. No differently did Atreus rage and swell with anger. Holding the blade stained with the blood of his twin slaughter, oblivious towards whom he was directing his rage, he violently drove it straight through the body. No sooner was the sword in the boy's chest than it stood protruding from his back: he fell, snuffing out the altar's fires with his blood, and he poured out his life through both wounds.

CHORUS: What a savage crime!

MESSENGER: Does this make you shiver? If the wickedness stopped there, you would consider him a devoted brother.

CHORUS: What greater or more horrible crime could there be?

MESSENGER: You think it is the end of the crime? It is but a step.

CHORUS: What more could he have done? Forbid cremation? Expose the bodies to wild beasts?

MESSENGER: If only he had! If only the bodies had been denied cremation! If only they were cast out to be a grim feast for birds and savage beasts! Under him, what is normally a punishment is something Thyestes would pray for: to see his children left to rot.

No age would believe this crime! Posterity would deny it!

The organs, ripped from the boys' living breasts, still throbbed.
The veins still pulsed. The hearts still beat. Atreus surveyed
the entrails, examined the signs and inspected the tissue of the
organs while they were still warm. When he was satisfied that
his victims were acceptable, he confidently turned his full
attention to his brother's banquet. He carved up the bodies
himself, removing limb from limb. He spread out their arms
and severed them where they met the trunk, cutting through
the tough sinews of the shoulders. Unfeeling, he stripped off
the flesh at the joints and cut through the bones. He preserved
only the heads and the hands, those recently given in good
faith. Some of the flesh he stuck on spits to drip over slow-
burning fires, some he boiled in cauldrons set over flame. But
the fire leapt around the feast above it. Atreus had to bring it
two, three times back into the quaking hearth, forcing it to
accept the burden above. It burned reluctantly. The liver on
the spits sizzled. It's hard to say whether it was the bodies or
the flames that groaned, but groaning there was. The fire
turned into pitch-black smoke, but the smoke itself, a gloomy
and heavy cloud, did not rise straight up and hang along the
ceiling, but settled down around the household gods in a hideous cloud.[14]

Phoebus, you allow too much! Though you turned back to
bury the light stolen from mid-sky, you have set too late! A
father now rends his children and devours the flesh of his own
brood with a grisly mouth! And he beams, oh, how he beams,
smiling, heavy with wine, his hair drenched with perfumed
oil. How often food got caught in his throat! There is one
fortunate aspect of your misfortune, Thyestes: you are not
aware of your troubles. But this, too, will pass. Though the
Sun-god has turned back and led his chariot along a course
to meet himself, though an oppressive night rises from the
east in daylight's hours and covers this gruesome deed in
unnatural shadows, it will come to light. The whole crime will
be revealed.

[MESSENGER *leaves*]

CHORUS IV: The Collapse of the Heavens

Where, lord of earth and heaven's vault,
whose rising scatters darkling night's
luminous stars, where are you turning,
forsaking day at noon-time, mid-sky?
Phoebus, why hasten from our sight?
Not yet has Vesper, the twilight-herald,
summoned the fires of the night,
nor has your chariot yet reached
its western mark, where you unyoke
your tired team whose job is done,
nor has the trumpeter yet issued
his third loud call as dusk approaches –
ploughmen, their oxen not yet weary,
are stunned that supper's come so soon.

What cause diverts you from your course
through heaven's dome? Why has your team
veered sharply from their routine path?
Have Giants broken through the gates
of hell? Do they threaten war again?
Has the old flame of hate rekindled
in Tityus' weary, wounded breast?
Has Typhon heaved aside the mountain
and stretched his massive limbs out full?
Have Phlegra's army wrought a path
to heaven, placing Thracian Ossa
on Thessaly's Mount Pelion?[15]

Heavenly cycles are no more!
Sunrise and sunset, gone for good!
The dewy mother of the dawn,
so used to passing off the reins
to the Sun-god in the east, is stunned
to see such chaos at her doorstep.
She knows not how to douse the weary
team, how to plunge their sweaty manes,

steaming like smoke, into the sea.
The Sun himself, disturbed by such
a strange reception, stares at Dawn
as he sets, and he commands the shadows
to rise, but night is not yet ready.
No stars arise to take his place,
no fires shine in heaven's vault,
no Moon dispels the eerie darkness.
Whatever it is, may it be night!
Our hearts are pounding, pounding hard;
our bones and bodies shake with dread!
May the whole cosmos not give way,
collapsing as ordained by Fate;
may shapeless Chaos not envelop
both gods and men a second time;
may Nature not engulf the earth,
the circling seas, the constellations
drifting throughout the spangled sky![16]

No longer will the lord of stars,
who ushers in the march of ages,
offer the signs of wintertime
and summertime with each day's sunrise.
No longer will the Moon, illumed
by Phoebus' flames, dispel the night's
fears and outrace her brother's team,
speeding along a shorter orbit.

All the divine celestial bodies
will plunge into the same abyss;
the Zodiac, along whose track
heavenly stars do make their way,
which carves a slanted path through heaven's
zones as it turns the long years through,
will watch the falling constellations
as it falls itself.
                    First Aries, herald
of springtime's early months, returning

the warm west winds to sails, will plunge
headfirst into the sea through which
he bore young Helle to her horror;[17]
then Taurus, who displays the Hyades
before his gleaming horns, will bring
the Gemini and Cancer's curved
claws crashing down along with him.
Then Hercules' great glory Leo,
bringer of scorching summer flames,
will fall from heaven's heights once more.[18]
Virgo will fall to the earth she left.
The scales of righteous Libra will fall,
pulling down stinging Scorpio, too.
The Archer, aged Chiron, who notches
winged arrows to Thessalian bowstring,
will drop his shafts, his bowstring snapped.
Now Capricorn, the frosty herald
of wintry months, will fall and shatter
your urn, Aquarius, whoever
you are. With you will Pisces, heaven's
last constellation, take its leave.
And those behemoths in the sky
that never sink beneath the waves
the all-consuming flood will swallow:
the one that segregates the Bears,
the Serpent, winding like a river,
and Ursa Minor, dwarfed by Draco,
frozen beneath the northern pole,
and Arctophylax, slow to set,
will fall, no longer fixed in place.

Are we of all the generations
in human history judged worthy
of being crushed by the world's collapse?
Is ours the final age of man?
For how harsh a fate were we created!
In our misfortune we have lost
the sun – or driven it away.

No more complaints; banish your fears.
You cling too avidly to life
if, as the world around you dies,
you do not wish to die yourself.

ACT V

[ATREUS *enters from the palace with his attendants*]

ATREUS: I walk among the stars! My head grazes against the heavens! I tower over the entire world! Now I possess the emblems of kingship and my father's throne. Gods, you are dismissed! I have attained my every wish. It is enough, plenty – yes, enough even for me. But why should it be enough? No, I will go on and stuff the father full of his children's deaths. So that shame cannot stand in my way, the watchful eyes of the Sun have withdrawn! Go on, while heaven is empty. How I wish I could have kept the gods from fleeing and dragged them all here by force to witness my feast of vengeance. But it will suffice that the father sees it.

Yes, Thyestes, though the day refuses, I will dispel the shadows that conceal your misfortunes. For far too long now have you reclined at my table as a carefree and merry guest. Enough food! Enough wine! I need Thyestes sober for suffering so great. Slaves! Open the temple doors![19] Let the festive house come into view. I want to see the colours he turns when he looks upon his sons' heads, what words spill out at that first moment of grief, how his body stiffens as he feels the shock. This is the fruit of my efforts: I do not want to see him miserable. I want to see him *becoming* miserable.

[*The doors are opened and the* exostra* *is brought forth with* THYESTES *reclining on a couch with a table of food before him*]

Ah, the halls are open and illuminated with the light of many torches. There he is, reclining upon purple and gold, left hand propping up a wine-heavy head. He belches! Highest of

the gods am I, king of kings! I have surpassed my every wish:
he is gorged.

Look, now he draws the wide silver cup full of wine to his
mouth. Do not hold back, Thyestes. Drink! The blood of so
many victims remains. The dark hues of well-aged Bacchus
will camouflage it. This is a fitting drink to cap off the main
course, yes, fitting indeed! Let the father drink the brew of his
own children's blood – he would have drunk my sons' blood.
Look, now he's breaking out into a festive song. He's tipsy!

THYESTES [*singing*]

O heart, long beaten down by woes,
now banish all your cares and worries!
Let sadness flee, let terror flee,
let poverty, that grim companion
of anxious exiles, flee as one.
It matters more how far you fall
than where you land. How great it is,
when you have fallen from your lofty
perch up on high, to plant your step
on solid ground. How great, when you
are crushed beneath the weight of hardship
and ruin, to bear on neck unbent
a broken kingdom's massive weight,
to shoulder that enormous load,
unbroken, undiminished, upright.
Come now, Thyestes, drive away
those clouds of savage fate that hang
above your head, and banish now
all memory of wretched days.
Now there is merriment! Allow
yourself to smile and sing – dismiss
the old Thyestes from your mind.

All hapless men are haunted by
a fault unknown to other folk:
they never trust in happy times.
Although good fortune may return,
they feel uneasy in their joy.

O grief, arising without cause,
why seek me now, forbidding me
to celebrate this holiday?
Why order me to weep and cry?
What keeps my locks from being crowned
in graceful flowers? What, pray tell, what?
Roses of spring slip off my head;
my locks, though wet with lustrous oils,
now stand on end with sudden chills.
Rain pours from my unwilling eyes,
and groans intrude upon my song.
Gloom loves the tears it knows so well;
the wretched feel a strange desire
to weep. I yearn to voice ill-omened
complaints; I yearn to tear these robes,
these that imbibed the rich red dyes
of Tyre – how I yearn to wail!
My mind foresees more grief to come,
sure signs that evil lurks about.
As sailors know, wild storms approach
when seas are swelling without wind.

This grief, these fears are nothing more
than figments of your raving mind!
Offer your brother a trusting heart:
whatever fear you have, that fear
is either groundless – or too late.
I do not choose to be unhappy,
yet terror wanders in my breast.
My eyes pour forth these sudden tears;
I know not if from grief or fear –
or could it be great happiness?

ATREUS: [*approaching* THYESTES] A day of celebration, brother!
Let us rejoice in mutual harmony. This is the day that will
strengthen my reign and affirm our pledge of unshakeable peace.

THYESTES: I have had my fill of food, my fill of Bacchus. One
final touch would make my pleasure complete, if I could share
my good fortune and joy with my children.

ATREUS: Faith, brother. Believe me when I say your children are in their father's embrace. They are here and always will be! No part of your brood will ever be taken from you. Soon I will show you the faces you long for, father, and glut you with your children. You will be fulfilled, don't worry. Right now your children are mingling with mine at the pleasant rituals of the children's table. But I will summon them. Here, take our family cup filled with Bacchus.

THYESTES: I accept my brother's banquet gift. First, let wine be poured as an offering to our paternal gods. Now, let us drink it down. What is this? My hands refuse! The cup grows heavy and weighs down my hand. I bring the wine to my mouth, but it flees from my lips, running down my chin and jaws, cheating my gaping mouth. Look, the table jumps as the ground quakes! The fire grows faint! Even the skies loom heavily, deserted, stuck between night and day. [*Looking up*] What now? Heaven's dome rumbles ever more violently, tottering this way and that! A dark fog has formed, darker than thick shadows – night has buried herself in night. Every star is in retreat! Whatever is happening, I pray that my brother is spared – and our sons! May this maelstrom spend its whole force on this vile head of mine. Bring me my children now!

ATREUS: I will, and they will never be taken from you.

THYESTES: What is this convulsion that wreaks havoc in my belly? What is this rumbling within? It feels like some restless weight inside. My chest groans, but the groaning is not my own. Come, children! Your unhappy father calls you, come! Your faces will relieve me of this pain – [*hearing noises*] where are those noises coming from?

ATREUS: [*a slave brings a basket forward*] Open your arms, father. They're here. [*Uncovering the heads and hands of* THYESTES' *children*] Surely you recognize your children?

THYESTES: I recognize my brother. Mother Earth, how can you continue to support such villainy? Why do you not split open and plunge both yourself and us into the Stygian shadows of hell? Why do you not open up some vast fissure and fling both king and kingdom into the gaping underworld void? Why do you not wrench Mycenae's structures from the earth and bring them crashing to the ground? Long before now both Atreus and I should have taken our rightful place next to Tantalus. Tear open your seams, cleave them open here and there, extend your vast chasm down to the land beneath our ancestors in Tartarus – if that place exists. Bury us beneath hell. Let guilty spirits roam above my head; let fiery Phlegethon drive its torched sands along its burning bed above my place of eternal exile. Why, Mother Earth, do you lie motionless, a listless weight? The gods have abandoned us!

ATREUS: Oh, come now, be happy! Receive into your hands what you've been seeking for so long. Your brother does not stand in the way, so enjoy them, kiss them. Divide your embraces among the three of them.

THYESTES: Was this the deal we struck? Is this your idea of good will and brotherly trust? Is this how you put aside your grudges? I'm not asking you to return my sons to me, their father, whole. No, brother to brother, I ask only that you grant me what you can without diminishing your crime or your hatred: let me lay them to rest. Give them back, and you'll see them burned immediately. I'm not asking you for anything to keep, but to lose.

ATREUS: You have whatever remains of your sons. You also have what does not.

THYESTES: What? Are they lying exposed in the open, fodder for savage birds? Devoured by monstrous beasts or wild animals?

ATREUS: No. You dined on your sons at this unholy table.

THYESTES: So this is what the gods were ashamed of! This is what drove the day back where it rises. What words do I have for this . . . what complaints? How can I express my – I . . . I gaze at severed heads, cut hands, feet torn from broken legs! Is this all that a gluttonous father could not consume? Their flesh churns inside me, an abomination fighting to escape, without exit, without release. Give me your sword, brother – it has spilled so much of my blood already. With it I'll carve a way out for my sons. Do you deny me this? Then my hands must pound my chest with blows of mourning! No, check your hand, you poor fool. Be merciful to your sons' ghosts.

Has anyone ever witnessed such evil? Heniochian outlaws who live on the rough crags of inhospitable Caucasus? Or Procrustes, villainous threat to Athenian lands? No, not even they! Behold, I am a burden to my sons, and they to their father. Surely there must be some limit to crime!

ATREUS: Yes, when a crime is committed. But this, this is vengeance! What I have done so far is still not enough for me. I should have poured the warm blood into your mouth while the wounds were still fresh, forced you to swallow the gore while they were still alive. But in my haste I cheated my anger out of its due. Yes, I dealt their wounds, pressing the sword into their bloody flesh. I sacrificed them at the altar and stained my hearth with votive slaughter. I cut and carved their limbs, their small corpses into morsels, dropping some into boiling cauldrons and forcing others to drip slowly over fires. I severed their limbs and sinews while they still breathed. I watched as the flesh on the slender spits groaned; I stoked the flames with my own hands. Yet, all of this would have been better done by their father. My pain has come to nothing! Although you rent your own sons in your unholy mouth, you did not know it . . . they did not know it.

THYESTES: Seas enclosed by curving shores, listen to this crime! Gods, wherever you took refuge, listen! Dead shades! Mother Earth! Night, heavy with hellish dark clouds, hearken to my words! Your dark void is all I have left. You are the sole witness to my misery. You, too, have been abandoned, by your stars. I will make no greedy prayer. I seek nothing for myself. What could I possibly want for me? No, my prayers are made with you in mind.

[*Raising his arms aloft*] You, mighty ruler of the sky, lord and master of heaven's palace, swathe the whole world in bristling clouds, rouse up wars of winds on every side, thunder furiously from every direction! Do not employ the lesser bolt you use when assailing innocent houses and homes. No, release your full fury, use the force that destroyed the three mountains piled on each other and the Giants that stood equal to them. Unleash your weapons, hurl your fires! Avenge the lost day. Cast your fiery bolts. Replace the light that was stolen from heaven with your lightning strikes! Do not wait: we are both guilty. At least consider *me* guilty and attack *me*. Send your three-forked weapon, that flaming torch, right through this chest of mine. If I want to fulfil my fatherly duty, to cremate my children and lay them to rest, *I* must be cremated. If nothing moves you, heavenly gods, if no divine power assails the wicked with weapons of vengeance, let a permanent night prevail here on earth and conceal these monstrous crimes in everlasting shadows. I have no complaint, Sun, if you continue to flee.

ATREUS: Now I praise my actions, now victory is truly won. My deed would have been fruitless if you did not grieve so deeply. Now I believe that my children are mine. Confidence in my sons' paternity and my wife's fidelity is now restored.

THYESTES: What did my children do to deserve this?

ATREUS: They were yours.

THYESTES: But sons . . . to their father . . .

ATREUS: Yes, and, what delights me, they were yours.

THYESTES: I call upon the gods who protect the righteous!

ATREUS: What about those that protect marriage?

THYESTES: But to heap crime upon crime!

ATREUS: I know what you are complaining about: you're upset that the crime was snatched from your fingertips. You're not distraught because you devoured these horrific feasts, but because you weren't the one who prepared them! It was your game all along to lay out a similar feast before your unwitting brother and attack his children with the help of their mother, to strike them down just like I did yours. But one thing stood in the way: you thought *you* had fathered them.

THYESTES: Gods, avenging gods, will soon come for you. My prayers deliver you to them for punishment.

ATREUS: And I deliver you to your sons for your punishment.

All leave

OCTAVIA

Preface to *Octavia*

Octavia, the only historical drama on a Roman subject to survive complete, dramatizes a three-day period (a unique structure in the Senecan corpus) in the year AD 62, during which four main events unfold: 1) Nero's divorce of Octavia; 2) Nero's marriage to Poppaea; 3) the popular uprising against Nero in support of Octavia; and 4) Octavia's exile and sentence of death. Because the author of *Octavia* views this critical period as the culmination of a long line of imperial crimes, he constantly refers back to the scandalous imperial history leading up to Octavia's divorce. Instead of 'constantly' one might more justly say *ad nauseam*: Britannicus' death is mentioned or alluded to thirteen times, Agrippina's eight times, and Claudius' and Messalina's six times each. Given that the references to these events in the play are often obscure – for instance, neither Messalina nor Agrippina is named – an overview of the domestic history of the reigns of Claudius (AD 41–54) and Nero (AD 54–68) is in order.

Claudius, perhaps the most unlikely of all Roman emperors, was considered unfit for a public life by no less a figure than the first emperor Augustus (reigned 31 BC–AD 14), although Claudius was the grandson of his second wife Livia. But after murdering the tyrannical Caligula in AD 41, the Praetorian Guard (the emperor's personal bodyguard) discovered Claudius hiding behind curtains in the imperial palace and proclaimed him emperor. Although modern historians are rightly more balanced in their views of Claudius' reign, their ancient counterparts were decidedly hostile, accentuating his physical defects and wanton cruelty, his dependence on imperial freedmen, and – most importantly for our purposes – his obliviousness to his wives' machinations. His third wife Messalina, whom he married in AD 38 or 39, bore him his only son, Britannicus (so named in honour of Claudius' victories in Britain), and a daughter, Octavia. Messalina, however, was notorious for her promiscuity, which reached the point of absurdity in AD 48 when she went through with a mock wedding to one of her lovers, Gaius Silius, a leading aristocratic figure who may have been plotting with her to overthrow the emperor. Modern historians are at a loss to explain Messalina's motives, but, whatever her reasons, Claudius had Messalina and Silius killed. There ensued a competition to replace Messalina. The winner was Agrippina the Younger, a woman of imperial blood, the daughter of the extremely popular general Germanicus and the great-granddaughter of Augustus on her mother's side. They married in AD 49.

Agrippina was remarkably ambitious. After her marriage to Claudius, she unabashedly went about installing her own son from her previous marriage, Lucius Domitius Ahenobarbus, on the throne, although there was a legitimate heir in Britannicus. In AD 49 she recalled Seneca to act as her son's tutor and prepared the way for her son, eleven years old at the time, to wed Octavia (aged eight) by engineering the removal of Octavia's fiancé L. Junius Silanus through a trumped-up charge of incest. In AD 50 Agrippina convinced Claudius to adopt her son, who now took the name Nero Claudius Drusus Germanicus Caesar (or, as he is known today, 'Nero'), while she herself assumed the title *Augusta* ('Empress'), the first woman to take this title while her husband was still in power. In AD 51 she installed her loyal associate Burrus as the head of the Praetorian Guard.

Now that her son was officially heir to the throne, having married Octavia in AD 53, and she had allies in high places within the imperial court, Agrippina undertook in 54 to hasten her husband's death with poisoned mushrooms and secured the sixteen-year-old Nero's position as emperor against the more legitimate claim of Britannicus. In the following year Nero, under pressure from his mother to eliminate his stepbrother, had Britannicus poisoned at a banquet in the presence of his sister Octavia. Despite Britannicus' murder, the first five years of Nero's rule

were comparatively positive, with Seneca and Burrus guiding
Nero's policy and restraining Agrippina's influence. As Nero
grew older, however, he came to resent his mother's domineering
influence and sought to rid himself of this nuisance; she
responded, according to the historian Tacitus, by increasing her
affections – so much so that rumours of incest arose. In AD 59
Nero tried to dispatch her by putting her on a ship that was
rigged to collapse at sea. Ever resilient, Agrippina survived, swimming ashore and reaching her villa, where she was ultimately
killed by a henchman sent by Nero to finish the job. Seneca, as
Nero's official speechwriter, composed a letter to the senate
narrating a false story: there had been a boating accident, an
attempt by Agrippina on Nero's life, and her inevitable death.
A long list of her previous crimes followed.

In AD 62 Nero divorced Octavia on the grounds of sterility
and married Poppaea, the beautiful aristocratic woman who had
been his mistress since 58. Poppaea was probably behind Nero's
murder of his mother and certainly behind Octavia's divorce,
exile and execution. Poppaea was already pregnant when she
married Nero (as he informs us in the play) and gave birth to a
daughter in 63, but the child lived only four months. Poppaea,
again pregnant with Nero's child, died in 65 when he kicked her
in the belly out of anger. In the same year Nero ordered Seneca,
implicated in a conspiracy against him, to kill himself. In 68
Nero, facing the mutiny of his armies, the revolt of the Praetorian
Guard and a hostile senate, fled from Rome and ultimately took
his own life. He died childless.

Of the ten plays that have been transmitted down to us as
written by Seneca, *Octavia* is unique in that it concerns a historical subject. It is also not by Seneca. Although advocates of
Senecan authorship could be found in the middle and late twentieth century, no scholar to my knowledge still believes that
Seneca wrote it. There are many reasons to doubt its authenticity: the play alludes to events after Seneca's death (not least
Nero's death), Seneca himself appears in the play, and the
language of *Octavia* is often awkward and unworthy of Seneca's
plays. Since it seems to make use of written historical sources
but shows no direct familiarity with Tacitus' *Annals* the most

likely date of composition is during the late Flavian period, perhaps under Domitian (AD 81–96), but it could have been written any time before the thirteenth century, when the play is first found among Seneca's authentic plays and mentioned in the writings of Vincent of Beauvais.

Although not by his hand, *Octavia* is Senecan in one respect: the author was deeply influenced by Seneca's tragedies, borrowing whole scenes, concepts and phrases from Seneca's authentic plays (as well as from his prose works *Consolation to Polybius* and *On Clemency*). To name but a few: the opening speech by Octavia's Nurse recalls Hecuba's opening speech in *Trojan Women*; the debate between Octavia and her Nurse on the nature of Love is indebted to that between Phaedra and her Nurse in Act II of *Phaedra*; Octavia's position is compared to that of Juno at the beginning of *Hercules Insane*; and the debate between Nero and Seneca on the boundaries of a king's power (Act II) is clearly derived from the debate between Atreus and his Adviser in Act II of *Thyestes*. The author also often borrows specific language from Seneca's plays and not infrequently employs it in the same metrical position. It seems an inescapable fact that the author of *Octavia*, whoever he was, saw the historical moment he chose to dramatize *as a Senecan tragedy*.

The author's dependence on Seneca's tragedies – and further on Greek tragedies such as Sophocles' *Electra* and *Antigone* – makes it difficult to ascertain *Octavia's* place within the Roman dramatic tradition. Although the Romans had borrowed and adapted mythological tragedies from the Greeks, there also arose performances that dramatized events in their own history, called *praetextae* after the distinctive Roman garment that aristocrats and priests wore (*toga praetexta*). These *praetextae* – all lost except for some fragments – seem to have aimed at celebrating living or recently deceased members of the Roman elite, providing dramatized examples of patriotic action for the moral edification of the young, or (particularly in the empire) serving as vehicles for political criticism. But we are at a loss about the overall structure and form of those plays. Perhaps the non-Senecan structure (it does not adhere to the typical division into five acts) and the multiple-day format are influenced by that genre;

but these violations of dramatic unity and structure may just as easily be signs of the playwright's ineptness at handling his medium, experimentation with dramatic form, or the awkward result of trying to force too much history into a single play. Indeed, the play is, from a literary point of view, not very satisfactory. It is repetitive; we have two female protagonists, two nurses, two dream sequences and two choruses, all constructed in a similar fashion and framed around a central act (the rising of Agrippina's ghost and Octavia's exit from her father's palace). The language is also quite awkward at times. While we cannot rule out *praetextae* as an influence, the handling of the play seems to indicate that the poet was trying to mimic Seneca's authentic tragedies and was only partially successful.

Octavia intriguingly transmits some historical facts that are not otherwise found in our sources. Some contend that this proves that the author was an eyewitness to the events he dramatizes. But an analysis of the way in which the author employs historical data points to a heavy dependence on *written* historical documents; *Octavia* is full of dramatically unmotivated historical details. Because of the unique nature of the play and the numerous historical figures found within it, the annotation to this play is fuller than in the other plays (where the glossary will provide such information).

In the Middle Ages and the Renaissance *Octavia* was thought to be by Seneca and was as influential on early modern drama as Seneca's authentic plays – perhaps even more so. One finds this influence in, among many others, Richard Edwards' *Damon and Pithias* (1564), John Marston's *Antonio's Revenge* (1599–1600), Matthew Gwinne's *Nero* (1603 in Latin), Jean Racine's *Britannicus* (1669 in French), and G. F. Busenello's historical opera *L'incoronazione di Poppea* (1642–3 in Italian). As the only Roman historical drama, *Octavia* naturally served as a model for many early modern historical dramas set in Rome.

Characters

OCTAVIA, *daughter of Claudius, wife of*
the Emperor Nero
NURSE *of Octavia*
SENECA, *Nero's adviser*
NERO, *Emperor of Rome*
CAPTAIN *of Nero's guard*
GHOST OF AGRIPPINA, *mother of Nero, wife of Claudius*
POPPAEA, *Nero's mistress and later wife*
NURSE *of Poppaea*
MESSENGER
CHORUS *of Roman citizens, supporters of Octavia*
CHORUS *of Poppaea's supporters*
NERO'S SOLDIERS (Mute)

ACT I

[OCTAVIA *appears above the stage on a balcony*]

OCTAVIA:
Look, shining Dawn now sets to flight
the roaming stars in heaven's dome;
the Sun-god rises, crowned in sunbeams,
restoring daylight to the world.
O light, you always bring me sorrow![1]
Octavia, come, sing your dirge,
repeat your mournful lamentations –
so many troubles weigh you down.
Surpass the halcyons, sea-dwellers,[2]
surpass Pandion's winged daughters.[3]
Your lot is more lamentable.
Mother,[4] for whom I'll always mourn,
who set my woes in motion, hear
your daughter's doleful protestations –
if souls retain their consciousness!
Would that the aged spinster Clotho
had snapped my life-threads with her hands
before I saw your wounds, your face
covered in gruesome gore – how sad![5]
Since then the light has been more hateful
to me than shadows or darkling night:
I've done the bidding of my cruel
stepmother, borne her animosity,
endured her dark and brooding looks.
She was the one who led my bridal
procession, a grim Fury she,

lifting up torches fit for hell;
and she extinguished you, poor father,
you, once the master of the world
and all that lies past Ocean's waves;
before your might the Britons fled,
a race unknown to us before,
a free and independent people.
But now, dear father, you lie dead –
oh god! – ensnared by wifely guile;
your house and children are tyrant's slaves!

[OCTAVIA *returns inside. Enter* NURSE *from one of the wings*]

NURSE: All of you who are captivated and star-struck by the outward shine of power, a blessing so brittle, sure to disappear, look here![6] Fortune, lying in ambush, overturned Claudius'[7] mighty house and line with a sudden blow. Just now the whole world was subject to his power; Ocean, flowing unchained for so long, submitted to him and allowed passage to ships against its will. And now? The man who first vanquished the Britons, who blanketed unknown seas with mighty fleets, who amid barbarian tribes and on savage seas remained free from harm – yes, he was laid low, by his wife's wickedness. But soon she, too, by her son's. And his brother's life was extinguished by poison, and now his ill-starred sister-wife mourns, unable to conceal her deep anguish despite angry threats from her heartless husband.[8] I try to calm her grieving mind out of loyalty and devotion, but it's no use – her unrelenting pain prevails over my advice. That wilful spirit of hers, born out of nobility, cannot be reined in but only grows stronger with her suffering. What a sinking feeling I have that some unspeakable deed will come from this. May some divine power ward it off!

OCTAVIA: [*from inside*]
No suffering can match my lot,
beset by troubles and despair,
though I repeat your woes, Electra:[9]
for all your grief, at least you could
weep for your father and behold
the vengeance taken by your brother,

the one you rescued from the foe
and hid out of loyalty and devotion.
But I am kept from mourning over
my parents, who were torn from me
by Fate, that cruel divinity,
and grieving for my murdered brother.
All of my hopes I placed in him,
solace short-lived for a troubled life.
Behold, a woman spared to live
a sorry life, alone, in sadness,
a silhouette of a mighty name.

NURSE: [*hearing* OCTAVIA's *laments*]
Ah! My dear darling's sorrowful
voice pricks these ancient ears of mine!
Will you, old woman, let your age
keep you from your lady's room?

OCTAVIA: [*entering*]
Receive these tears of mine, dear Nurse,
you faithful witness to my sorrow.

NURSE:
Such misery! What day, dear girl,
will give you leave of such distress?

OCTAVIA:
The day I reach the shadows of hell.

NURSE:
Keep such ill-omened thoughts away!

OCTAVIA:
Your prayers govern not my life –
the Fates do.

NURSE:
                        Though you suffer now,
some kindly god will grant you better
days, but you must relent and try
to win your husband over with
subservience and flattery.

OCTAVIA:
More easily would I win over
violent lions and vicious tigers

than I would that savage tyrant's heart.
He loathes all those of noble blood,
he scorns the gods and men alike,
he cannot handle his great fortune,
the gift bestowed upon him by
his monstrous mother's wickedness.
However much that ingrate tries
to cover up his path to power –
his dreaded mother's splendid gift,
a splendid gift repaid with death –
forever this distinction will
be hers, a woman's, yet in death.

NURSE:

Stop ranting like some madwoman;
stifle these words so rashly spoken!

OCTAVIA: Although I will endure what I must, my suffering will never come to an end except through grim death. My mother was slaughtered. My father was villainously taken from me. I've lost my brother. I drown in a flood of sorrow, misery, grief. My husband hates me. My slave girl lords over me. Light brings me no joy. My heart never stops trembling – I'm not afraid of death, but of some wickedness. Provided that no slander comes to my good name, I'll gladly welcome death. After all, execution would be better than facing that tyrant's arrogant and menacing looks, kissing his hateful lips and fearing his every whim. I can't stand bowing to his desires ever since that day my brother was villainously murdered – the pain is too much! And now the author of that heinous murder possesses the power that belongs to him and revels in his death!

How often the sad ghost of my brother appears before me when rest loosens my limbs and sleep shuts my eyes weak from weeping! Sometimes he arms his powerless hands with black torches and viciously assails his brother's eyes and face. At others he's just a frightened boy seeking refuge in my bedroom – but his enemy is always hot on his heels, and as we sit, holding each other close, he brutally thrusts his sword through the both of us. I bolt from sleep in violent convulsions of fright; sorrow and fear once again come washing over me.

Now add to all of this an insufferable whore,[10] who parades around our house glittering in the spoils of *my* family. In order to please her, Nero put his own mother on a ship of death. This she survived, escaping the sea's clutches after a horrific shipwreck, only to be slain by cruel steel on orders from her son, who is more unfeeling than the barren seas. What hope have I for salvation, when he could perpetrate such a monstrous crime as that? Exulting in this victory, his whore now eyes my marriage with malice, her hatred stoked to flames. She demands, as the fee for adultery, the head of his lawfully wedded wife – me!

Father, rise up from the dead! Bring help to your daughter who calls upon you! Otherwise, break open the earth, lay bare the chasms of hell so that I can hurl myself into it!

NURSE: It's no use, calling upon your father's ghost, poor girl, no use at all. He has no concern for his living kin in death. Remember, this is the man who could dispossess his own son in favour of someone from another bloodline, and who was so smitten by his niece[11] that he took her to wife, an abominable coupling beneath a torch of woe. From this marriage there arose a long series of wickedness: slaughter, treachery, lust for power and inhuman bloodthirstiness. His would-be son-in-law Silanus[12] fell, a victim sacrificed for his own marriage, to prevent him from growing too powerful through his marriage to you. What a horrific crime! Silanus' life was a woman's wedding-gift; he defiled his ancestral home by spilling his own blood, accused and condemned on a trumped-up charge.

It was then that the enemy – O the horror! – set foot in a house that had already been captured by your stepmother's subterfuge. At one and the same time Nero became the emperor's son and son-in-law, a young man of monstrous character, capable of every crime. His mother, that fell woman, lit the bridal torch and joined you to him in marriage, against your will, despite your fears.

Triumphant, and made all the more bold because of her

success, that woman then set her sights on dominion over the whole blessed world. Who could describe all of that woman's villainy, all her wicked aspirations, all her seductive machinations as she employed every kind of crime in her march towards the throne? It was then that family Devotion, that hallowed goddess, walked out on us with shaking steps, and a vicious Fury entered the palace in her stead, leaving a trail of death as she moved. She desecrated the sacred household gods with her Stygian torch, and in her madness she broke the laws of nature and all that is right: wife stirred poison into her husband's dish, only to succumb herself to her son's wickedness. And now you, too, lie dead, Britannicus,[13] luckless boy, your life extinguished, your death bringing eternal sadness to me. You were once a bright star, the pillar of the Emperor's house, but now – alas! – you are nothing but light ash and a grim shadow. Even your cruel stepmother shed tears as she placed your body on the pyre and the crackling fires began to consume your flesh, your beautiful features, so like the winged god's –

OCTAVIA: [*interrupting*] Nero will have to kill me, too, or else die at my hands!

NURSE: Nature hasn't given you enough strength to do that.

OCTAVIA: Then pain, anger, sorrow, misery, grief will provide it.

NURSE: No, win over your cruel husband by giving in to him.

OCTAVIA: Will that restore my murdered brother to me?

NURSE: No, but you'll safeguard your position and restore your father's fading line by providing an heir from your blood.

OCTAVIA: The emperor's expecting an heir from another quarter. As for me, I'm destined to meet my brother's fate.

NURSE: Take courage from the public's deep support.

OCTAVIA: Some comfort, that, but it does not eradicate my misery.

NURSE: The people's power is great.

OCTAVIA: The Emperor has more.

NURSE: He'll look out for his wife –

OCTAVIA: His whore won't allow it.

NURSE: You mean the one everyone hates?

OCTAVIA: My husband adores her.

NURSE: She's not his wife yet.

OCTAVIA: Oh, she soon will be, and a mother, too!

NURSE: Darling, a young man's passion might flare up when
first ignited by desire, but it's destined to fade quickly when
it's the sordid kind of love, just like the heat of a fickle flame.
But love for a chaste wife, well, that endures for ever. Remember your husband's slave girl,[14] the one who first dared to
violate your marriage bed, the one who caught her master's
fancy and held on to it for a good while? This same woman
is now racked with fear. Of what? The woman Nero now
prefers to her. His old love has been knocked from her perch,
humiliated, and in desperation even sets up memorials that
attest to her fear. His new mistress, too, will be abandoned by
that capricious god, winged Cupid. No matter how stunningly
beautiful she is, no matter how wealthy and proud, her joy
will be short-lived. [*Turning to song*]
The mighty queen of the gods herself
did weather heartache like your own,
when heaven's lord, the gods' great father,
transformed himself into every shape,
assuming now the wings of a swan,[15]
now a Sidonian bullock's horns,
or flowing down as golden rain.
Leda's twin sons now shine in heaven,
Bacchus resides on Olympus' heights,
now Hercules has Hebe's hand,
in fear of Juno's wrath no more:
her foe is now her son-in-law.
Yet prevail she did, by giving in
and wisely stifling her pain.
Now mighty Juno, carefree, holds
the Thunderer in heaven's bed,
and Jupiter does not desert
his lofty palace, captivated
by the sweet spell of mortal beauty.
You, be a Juno here on earth,
the Emperor's young sister-wife,[16]
and bravely bear this heartache, too.

OCTAVIA: Sooner will savage seas unite with stars, fire with
water, heaven with dismal hell, nourishing light with shadows,
day with dewy night, than I would unite my heart to that of
my wicked husband. I cannot forget my brother's death. O
how I hope that the ruler of heaven is preparing to unleash
his fires against our dreaded emperor and obliterate him! For
a long time now he has been ceaselessly rocking the earth with
violent thunderbolts, instilling terror deep in our souls with
sacred flames and strange portents. He is preparing something.
Have you seen the bright streak of light in heaven, an ill-
omened comet with a blazing trail,[17] where the Wagoner in
the chill northern skies slowly drives his cart in the dark night
hours? See, even the heavenly skies are infected with the contagion of our brutal leader – the stars threaten renewed
slaughters for whole nations, perpetrated by our godless
leader! Not even Typhon was so destructive, whom Mother
Earth bore in anger as an affront to Jupiter. But *this* scourge,
Nero – he is more oppressive than that monster! Enemy of
both heaven and earth, he has driven gods from their temples
and people from their countries, taken away his brother's life
and even drained the lifeblood from his mother. And yet he
looks upon the light of day and lives a happy life, even as he
draws in his poisonous breath.

O Father, who art on high, why do you so often hurl your
inexorable bolts from that majestic hand at random? Why
have you not taken aim at that most guilty of men? I pray
Nero will someday face reckoning for his wickedness, that
son of Domitius who has been grafted on to our family, that
tyrant terrorizing the world, keeping it oppressed beneath a
shameful yoke, and besmirching the good Augustan name
with his wicked ways.

NURSE: Fine, I admit he doesn't deserve to call you wife, but I
beg you, darling, give in to your fate and fortune. Don't
provoke your violent husband's anger. Perhaps some avenging
god will rise up to set you free and bring back happier days.

OCTAVIA: Long now has the unforgiving wrath of the gods
haunted our family, ever since hard-hearted Venus threw my
poor mother into a fit of mad lust.[18] Though already married,

she mindlessly married again beneath an adulterous wedding
torch, forgetful of her children and husband, paying no heed
to the laws. An avenging Fury, with hair let loose and hissing
serpents all about her, came to that sinister marriage bed,
violently seized the torches, and snuffed them out with blood.
Then she set the Emperor's heart afire with angry thoughts of
unspeakable bloodshed. My ill-starred mother was put to the
sword, her death drowning me in a never-ending flood of grief,
and she dragged her husband and son down with her into the
shadows of death. She brought the whole Claudian house
crashing down.

NURSE: Do not renew your grief and tears for your loved ones,
nor disturb your mother's ghost – she's already paid a heavy
penalty for her mad lust.

[OCTAVIA *and the* NURSE *enter the palace. Enter a* CHORUS
of Roman citizens, supporters of OCTAVIA *and the Claudian
house*]

CHORUS I: Ode to Roman Courage

How grim the rumour that I hear!
May it come to nothing, no more
than widespread gossip, empty talk!
May no new bride in matrimony
enter the Emperor's grand bedroom;
may Claudius' fair daughter keep
her marriage and her rightful home,
may she bear children, guarantors
of peace and rightful heirs to power,
so that the tranquil world can prosper
and Rome retain eternal glory!

Great Juno still enjoys her brother's
bed that she won so long ago –
but the sister-wife of our Emperor,
why must she leave her father's halls?
What good did her devotion do,
what good her father made divine,

her purity and modesty?
Have we forgotten who we are
after our leader's death, betraying
his daughter, paralysed by fear?

Our forefathers exhibited
real Roman courage. Through them coursed
the blood and pedigree of Mars.
Such men drove haughty kings away
and forced them from our city's walls.
They rightfully avenged your death,
O maiden slain by your father's hand,
lest you endure harsh slavery,
lest rotten Lust prevail and carry
you off as its ill-gotten spoils.[19]
Grim war did follow your death, too,
Lucretia,[20] death that roused our pity,
self-sacrificed by your own hand,
after a savage tyrant's rape.
Tarquinius paid the price for his
appalling crimes; his wife did, too,
Tullia,[21] heartless daughter she,
who drove a chariot across
her parent's lifeless limbs and left
the mangled old man's limbs to rot.

Our generation too has witnessed
a son's great crime: our emperor
ensnared his mother in a ruse
and sent her on Tyrrhenia's sea
upon a ship that sailed for death.
Quickly the sailors left the safety
of port; they had received their orders.
The seas resounded with strokes of oars,
the vessel passed into open water –
then timbers came undone, the ship
buckled, a hole in the hull gaped
and gulped the sea – the ship was sinking!

A dreadful din of shouts erupted,
as women wailed and beat their breasts.
Death flashed before their very eyes.
They panicked – every man for himself.
Some clung to wreckage, planks of wood,
and, clothes stripped off, cut through the waves,
while others made for shore by swimming,
but most encountered doom at sea.
Queen Agrippina tore her dress,
pulled at her hair and drenched her cheeks,
sending down streams of sorry tears.
When it dawned on her no hope was left,
crushed by despair, she flared in anger
and cried out, 'Is this how you repay me,
the thanks for my magnificent gift?
This ship, I admit, is just deserts:
I gave birth to you; I gave you light,
an empire, and the name of Caesar –
mindless and mad must I have been!
Come, come, my husband,²² rise from hell,
watch and drink in my punishment:
see, I, who caused your death, poor man,
who engineered your son's demise,
am coming to your ghost as I
deserve, unburied, with no tomb,
yes, swallowed by the heartless sea!'
But as she spoke waves lashed her mouth;
she plunged beneath the sea and sank,
that drowning woman – but she resurfaced,
flailing her arms for fear of death,
but soon exhaustion took its toll.
Unspoken loyalty yet abided
in the hearts of men: many scorned death
and dared to help the struggling queen,
wholly exhausted, wholly spent;
though she could barely drag her arms,
they cheered her on or held her up.

What did it matter, this escape
from the clutches of the raging sea?
Doomed, you, to die by your son's sword,
a deed posterity and future
ages will hardly judge was true!
Aggrieved he was, enraged that his
mother escaped the sea and lived;
that fiend renewed his wickedness.
He rushed to bring his mother to ruin
and suffered no delay in crime;
a henchman carried out his orders,
unsealing our queen's chest with steel.
As she lay dying, luckless, doomed,
she begged her executioner
to plant his baleful sword in her womb.
'Stab your sword here, yes here,' said she,
'where I bore such a monstrosity!'[23]
And with these words, with one last groan
she freed, at last, her wretched soul
and sorry life through savage wounds.
        [CHORUS *leaves*]

ACT II

[*Enter* SENECA *from the palace*]

SENECA: Fortune, how wilful you are! Why, why did you seduce me with your deceptive smiles and raise me up on high, when I was content with my lowly lot? So that I might fall more heavily from this lofty pinnacle? So that I could have a clearer view of all there is to fear? How much better it was when I was an exile among the stony cliffs of the Corsican Sea,[24] far removed from the barbs of Envy! There my mind, unfettered and unbound, was ever free to pursue its studies. How pleasant it was to contemplate the cosmos, that marvellous work produced by Mother Nature, the architect of the boundless universe: the heavens, the sacred pathways of the sun, the movements of the world, the ebb and flow of night, and Phoebe's orb, shining far and wide, that great glory of the heavens encircled by a ring of roving stars.

If this great vault of heaven is growing weary with age, destined in all its vastness to plunge into shapeless Chaos again, then the last day of the world is at hand – that day which will destroy this godless race of men by bringing heaven crashing down, so that a better world may be reborn and produce a new stock of men.[25] Yes, a better world, just like when our world was young, when Saturn held sway over heaven. At that time fair maiden Justice, a goddess of great power, was sent down from heaven along with holy Loyalty to rule the human race on earth with gentleness. Men knew no wars; there was no harsh call of the war-trumpet, no weapons, no city walls. Everyone could go as they pleased, everything was held in common for all to use. Mother Earth herself happily opened up her fertile bosom of her own accord, a fertile parent looking out for her dutiful nurslings.

But a second brood arose, much less kindly than the first <gap in the text>[26] Then a third generation emerged, cunning and inventive, but righteous nonetheless. They soon grew restless: they bravely hunted ferocious animals, caught fish that hid beneath the waves with weighted nets or a slender reed-pole, trapped roving birds with wicker traps or fine-meshed snares, domesticated wild bulls, submitted them to the yoke, and cut furrows into Earth, she who had never before felt the sting of the ploughshare. Wounded, Mother Earth sent forth her fruits with a heavy heart, but her vast riches she buried deep within her sacred bosom.

But a more degenerate age delved into the bowels of its mother and violently gouged out of her heavy iron and gold. Soon they had outfitted their savage hands for war, marked off territories and established kingdoms, erected the first cities, and with weapons of war defended their own homes and attacked those of others, bent on plunder. Fair maiden Justice, no longer revered, fled the earth and the savage ways of men, their hands foully stained with bloodshed; she now shines in heaven as Virgo, a great and glorious star. Lust for war and hunger for gold spread across the whole world like wildfire. Then the greatest sin of all reared her head, Excess, a seductive plague allowed to grow and thrive because of our profound foolishness for so many years.

And now, all the vices accumulating over so many generations are washing back over us in a flood. We struggle beneath an oppressive age, one in which Crime is king, Wickedness rages furiously, Lust plays lord and master alongside shameful Sex, and Excess greedily snatches up the world's boundless riches with predatory hands, only to squander them.

But look, here comes Nero, grim-faced, marching furiously. I shudder to think what this means.

[*Enter* NERO *and the* CAPTAIN *of the guard from the palace*]

NERO: [*to the* CAPTAIN] Carry out my orders – send someone to kill Plautus and Sulla and bring me back their heads.[27]

CAPTAIN: I shall waste no time in executing your commands –
  I'm off at once to the barracks. [CAPTAIN *exits*]
SENECA: It's not right to pass judgment on kin rashly.[28]
NERO: It's easy to think of justice when you've got nothing to
  fear.
SENECA: Mercy's a great cure for fear.
NERO: Exterminating enemies is a leader's chief task.
SENECA: The Father of the Country[29] should be *protecting* his
  people.
NERO: Soft old man, you should be instructing children!
SENECA: Hot-headed young men need more reining in.
NERO: I have enough judgement at my age, I think –
SENECA: – what, for the gods to approve your every action?
NERO: I'd be a fool to fear the gods, since I *make* them.[30]
SENECA: Your great power is all the more reason to fear them.
NERO: Fortune's been good to me – I have *unlimited* power.
SENECA: When Fortune favours you, be suspicious. She's a fickle
  goddess.
NERO: Only a pathetic ruler does not know his power.
SENECA: It's commendable to do what's right, not what's possi-
  ble.
NERO: The mob walks over the weak.
SENECA: And crush what they hate.
NERO: Swords protect the emperor.
SENECA: Loyalty better.
NERO: Caesar should be feared.
SENECA: But loved even more.
NERO: They'll be forced to praise . . .
SENECA: [*interrupting*] What you wring from them is painful.
NERO: [*ignoring* SENECA] . . . and obey my commands.
SENECA: Then make your commands just.
NERO: I'll decide that –
SENECA: – such that consensus would ratify them?
NERO: A drawn sword will push them through.
SENECA: God forbid!
NERO: So I'm supposed to let them keep coming for my blood?
  Let them kill me in a sudden coup, despised and without
  retribution? Exile in a far-off land didn't break Plautus and

Sulla. No, their madness abides; they are arming conspirators to cut me down while there remains widespread support for them in the city, feeding the exiles' hopes. I must put all suspected enemies to the sword. My hateful wife, too, must perish and follow her dear brother to the grave. Whatever is lofty must be brought down!

SENECA: The virtuous path is to be preeminent among illustrious men, to help one's country, to show mercy to the downtrodden, to refrain from ruthless bloodshed, to act rationally and not out of anger, to give tranquillity to the world and peace to one's generation. This is the highest virtue. This is the path to the stars.

This is how the first Father of the Country, Augustus, attained heaven. This is why he is worshipped at our temples as a god. Yet Fortune long buffeted him on land and sea through the difficult vicissitudes of war until he crushed his father's enemies. But you, well, Fortune smiled on your reign, readily gave you the reins of power, and brought the lands and sea beneath your sway – without bloodshed. Disagreeable spite gave way to harmony and loyalty in the Senate; the equestrian class zealously supported you. Chosen both by the votes of the people and by the judgement of the senators, you, the author of peace, the arbiter of the whole human race, rule the world with your divine breath. You are the Father of the Country! Rome bids you to uphold this name, take her citizens in your arms, and protect them.

NERO: It is the gift of the gods that Rome herself and the Senate serve me, and that the people's fear of me wrings entreaties and submissive words from them. Protecting citizens hostile to their emperor and country, puffed-up with the pride of their pedigree – what kind of lunacy is that, when you can dispatch suspected conspirators to death with but a single word? Brutus took weapon to hand and slew Caesar, the leader who had spared him earlier. This man, unconquered in battle, the vanquisher of nations, the man who climbed a series of lofty honours to stand equal to Jupiter – yes, *Caesar* was struck down by his citizens in an unspeakable crime![31]

How much of her own blood did Rome see then, so many

times torn apart! Even that man who earned a place in heaven because of his virtuous dedication, divine Augustus – how many noble men did he exterminate? Young and old alike, men who had scattered all over the world, driven by fear of death from their ancestral homes, fleeing the triumvirs' steely swords, condemned to execution in their death-lists![32] The heads of the slain were displayed on the Rostra.[33] Mournful fathers came to see, but were not allowed to weep or grieve over their sons as they stood in the forum, festering as it was with grisly decomposition, the faces of men dripping with the foul ooze of decaying flesh.

But this was not the end of the bloodshed. Carrion birds and wild animals glutted themselves on the flesh of those who died on Philippi's battleground.[34] The Sicilian Sea then swallowed fleets along with their crews, frequent butchers of their own countrymen.[35] The whole world shuddered beneath the mighty armies of generals. Defeated in battle, Antony made for the shores of the Nile on ships prepared for flight, only to die soon after; for a second time unchaste Egypt drank deep a Roman leader's blood and now shrouds his weightless shade.[36] There the war, that detestable war trafficking in citizens' blood, was finally laid to rest. Only then did the victor, in utter exhaustion, sheathe his sword, dulled as it was by countless wounds. Fear enforced his authority. Protected by military strength and his soldiers' loyalty, he was made a god by his son's exceptional devotion, deified after death and enshrined in temples.[37]

Heaven awaits me, too. But first I, too, must mercilessly execute whoever threatens me before they reach me, and secure my legacy with a worthy heir.

SENECA: The glory of the Claudian line, Octavia, born of a god[38] and allotted her brother's bed like Juno – let her fill your palace with the stock of gods.

NERO: Her adulterous mother makes her lineage suspect, and besides, Octavia was never close to me.

SENECA: Chalk that up to her tender age, when one's affections are hardly clear, when love, overcome by modesty, conceals its flames.

NERO: I for my part did believe this was the case for a long time – despite clear signs otherwise. Her glares and cold attitude betrayed her hatred. My pain flared up and my anger boiled – in the end I decided to gain my revenge. So I found a wife who deserved my bed, high-born and beautiful, to whom Venus, the fierce goddess of war, and Jupiter's wife would all admit defeat.[39]

SENECA: A husband should be concerned about his wife's uprightness, loyalty, behaviour and modesty. Only the unassailable virtues of the mind and soul last for ever. Every day wilts the flower of beauty.

NERO: A god brought all the good qualities together in one woman. The Fates deemed such a woman be born for *me*.

SENECA: Don't put too much faith in love – it *will* desert you.

NERO: You mean Love,[40] the god that the lord of the thunderbolt could not escape? You mean the one who terrorizes heaven, who works his way into the savage seas and the realm of Dis, who induces the gods above to desert heaven?

SENECA: Human ignorance is responsible for the creation of that winged, heartless god they call 'Love'. They put a bow and arrows in his sacred hands, outfit him with a cruel torch and imagine that he's born of Venus by Vulcan's seed. 'Love' is nothing more than a powerful force at work in one's mind, a warm, scintillating tingle in the soul. It arises in one's youth and is nourished by excess and indolence and all the other plush boons of Fortune. But once you stop fostering and nourishing it, it quickly fades away and burns itself out.

NERO: Love's the primary force behind life, I think, since pleasure arises through him. The human race survives extinction because it continually reproduces under the influence of sweet Love, who tames even vicious beasts. May *this* god bear my wedding torch and join Poppaea to me under his flame!

SENECA: The people's indignation would scarcely put up with this marriage and sacred Devotion would not allow it.

NERO: Will I alone be forbidden what is permitted to all others?

SENECA: The people always hold their kings to higher standards.

NERO: Let us test them. Let us see if the people's ill-conceived support crumbles once it is broken by my might.

SENECA: You should rather give in to your people's wishes.

NERO: It's bad policy to let the mob rule its leaders.

SENECA: When entreaties are rejected, they have a right to
protest.

NERO: So extortion's just when entreaties are ineffective?

SENECA: It's harsh to say no.

NERO: And wrong to force the Emperor's hand.

SENECA: He should relent first.

NERO: Gossip will call it surrender.

SENECA: That's just empty talk.

NERO: Even so, it's blackened many.

SENECA: It fears the lofty.

NERO: But disparages them just the same.

SENECA: We can easily quash the rumours. Now, think of your
divine father's accomplishments and your wife's age, her
uprightness, her modesty!

NERO: Enough! You've become loathsome – I'll do exactly what
Seneca disapproves! I've been putting off the people's prayers
for far too long now as it is, since Poppaea now carries an
heir in her womb, a part of me. Indeed, why don't we settle
on tomorrow for the wedding?

　　[SENECA *and* NERO *enter the palace*]

ACT III

[*The* GHOST OF AGRIPPINA *enters through a trapdoor. Though no time is announced, this scene takes place during the night of Day 1, before the wedding of* NERO *and* POPPAEA *that is to take place on Day 2 (which is not drama- tized in the play)*]

GHOST OF AGRIPPINA: I have cleaved apart the earth to emerge from hell, bearing in my blood-stained hands a Stygian torch to usher in this abominable wedding. Let Poppaea marry my son beneath *this* flame, which these avenging hands, driven by a mother's pain, will turn to light funeral pyres. Even in death the memory of my murder remains alive and tortures my still unavenged soul. All my services to my son? Repaid with a ship of death. My reward for bestowing an empire on him? That grim night during which I shed tears after being shipwrecked. I had wanted to mourn the deaths of my friends, the wickedness perpetrated by my heartless son, but no time was allowed for tears. No, he renewed his wickedness: though rescued from the sea's clutches, I was brutally slain and mutilated by the sword, and I poured out my sorrowful spirit in the sanctity of my own house. Even so my blood did not extinguish my son's hatred. That unbridled tyrant raged even against his mother's name. He wanted my favours covered up; he had my statues and the inscriptions that bore my name destroyed the world over – the same world that my cursed love had given him, still a boy, to rule, only to end in my ruin.

My dead husband angrily torments my ghost, assailing my guilty face with torches. He hounds me, threatens me, blames me for his death and his son's murder. He demands the murderer's head!

Patience, my husband, patience – he *will* pay. I ask only a little time. An avenging Fury is preparing a death worthy of that tyrant's iniquity: floggings, cowardly flight and torture transcending Tantalus' thirst, Sisyphus' trying toil, Tityus' bird and the wheel that wrenches Ixion's limbs. Go ahead, son: in your arrogance erect a palace overlaid in marbles and gold and place armed guards before your door; let the world, stripped bare, send to you its boundless wealth as tribute; let the Parthians bow before you and seek your murderous hand in supplication; and let great kingdoms bring you all their riches – there will come a day and time when you will atone for your wickedness by yielding up your guilty soul. You will offer your neck to the enemy, deserted, destroyed and wholly destitute.

[*Sighing, pitying her son*] Is this what my toil, is this what my prayers have sunk to? Has your unbridled madness, has your destiny brought you to such misery that even the mother you murdered might relinquish her wrath in the face of such a terrible plight? How I wish wild beasts had torn open my womb before I brought your tiny body into the world and suckled you. Then you would have perished without the stain of crime, without consciousness, an innocent babe all my own! In a quiet corner of the underworld, forever fast in my arms, you would gaze upon your father and forefathers, men of a mighty line. But now, only eternal shame, eternal sorrow await them because of you, you abomination, and me, because I bore you such.

Why do I, a stepmother, wife and mother ruinous to my kin, hesitate to retreat and bury my shameful face in hell?

[*The* GHOST OF AGRIPPINA *leaves through the trapdoor*]

ACT IV

[*The* CHORUS *of* OCTAVIA's *supporters files in from the wings.* OCTAVIA *enters from the palace and walks through them as she departs. The time is the morning of* NERO *and* POPPAEA's *wedding, Day 2*]

OCTAVIA: [*to the* CHORUS]
Refrain from tears this festive day,
a day of public celebration,
lest your great love and support for me
incite our leader's bitter rage
and I become the source of your ills.
My heart has felt the wounds of sorrow
before – much worse have I endured.
This day will bring an end to my
anguish and pain, be it by death.
No more will I be forced to suffer
my husband's dark and hateful looks,
or cross the threshold of my slave
girl's bedroom, that revolting place.
I will not be the Emperor's
wife – I will be his sister only.[41]
Just keep away the threat of death,
the threat of dreadful punishment.
Fool! Can you really hope for this,
knowing your dreadful husband's deeds?
He's let you live this long to be
sacrificed now for these wedding rites,
a deathly victim, last of your line.
Why turn to gaze at your father's house,

with troubled look and tear-filled eyes?
Move from these walls in haste, leave now
the blood-stained halls of your Emperor.
    [OCTAVIA *leaves through one of the wings*]

CHORUS II: Time for Action

Behold, that dreaded day has dawned,
so often rumoured to be near:
Claudius' daughter yields her place,
divorced from evil Nero's bed.
Poppaea holds this now, triumphant,
while our devotion flags, subdued
by fear, and our pain is slow to act.
Where now the Roman people's nerve?
We once defeated famed generals,
imposed decrees on our unconquered
nation, bestowed supreme command
upon those few who earned it well.
Our might decided war and peace.
Our might once tamed barbaric peoples
and shut their captive kings in prison.

But now – what an oppressive sight!
Poppaea's image joined to Nero's –
great statues gleaming everywhere!
We must with violence smash to ground
those statues bearing her haughty likeness,
then drag that woman from her couch
and storm with flames and stones and wrath
the palace of our brutal tyrant!
    [CHORUS *leaves through one of the wings*]

ACT V

[POPPAEA *enters from the palace, followed by her* NURSE. *The time is the night after* OCTAVIA's *divorce and the wedding of* NERO *and* POPPAEA]

NURSE: Where are you going, dear girl? Why do you leave your husband's bedchamber all atremble? Why do you seek privacy? You look upset – why are your cheeks wet with weeping? Surely the day we've all been praying and hoping for has dawned: you were joined to your Caesar beneath the nuptial torch, the man you captured with your beauty, the one Venus, Love's mother, the mightiest of divinities, bound and delivered to you as a reward for your dutiful reverence towards her. How beautiful, how majestic you looked reclining on that lofty couch within the palace! The Senate gazed in awe at your beauty as you offered incense to the gods and sprinkled the sacred altars with thank-offerings of wine, a delicate saffron veil covering your brow. And Nero himself, brimming with pride, was joined arm in arm with you, parading himself amidst the happy shouts of well-wishers and radiating happiness on his face and in his gait. Just so did Peleus beam with joy when he received his wife Thetis as she emerged from the sea-surf. Their marriage, they say, all the heavenly gods and sea divinities celebrated in mutual harmony.[42]

But what has caused your face to change so drastically? Tell me the reason for your tears and ashen complexion!

POPPAEA: I'm carried away by a troubled mind, Nurse, disturbed by a grim and fearful vision I had last night. I am at my wit's end. After that joyous day yielded to darkling stars and the bright heavens to night, I succumbed to sleep, held fast in my

Nero's embraces. But I did not enjoy a restful sleep for long.
I had a vision – a sorrowful group of mourners had thronged
to my wedding room; Latin matrons, their hair let down in
mourning, were tearfully beating their breasts. Suddenly,
amidst the fearful droning of funeral trumpets, my husband's
raging mother appeared, her face breathing menace, her hand
brandishing a blood-soaked torch. As I followed her, spellbound in the grip of fear, the earth suddenly gaped wide open
beneath me, a huge chasm, and I plunged headlong into it.
There, to my amazement, I found my wedding couch, on which
I lay down in exhaustion. Then I saw someone coming towards
me, attended by a huge crowd. It was my former husband
Crispinus,[43] followed by our son. He quickly rushed to my
embraces and the kisses he long had missed. Suddenly, my
husband Nero, shaken, burst into my room and buried a cruel
sword in his neck.[44]

   At last I started awake in great terror. Violent shuddering
shook me inside and out, my heart pounding, and fear had
stolen my voice. But now your loyal devotion has drawn it
out of me. Tell me, what do the ghosts of the dead bode for
me? What does this dream of my husband's blood portend?
NURSE: The same things your waking mind consciously dwells
upon, a sacred, mysterious and swift-working faculty recalls
during your sleep. Are you really surprised you saw your
husband, bedroom and wedding couch while you were held
in your new husband's arms? And are you disturbed by the
beating of breasts and the hair let down on your joyous day?
They were mourning Octavia's divorce within the hallowed
halls of her brother's and father's house. That torch carried
in the hand of Nero's mother, the one you followed? It fore-
casts that out of envy an illustrious name will be imparted to
you. That all of this took place in the underworld promises a
marriage forever stable and a line eternal. As for your dear
Emperor's burying a sword in a throat – well, this only means
that he will not incite wars but bury the sword in peace. Gather
yourself. Be happy, I beg you. Put aside your fear and return
to your chamber.
POPPAEA: The sacred shrines and altars – I'm determined to visit

them, to propitiate divine will with sacrificial victims so that
the threatening omens of my nocturnal dream may be averted
and that this paralysing fear may rebound on to my enemies.
But you, go, entreat the gods on my behalf with vows and
venerate them with reverent prayers, so that my fears may
come to nothing.

[NURSE *and* POPPAEA *leave.* CHORUS *of* POPPAEA's
supporters enters]

CHORUS III: Poppaea's Beauty

If windy Rumour's tales are true
of Jupiter's delightful trysts –
how once he nestled in Leda's lap
covered in feathers and white down,
how once he whisked Europa across
the high seas as a fierce-eyed bull –
he will desert his astral kingdom
for your embraces, too, Poppaea.
Yes, you would he prefer to Leda,
or Danae, who watched in awe
as he rained down as tawny gold.
Let Sparta boast of Helen's beauty,
let Paris boast of his shapely prize:
Poppaea will surpass the beauty
of Tyndareus' far-famed daughter, she
who roused horrific wars and strife,
and brought Troy's kingdom to the ground.
[*Enter* MESSENGER]
But look, here comes a man in panicked
steps, breathing hard! What news brings he?

ACT VI

MESSENGER: All soldiers manning a post along our emperor's
walls, defend the palace! The people's uprising threatens to
destroy it! Look! Terrified captains are drawing up platoons
to safeguard the city, but the mob's reckless fury does not
abate in the face of fear. It only grows stronger.

CHORUS: What madness, this, that drives them to rebel?

MESSENGER: Support for Octavia spurs on the massive crowd.
They're running rampant, reckless in their violence.

CHORUS: Tell us: what bold deed have they done, what now
their plans?

MESSENGER: They mean to restore Claudius' daughter to her
divine father's home, to her brother's bed, to her rightful share
of the empire!

CHORUS: All that Poppaea now possesses in a mutual bond of
trust?

MESSENGER: This is precisely what kindles their anger, this
fanatical support of Octavia. This is what drives them into
a blind rage. Every statue that once stood bearing Poppaea's
likeness, whether gleaming ivory or bronze, lies on the
ground, dashed down by the mob's hand, toppled by pitiless
steel. With ropes they drew and quartered them, breaking
off the limbs. Then they trampled on them and drove them
into the foul mud. Their insults matched their brutality, but
modesty prevents me from repeating what they said. Now
they are preparing to engulf the Emperor's residence in
flames unless he yields, surrenders his new wife to the
people's anger and returns Claudius' daughter to her rightful home. I must personally inform him about the citizens'

revolt – I must carry out the captain's orders at once.
[MESSENGER *exits*]

CHORUS IV: The Power of Love

No use, inciting savage warfare –
invincible are Cupid's arms:
his flames will beat your firebrands.
They overwhelmed the thunderbolts
of Jupiter and drew him down
from heaven's heights against his will.
You'll feel the Love-god's searing sting,
your blood the punishment for scorn.
He is hot-tempered and quick to wrath,
that wilful god. He bade Achilles
to strum the lyre despite his rage;[45]
he broke the Greeks and Atreus' son;
he toppled Priam's realm and brought
illustrious cities to the ground.
And now? I shudder just to think
what that cruel god will wreak today.
     [*The* CHORUS *leaves*]

ACT VII

[*Enter* NERO *from the palace*]

NERO: How slow my soldiers are to act! How tolerant my
wrath in the face of such mutiny! Else now those torches lit
for my destruction would have been extinguished by the
people's blood, and Rome, who bore such men, would be
dripping with the massacre of citizens and reek of death. But
punishing their insubordination with death is not enough.
No, this rabble's treasonous crime deserves greater punishment. Ah, yes, that woman whom the citizens in their rage
would elevate above me – my sister-wife, the one I've long
suspected of subversion – must at long last yield up her life
for my pain and quench my anger with her blood. Then, ah
then, the city's structures must sink beneath my flames;[46] that
guilty mass of mutineers must be humbled by fire, ruin, abject
poverty, severe hunger, grief. They all, that whole rotten
bunch of them, live wayward lives, spoiled by the prosperity
of my reign. They cannot truly grasp my clemency. Ingrates!
Peace is not enough for them. No, they grow restless, seized
on one side by audacity, carried away on the other by temer-
ity. We must tame them with punishment and keep them
oppressed beneath a heavy yoke. They must never again
attempt such insubordination – or even dare to lift their eyes
to meet my wife's holy face. I'll break them with fear and
punishment – *this* will teach them to obey their Emperor's
every whim.

[*Enter* CAPTAIN]

But here comes the man whose outstanding loyalty and
devotion earned him the captaincy of my guard.

CAPTAIN: The crowd's rage has been brought under control by putting to death those few who foolishly resisted.

NERO: And you think this sufficient? This is how you follow your leader's orders? You *reined* them in? This is hardly the retribution I deserve!

CAPTAIN: But the leaders of the rebellion were put to the sword!

NERO: And what about the mob that dared to assail the palace with flames, to dictate the Emperor's actions, to drag my dear wife forcibly from our bed and desecrate what they could with filthy hands and abusive words? They've not yet got what they deserve!

CAPTAIN: You'll let a personal grudge influence how you punish citizens?

NERO: Yes, and no age will ever forget it.

CAPTAIN: Your anger should subside, our fear will not.[47]

NERO: My anger will be placated when she who caused it dies.

CAPTAIN: Tell us whom you demand; we will see it through.

NERO: My vile sister – I want her head!

CAPTAIN: Numbness runs through me – I am paralysed by dread.

NERO: Are you reluctant to obey?

CAPTAIN: You question my loyalty?

NERO: Yes, because you would spare the enemy.

CAPTAIN: Can a woman have that name?

NERO: If she plotted the revolt.

CAPTAIN: Do you have witnesses to her guilt?

NERO: The people's rage.

CAPTAIN: Who can control a mindless mob?

NERO: The one who incited it.

CAPTAIN: I hardly think anyone –

NERO: – a *woman* can! Nature gave them evil minds and outfitted their hearts with deception to do harm.

CAPTAIN: But it did not give her strength.

NERO: Yes, to prevent her from being wholly unassailable, so that fear of punishment might break her feeble strength! And now that punishment, though late in coming, will be exacted upon that condemned woman, guilty for so long. Enough of your advice and entreaties – carry out your orders! Put her

on a ship to some remote shore and have her killed. Only then
will the angry swell in my heart subside.

> [NERO *enters palace; the* CAPTAIN *exits from one of the*
> *wings. The scene is now Rome's docks; enter* CHORUS *of*
> POPPAEA's *supporters*]

CHORUS V: The Danger of Popular Support

How ruinous, the mob's support!
How many deaths it leaves in its wake!
It fills your sails with backing winds,
propelling you to open seas –
then, suddenly, the gusts subside,
deserting you on savage seas.

Cornelia wept for her two sons,
the Gracchi,[48] ruined by the mob's
excessive love and fierce support,
illustrious in lineage,
in loyalty and devotion,
famed orators with mettle plenty,
and forceful activists in law.
You, Livius,[49] were likewise sent
to death by Fortune's bitter blows;
neither your office nor your house
protected you – so many stories
I could tell, but present grief deters.

> [*Enter* OCTAVIA *in chains, led by mute members of* NERO's
> *guard*]

Behold, the queen our citizens
aimed to restore to her rightful home,
her brother's bedroom, is now dragged
to death before their very eyes,
sad-faced and weeping pitifully.
How well does Poverty lay low,
content with humble home and hearth –
it's lofty palaces that gales
batter and Fortune overturns.

ACT VIII

OCTAVIA

Where are you taking me? What land
of exile do tyrant and queen decree –
if she's relented, spared my life,
won over by my ceaseless hardships!
Or does she mean to crown my sorrows
with death? Then why does she so cruelly
begrudge me death in my native land?
No hope of deliverance remains –
I see my brother's boat – I'm doomed!
This is the ship on which his mother
once sailed, and now it will carry me,
his wretched sister and ex-wife.
What sway does sweet Devotion hold?
What sway the gods in heaven? None:
now a grim Fury rules the world.
Who has enough soft tears to mourn
my misery? What nightingale
could echo my plaints with equal sadness?
O how I wish the Fates had given
the nightingale's swift wings to me!
Then borne away on whirring wings
would I escape my miseries,
far from the rotten hordes of men
and the bloodshed of humanity.
Alone in an empty forest, perched
upon a slender branch, I could
pour forth my plaintive warbling,

my sounds of sorrow, songs of woe.
CHORUS
The mortal race is ruled by Fate.
Do not expect what seems secure
or lasting will abide for ever;
each dreaded day will pitch and toss
you through a thousand ups and downs.
Take courage from your family's past,
the women suffering punishment:
was Fortune more unkind to you?
You, daughter of Agrippa,[50] are
the first I name, the mother of
so many children, great Augustus'
daughter-in-law and Caesar's wife,[51]
whose celebrated name shone brightly
in every corner of the world.
Your fertile womb produced so many
pledges of peace – but soon you suffered
grim exile, floggings, brutal chains,
bereavement, sorrows and at last,
after long days of torture, death.
Livia,[52] blessed in her marriage
to Drusus and in children, rushed
headlong into her crime and death.
Julia was fated to join her mother;
many years passed, yet she was put
to sword, uncharged and innocent.
What power your own mother wielded![53]
She lorded over the Emperor's court,
dear to her husband, famed in children!
But she succumbed to her own slave,
felled by a heartless soldier's sword.
And Nero's mighty mother, too,
who dreamed of kingship and of heaven –
was she, the queen, not violated
by a band of sailors bent on death,
then slain with steel and mutilated,
the victim of her callous son?

OCTAVIA

Behold, that brutal tyrant sends
me, too, to join those shades in death.
Why do I cling to this wretched life?
    [*Addressing the guards*]
Take me to death at once, you henchmen
of Fortune, masters of my life.
I swear by the gods – fool, what use is this?
Do not invoke the gods in heaven
who despise you! Swear by Tartarus,
swear by the dark, grim goddesses,
avengers of crime, and by your father!
I swear I do not deserve this death,
but death, you I do not begrudge.
Now rig the ship! Unfurl the sails
and have the helmsman set his course
to make for Pandataria's shores.[54]

CHORUS

Light breezes, gentle Zephyrs, you
once rescued Iphigenia, sweeping
her from the savage virgin's altars,
swathing her in ethereal clouds:
now carry this girl far from death,
to Trivia's temple, I beseech you!
Our city proves more savage than
barbarous Aulis or the Taurians.[55]
There they appease the will of heaven
with the blood of foreign visitors,
but Rome rejoices in her own.

All leave

Notes

An asterisk (*) denotes an item
found in the glossary

HERCULES INSANE

1. *the Great Bear*: Callisto.* For the other loves of Jupiter* noted in this passage see Taurus,* Pleiades,* Orion,* Perseus,* and Gemini.*
2. *the wandering land stood still*: The island of Delos* was said to have stopped wandering the sea when Latona* gave birth on it to Jupiter's* twin children Apollo* and Diana,* who are here identified as the Sun and Moon respectively.
3. *Bacchus' mother reach heaven*: Semele.*
4. *made me a step-mother*: Juno* alludes to Jupiter's trysts in Thebes* with Antiope,* Semele,* and Alcmena.*
5. *beneath Ocean's waters*: Jupiter* was said to have removed a day and joined two nights together during intercourse with Alcmena.*
6. *its nearby flame*: In Homer the Ethiopians were said to inhabit the far east and west of the known world. The darkness of their skin was thought to be owed to their nearness to the sun when it rose and set; some Greeks etymologized the word as coming from *aithein* ('burn').
7. *Lion and Hydra*: Hercules* used the impervious skin of the Nemean Lion* as a shield and dipped his arrows in the poisonous blood of the Lernaen Hydra,* his first two labours.
8. *infernal Jupiter*: Dis* (or less often in Seneca Pluto*), god of the underworld, was sometimes referred to as 'infernal Jupiter'.
9. *his brother's realm*: Hercules' father Jupiter* and Dis* were brothers.
10. *Argolid, my cities*: Juno* had a particularly strong cult presence in Argos,* the city at the centre of the Argolid.*
11. *more stably upon Hercules' shoulders*: That is, more stably than it rested on the shoulders of Atlas.*

12. *even as I pressed down with all my weight upon it*: In order to fetch the golden apples of the Hesperides (his eleventh labour), Hercules enlisted the help of Atlas* and held heaven aloft while Atlas went to obtain the apples. The neat point that Juno pressed down with all of her weight upon the sky may be an inversion of the image on the metope of Hercules' labour on the Temple of Jupiter at Olympia,* where the goddess Minerva* is shown *easing* the burden of the sky as Hercules holds it up.

13. *causes the Doric lands to convulse and quake*: Seneca is probably referring to Typhon,* the immense child of Earth (Greek 'Giant' means 'Earth-born') who challenged Jupiter* for the kingship of heaven but was defeated and pinned beneath Mount Etna* in Sicily (a Doric land).

14. *has turned its cart, heralding Dawn*: The stars composing the Bear were also thought to form the Wagon, the turning of which around the North Pole marked the approach of dawn.

15. *famed for Cadmus' girls*: Agave* and her sisters tore apart her son Pentheus* on Mount Cithaeron,* while under the influence of the god Bacchus.*

16. *Thracian mistress preens*: Philomela (see Procne*).

17. *glorious golden horns*: For the following account of Hercules' twelve labours, see Hercules* and the next note.

18. *wide pathway for Ocean to rush in*: Hercules' opening of the Straits of Gibraltar is not normally included among his twelve labours, but in his 'side labours'. Seneca elevates this to the rank of one of his labours not only to keep the number at the canonical twelve (Cerberus* cannot be counted as the twelfth yet), but also to highlight Hercules' violent nature and the motif of Hercules' breaking through barriers.

19. *cut off along with his head*: Megara's* father Creon* – if Seneca is following Euripides' *Heracles* – is the same Creon as in the Oedipus* myth.

20. *swords drawn and at the ready*: See Cadmus* and Serpent Race.*

21. *a mighty upheaval*: Seneca here follows the account (again emphasizing the motif of Hercules' breaking through barriers) in which Hercules is responsible for the cleaving apart of Tempe* in Thessaly,* which allowed the Peneus river, which frequently flooded Thessaly, to flow out.

22. *the mindless dead*: Mindless because they drank from the river Lethe* ('Forgetfulness').

23. *long torches in secrecy*: See Eleusis.*

24. *Hercules' true sire clings to her side*: Lycus, attempting to elevate

his own position relative to Hercules, rejects the notion that Hercules is son of Jupiter.

25. *suffered or committed horrific crimes*: Agave,* Ino,* Jocasta.*

26. *their twin funerals*: Eteocles and Polynices, the sons of Oedipus* and Jocasta,* fought over the kingship of Thebes and died at each other's hands.

27. *those who defied them*: Referring to the Olympian gods' war with the Phlegraean Giants,* in which it was fated that a mortal – Hercules – had to fight to bring it to a close.

28. *shepherd flocks in Pherae*: Apollo,* born on Delos, was sold into slavery to the mortal Admetus,* king of Pherae, for having killed the Cyclopes,* the makers of Jupiter's thunderbolts.

29. *a wandering island*: Latona,* when pregnant with Apollo* and Diana,* was driven all over the earth by Juno* until she arrived at Delos (see note 2, above).

30. *as an infant*: Rhea* hid the infant Jupiter* on Mount Dicte on the island of Crete to keep him from his father Saturn,* who was devouring his children to prevent one of them from overthrowing him.

31. *shimmering Sidonian dress*: When Hercules was sold as a slave to Omphale,* the queen of Lydia,* she compelled him to dress as a woman and perform woman's work; there is also a hint of eroticism here.

32. *maidens he humped like cattle*: On his quest to conquer the Cithaeronian lion, Hercules was entertained by Thespios, king of Thespiae, who, recognizing the greatness of the hero, had his fifty daughters have sex with him to produce noble grandchildren – according to some accounts all on the same night.

33. *bearing no wound upon his body*: Seneca here conflates two figures named Cygnus,* one the son of Mars* killed by Hercules with a spear, and another, the son of Neptune,* who was invulnerable to weapons and killed by Achilles.*

34. *once gave a wife to Jupiter*: While Amphitryon* was away fighting the Teleboans, Jupiter* visited his wife Alcmena* disguised as Amphitryon himself. When he learned what had happened, Amphitryon acquiesced and raised the child, Hercules, as his own.

35. *one boatman*: Charon.*

36. *a wound so minute*: In Homer's *Iliad* (5.392 ff.) Hercules was said to have wounded Hades with an arrow at Pylos.

37. *vainly searched the whole world through*: Ceres* and Proserpina.*

38. *still wander in madness*: See Agave.* This is the only passage from antiquity where Cadmus' daughters were punished in the under-

world, although in *Oedipus* (Act III) Tiresias* does summon the daughters of Cadmus* and Pentheus* from the underworld.

39. *gap in the text*: Following Fitch, I have omitted the line, 'and the Lapiths burning for war because of too much wine', because it is likely a later addition prompted by the mention of the Centaurs,* whose battle with the wine-incensed Lapiths was legendary. While Hercules* did fight the Lapiths, they are human and are unlikely to be included in this catalogue of monsters that Hercules faced (a great part of which is likely lost).

40. *did not dare refuse*: Theseus* had been trapped in the underworld since his disastrous expedition to help his friend Pirithous* abduct Proserpina,* Dis' wife (a mission criticized by Phaedra in *Phaedra*, Act II).

41. *scatters the night before them*: Funerals for children in Rome were conducted at night.

42. *who hailed from Tyre*: Cadmus.*

43. *send it crashing into heaven*: Hercules* recalls the attempt of the Giants* to assault heaven by piling three mountains on each other. Hercules here is fulfilling Juno's prophecy in Act I that he will make an assault on heaven.

44. *Theseus*: Most of the manuscripts attribute these lines to Theseus,* but modern editors assign them to the Chorus, perhaps rightly, because Theseus' exit at the beginning of the act is signalled by Hercules'* command to venerate the founders of Thebes. In the interpretation (hesitantly) followed here, Theseus begins to leave but stops short of exiting when Hercules begins to hallucinate. This interpretation has the advantage of eliminating the problem as to when Theseus returns onstage; there is no natural opportunity for him to do so (perhaps during the choral ode?).

45. *better felt your shafts*: That is, better than the child he killed, a reference to the Stymphalian Birds,* which Hercules* shot down with arrows.

46. *savage team of horses*: see Diomedes 2.*

47. *lords of Libya*: Antaeus* and Busiris,* although the latter is Egyptian.

48. *with his hands or on his altars*: Eryx,* Antaeus,* and Busiris.*

49. *compassion and redemption*: Athens* in general and Theseus* in particular were known for offering sanctuary to those who had committed crimes elsewhere.

50. *again took weapons to hand*: Mars killed Neptune's son Halirrhothius (because he had raped his daughter Alcippe) and was brought to trial for murder by Neptune in Athens on the Areopagus

('Hill of Ares', where homicides were judged in historical times). Mars presented his defence of justifiable homicide and was acquitted of the charge.

TROJAN WOMEN

1. *the gods' toil*: Laomedon,* Priam's father, promised to pay Apollo* and Neptune* for building the walls of Troy, but refused to do so after the walls were built.

2. *seven-mouthed Tanais*: The Tanais here is probably a mistake for the Ister, (Danube), which formed the northern limits of the Thracian territory (the land of Rhesus) and had the epithet 'seven-mouthed'.

3. *squadrons of cavalry*: These last two episodes were recounted in the lost Greek epic *Aethiopis*, the sequel to the *Iliad*, although in that work Penthesilea* arrived before the Ethiopian Memnon* (Seneca also reverses the order in Act II). Both were killed by Achilles.*

4. *when I was pregnant*: Pregnant with Paris,* Hecuba* dreamed that she gave birth to a torch whose fires subsequently spread and consumed Troy.* When consulted, seers foretold that the son she carried in her womb would bring destruction to Troy and instructed her to kill the child. Her attempt to expose the infant failed and Paris survived to seduce Helen,* leading to the Trojan War and the destruction of Troy.

5. *twice captured by the Greeks*: Priam* was captured the first time when Hercules* sacked Troy* after his father Laomedon* refused to pay Hercules for saving his daughter; Priam* was ransomed by his sister Hesione and became king (as described in Andromache's song in Act III).

6. *ill-fated bow*: Troy* was sacked twice by Greeks, first by Hercules* himself (see previous note), then by Agamemnon's* forces, which were fated to take Troy if and only if they had Hercules' bow. The Greeks retrieved Philoctetes, the owner of Hercules' bow, whom they had earlier abandoned on the island of Lemnos after his snake-bitten foot had become foul-smelling and caused Philoctetes to howl in pain, disrupting the Greeks' sacrifices. Recalled, Philoctetes would kill Paris* with Hercules' bow.

7. *pageant shameful for a king*: Although the context is Greek, these lines allude to the Roman triumph, in which a victorious general

would parade a conquered king bound in chains and the captured spoils through Rome.

8.   *it cost them dearly*: As told in the *Iliad*, the Greeks suffered greatly because of Achilles'* withdrawal from the war.

9.   *by taking up weapons*: In an attempt to prevent her son Achilles* from going to war, Thetis* hid him among the young daughters of King Lycomedes* on Scyros.* When Ulysses* and Diomedes* came to Scyros to find Achilles, they planted weapons and armour among more feminine gifts and had a trumpeter sound the call to war. Achilles, unable to suppress his heroic nature, seized the weapons and betrayed himself.

10.   *was also gentle*: Achilles* wounded Telephus,* but later magically healed him with the rust of the spear that wounded him (see glossary for full details).

11.   *causing disputes among kings*: In the *Iliad* 1, Agamemnon* and Achilles* quarrel over the former's refusal to return his war prize Chryseis* to her suppliant father Chryses,* who hailed from the city of Chryse.

12.   *in front of his uncle's*: Both father and uncle here refer to Priam;* Memnon was the son of Tithonus, Priam's brother.

13.   *for Helen*: At the beginning of the war, Agamemnon* sacrificed his daughter Iphigenia* at the Greek port of Aulis* to appease Diana* and secure favourable winds so that the Greeks could sail to Troy.*

14.   *high and mighty descendants*: A reference to Achilles'* threats towards Agamemnon* in the *Iliad* 1.

15.   *savage acts committed last night*: When the Greeks finally sacked Troy,* many of them committed heinous acts: the lesser Ajax* raped Cassandra* while she clung to Minerva's statue, and Pyrrhus* killed Priam,* although he had taken refuge at the altar of Jupiter.*

16.   *fear of the enemy*: This alludes to the *Iliad* 9, where Agamemnon,* with the Greek army in desperate straits, sends Ulysses* (the Ithacan), Ajax 1* and Phoenix to ask Achilles* to rejoin the war. Agamemnon's response here is meant to insult Achilles, who was found strumming the lyre when the embassy arrived at his tent.

17.   *for Hector's father*: In the *Iliad* 24 Priam* steals into Achilles'* tent to ransom his son Hector's* body. Achilles treats the man kindly and allows him to take Hector's body home and bury it.

18.   *sacrifice virgins*: Another allusion to Agamemnon's* sacrifice of his own daughter Iphigenia* before the war in order to secure favourable winds.

19. *related to me*: Pyrrhus* is related to the sea through his father's mother Thetis,* the sea-goddess who is herself daughter of the sea-god Nereus.*

20. *he'd become a man*: A reference to Achilles'* dalliance with Deidamea, the daughter of King Lycomedes,* while he was in hiding among the king's daughters on Scyros. Their union produced Pyrrhus.*

21. *to fight in person*: An allusion to the *Iliad* 20, where neither Neptune* nor Apollo* dares to attack Achilles.*

22. *a price they paid before*: Another allusion to Agamemnon's* sacrifice of his daughter Iphigenia* at the port of Aulis* (See note 13 above). Iphigenia had been summoned under the pretence of marrying Achilles* and was sacrificed while dressed in bridal attire – just as Polyxena* will be in Act IV.

23. *counterfeit Achilles*: Achilles'* close companion Patroclus donned Achilles' armour in his absence and drove back the Trojans from the Greek ships until Hector* met and killed him (*Iliad* 16).

24. *shrouded his face*: The description of Hector* in Andromache's* dream recalls the description of him in Aeneas' dream in Vergil's *Aeneid* 2. There Hector, bloody and beaten, urges Aeneas to awaken and save the sacred icons of the Trojan gods – similar to his message to Andromache here.

25. *dread even his offspring*: In the *Iliad* 6 Hector* expresses his hopes that Astyanax* will live up to his name ('lord of the city') and become the champion of the next generation of Trojans.

26. *once suffered before*: This refers to Agamemnon's* sacrifice of his daughter Iphigenia.*

27. *those mothers were goddesses*: Thetis'* attempt to save her son; see note 9 above.

28. *that the lifeless are owed*: Andromache's* oath to Ulysses* is strictly true, since Astyanax* does, in fact, reside among the dead and has been interred in a tomb. This is a ruse worthy of her cunning opponent Ulysses and has the immediate though temporary effect of convincing him that Astyanax is dead.

29. *you Greeks ransomed*: See note 17 above.

30. *on your return*: An allusion to Homer's *Odyssey*, in which Ulysses* does return home to Ithaca* after ten years of wandering after the Trojan War. Andromache's* prayers do come true despite Ulysses' pitiless treatment of her here.

31. *with more honour*: Laomedon,* Priam's* father, reneged on his promise to pay Hercules* for saving his daughter Hesione from a sea monster.

32. *all that you prize*: See note 6 above.

33. *your malicious mind*: Ulysses* engineered the death of Palamedes, his Athenian (and so Greek) rival in cunning, who had seen through Ulysses' ploy of acting insane to avoid fighting in Troy;* in retaliation Ulysses contrived a scheme that incriminated Palamedes of conspiring with the Trojans. Believing him, the Greeks killed Palamedes.

34. *in the light of day*: Ulysses* twice went on covert operations with Diomedes 1* at night, first on a raid against the Trojan forces, killing Dolon and Rhesus* (*Iliad* 10), and later when they slipped into Troy and stole the sacred Palladium, the magical icon that protected the Trojans.

35. *Trojan Games*: The Trojan Games were a Roman festival that featured an equestrian parade and manoeuvres performed by leading young men of the state. This festival was especially prominent in the reigns of Julius Caesar and his heir Augustus, who traced their lineage back to Venus* through the Trojan son of Aeneas, Iulus (= Iulius), who in Vergil's *Aeneid* (Book 5) led the first such cavalry manoeuvres during the funeral games of his grandfather, Anchises.

36. *the gates of heaven*: When the Giants* were making their assault against Jupiter* in heaven, they were said to pile Ossa* on Olympus and then Pelion* on Ossa.

37. *renowned for its savage beast*: The Calydonian Boar, which Diana* sent to ravage the lands because King Oeneus forgot to sacrifice to her.

38. *call you daughter*: Achilles'* parents were Peleus* and Thetis,* the daughter of the sea-divinities Nereus* and Doris, the latter of whom is the daughter of two other sea-divinities Ocean* and Tethys.* Helen* slips here, since only if Polyxena* is given to *Achilles* in marriage would Peleus* be able to call her 'daughter-in-law', but the Trojan women in their grief do not catch on.

39. *arrange it into braids*: This alludes to the Roman bridal ritual of parting a bride's hair into six separate locks using a bent spear.

40. *Paris' blow*: Achilles'* death by Paris* was something of an embarrassment given the former's might and the latter's moral failings and relative martial weakness – here noted by his own mother. Compare Agamemnon's* retort to Pyrrhus* in Act II: 'You mean the Achilles who was felled by *Paris'* hand?'

41. *Andromache*: I follow Fitch in attributing these lines to Andromache. They are given to Hecuba* in the manuscripts.

42.   *the possessor of Achilles' armour*: After Achilles'* death, Ulysses*
       and Ajax 1* – both of whom rescued Achilles' body from being
       captured and defiled by the Trojans – put in a claim for Achilles'
       divine armour, which Ulysses won.

43.   *should be just right for you*: Pyrrhus* had brutally slain the elderly
       Priam* on the altar before Hecuba's own eyes. Hecuba,* herself
       old, mocks Pyrrhus for his penchant for killing the elderly – a
       heinous crime in the eyes of the Greeks and Romans (compare
       Priam's similar insults in Vergil's *Aeneid* 2).

44.   *when I set sail*: Many of the Greeks that set sail after Troy's* fall
       suffered shipwreck or some other disaster on the sea. Although
       Hecuba's* curse here suggests that she will meet shipwreck, in no
       other account does this occur; rather, she is changed into a dog,
       either at Troy, in Thrace,* or at sea. Ulysses,* however, to whom
       Hecuba is awarded, does become lost at sea, wandering for ten
       years until he returns home to Ithaca* (as told in Homer's *Odys-
       sey*).

45.   *a wedding such as this*: The Trojans' imprecation is ironic; Hermi-
       one,* the daughter of Helen* and Menelaus,* will, in fact, marry
       Pyrrhus.*

PHAEDRA

1.   *beneath Parnethus' crags*: All of the geographical references in this
       passage are to features of the Attic landscape around Athens.*

2.   *a ruse of fear*: These lines refer to the *formido* ('terror'), whereby
       hunters use cordons of brightly coloured feathers to 'scare' the
       prey into the nets.

3.   *virile goddess*: Diana,* goddess of the hunt, a typically masculine
       pursuit.

4.   *deer in Crete*: Following Fitch I have omitted the following line:
       'Now you shoot fleet-footed deer with a lighter touch.'

5.   *Arabia's rich forests*: The Arabs were known for their spices,
       particularly cinnamon, which the Romans thought grew on their
       trees, although the Arabs probably imported it from Indian trad-
       ers.

6.   *orders of a bold suitor*: The bold suitor is Pirithous,* Theseus'
       close companion, who, in return for helping Theseus abduct
       Helen,* asked him to help in his own quest to abduct Proserpina*
       from the underworld.

7.   *from Etna's vents*: A typical description of the symptoms of love;

although Phaedra nowhere explicitly reveals the object of her passion, a Roman audience would have immediately realized that it was for Hippolytus.*

8.   *sacred mysteries*: see Eleusis.*

9.   *the land awarded to her*: Minerva,* who contended with Neptune* over the patronage of Athens.*

10. *my wretched mother*: see Pasiphae.*

11. *in the embrace of her lover Mars*: When the Sun informed Vulcan* that his wife Venus* was having an affair with Mars,* Vulcan forged invisible chains, placed them on his bed, and caught his wife in the act. Because of this Venus bore a grudge against the Sun's descendants, one of whom was his daughter Pasiphae,* Phaedra's mother.

12. *involves some wickedness*: Phaedra alludes to her husband's mistreatment of her sister Ariadne,* whom Theseus* abandoned on the island of Naxos despite his promises to marry her.

13. *grandfathers who see everything*: Phaedra had a divine grandfather on both her maternal and paternal side: the Sun was her mother's father and Jupiter was her father's father.

14. *your brother's halls remain empty*: The brother here is the Minotaur,* Phaedra's half-brother, killed by Theseus.*

15. *heaven than to earth*: Phaedra refers to, among others, the affairs of Jupiter;* Mars'* and Vulcan's* relationships with Venus;* and Apollo's* unsuccessful affair with Daphne.* Seneca neatly chooses those gods who possessed weapons similar to Cupid's.

16. *impossible exits*: An allusion to Theseus'* escape from the labyrinth.*

17. *respond to entreaties*: I assign these words to the Nurse against recent editors. The distribution of speakers in this passage is rather confused in the manuscripts.

18. *Ariadne's mild-mannered father*: Phaedra alludes to the unwillingness of her father Minos* to pursue Theseus* after he seduced Ariadne* and convinced her to leave with him after defeating the Minotaur.*

19. *with unequal pan pipes*: Normally Apollo* is enslaved to Admetus* for killing the makers of Jupiter's* thunderbolts, the Cyclopes,* but Seneca follows a variant in which Apollo voluntarily serves Admetus for erotic purposes.

20. *than swans do at death*: Swans in antiquity were said to have sung most sweetly at their deaths, the origin of our phrase 'swansong'. The reference here is to his seduction of Leda* as a swan.

21. *cargo he was carrying*: Jupiter* abducted Europa* as a bull.

22. *Moon-goddess . . . burned*: An allusion to the Moon's affair with the mortal shepherd Endymion of Thessaly.*

23. *on whirling spindles*: An allusion to Hercules'* servitude to Omphale.*

24. *no shepherd win glory from you*: The Nurse repeats the previous ode's allusion to the Moon's affair with the mortal shepherd Endymion (see note 22 above).

25. *your Colchian stepmother*: Medea,* who hailed from Colchis,* persuaded her second husband Aegeus* to kill his son Theseus* with a poisoned drink. Just before Theseus took the first sip, Aegeus realized that he was his son by the sword he was carrying (his own) and knocked the cup from his hand.

26. *horn-sprouting head with a turban*: This portrait of Bacchus,* triumphantly returning from his eastern conquests on a chariot pulled by tigers and sprouting horns, became common in the wake of Alexander's conquests in the east (hence India here).

27. *preferred over Bacchus*: In Homer's *Odyssey* (11.321–5) Ariadne* was said to have chosen the mortal Theseus* over Bacchus* – a variant of the more commonly told myth that Bacchus rescued the abandoned Ariadne on Naxos.*

28. *drowning young beauties in fountains*: An allusion to the myth of Hylas, a handsome youth who joined the Argonauts as a companion of Hercules; he was pulled into a spring and drowned by Naiads* while drawing water in Mysia.*

29. *ancient Arcadia*: The Arcadians were considered the oldest people in Greece, born even before the moon.

30. *to offset them*: The blushing moon refers to a lunar eclipse, which was thought to be brought on by witchcraft drawing the moon down from heaven. Clanging together brass objects was used as a magical countermeasure to the witchcraft.

31. *stands balanced*: That is, Hippolytus'* death balances Theseus'* escape from the underworld.

32. *love or loathing for your wives*: Theseus'* father Aegeus* committed suicide when Theseus failed to put up the white sails indicating that he had survived his encounter with the Minotaur; Theseus' love for Phaedra caused Hippolytus'* death; and his loathing for his Amazon wife Antiope* compelled him to kill her. This may also be an allusion to Theseus' abandonment of Ariadne* on Naxos* on his way back from Crete.

33. *raising his hands to the heavens*: The metre here changes to trochaic tetrameter, which Seneca uses in solemn prayers involving the underworld.

34. *not for sex*: A reference to Theseus'* journey into the underworld to help Pirithous* abduct Proserpina,* a voyage that kept him from Phaedra for four years. See Introduction.

OEDIPUS

1. *scorching fires of the Dogstar*: The constellation Leo* is associated with summer heat because the sun passes through the constellation in late July and August. The star Sirius ('Scorcher'), or the Dogstar (because it was part of the constellation *Canis Maior*, 'Greater Dog'), rises in conjunction with the sun about the same time of year, heralding, as they were called in antiquity, 'the dog days' of summer.

2. *the grim riddle of that pitiless, winged monster*: The specifics of the riddle, given neither here nor in Sophocles' play, are found earliest and fullest in a text by Asclepiades, a scholar of the fourth century BC who studied the versions of myths found in Greek tragedies: 'Two-footed and four-footed and three-footed on the earth, it has but a single voice, and it changes form alone of all those on land or in the skies or in the sea. When it travels supported on three feet [some manuscripts have "most feet"], the speed of its limbs is most sluggish.' The answer is a human, which crawls on all fours as an infant, walks on two legs as an adult, and requires a staff in old age.

3. *Fool . . . Rule of the city!*: These lines are mistakenly attributed to Jocasta* in some manuscripts, probably in an attempt to expand her role in the first Act, which is curiously limited to her one speech, her rebuke of Oedipus'* manliness.

4. *The ferryman*: Seneca's description of Charon* echoes that of Vergil in *Aeneid 6*.

5. *in contorted words*: One of Apollo's* epithets was Loxias ('Crooked'), which reflected the fact that his oracles were typically ambiguous and frequently misunderstood by humans with their limited capacity to understand the gods.

6. *teasing out knotty riddles*: This is not only an allusion to Oedipus'* solving the riddle of the Sphinx* but also a play on one etymology of Oedipus' name, from Greek *oid-* 'know'.

7. *Creon*: The metre changes here to trochaic tetrameter, which is used in solemn invocations; Seneca reserves it for contexts in which the underworld is invoked (see also Theseus'* prayer in Act IV of *Phaedra*).

8.   *to Cadmus' Thebes*: Oracles, as the one given here, were delivered
      in dactylic hexameter (translated into iambic pentameter).

9.   *wedged between two seas*: Sisyphus* was the legendary king of
      Corinth,* the city from which Oedipus* had set out to consult
      the oracle at Delphi.*

10.   *at odds*: This is the first of many omens predicting the civil strife
      between Oedipus'* sons Eteocles and Polynices; according to one
      mythical tradition, after their deaths at each other's hands they
      were burned on the same pyre, but produced two plumes of smoke
      that travelled in opposite directions.

11.   *with serene expressions*: Roman blood sacrifice followed a very
      specific formula, a series of steps that required the assent of the
      animal for the sacrifice to be acceptable. The opposite reactions
      of the two sacrificial animals – the willingness of the heifer, the
      reluctance of the bull – are just one of many contradictory signs
      that highlight the convoluted nature of Oedipus'* crime and the
      reluctance of the gods to reveal the answer.

12.   *which will leave no doubt*: Extispicy was the investigation of
      divine will through the inspection of the entrails (*exta*) of sacrifi-
      cial animals. The liver was a particularly rich organ for divination,
      as can be seen from, for example, the bronze Liver of Piacenza.

13.   *twin protruding lobes of equal mass*: This portends the conflict
      between Oedipus'* sons Eteocles and Polynices over the kingship
      of Thebes.

14.   *none of them to return*: The seven veins prophesy the attack of
      the Seven against Thebes,* in which Oedipus'* exiled son Polyn-
      ices and six other generals from Argos make an assault on Thebes.
      Only one, Adrastus, the king of Argos,* returned alive, but his
      son would later die in a second attack on Thebes, thus fulfilling
      this prophecy.

15.   *in a strange place*: The meaning of this omen is not entirely clear,
      but the unnatural birth may allude to the incest between Oedipus*
      and Jocasta.*

16.   *foliage loved by Phoebus*: The laurel was the sacred tree of Apollo*
      and was used to make the crowns given to victors at the Pythian
      Games held in Delphi* every four years. Also implied here is
      Apollo's love of Daphne* ('Laurel'), who, when fleeing from the
      god, was turned into a tree of the same name.

17.   *Zalaces*: The manuscripts read either *Zalacum* or *Zedacum* here,
      but these peoples are not otherwise known. It is highly likely here
      that this word has replaced some other nation which Bacchus*
      conquered, but it is not clear which.

18. *Stepmother's presence there*: Argos* was a major cult centre for Juno;* the point here is that Bacchus'* sway had become so strong that he even eclipsed his hostile stepmother's considerable power there.

19. *with a better mate*: Theseus* abandoned Ariadne* on Naxos* on his way home from Crete* to Athens.* Bacchus* rescued her and made her his wife.

20. *as Bacchus approached*: A neat touch, since Bacchus'* mother Semele,* while pregnant with him, was consumed by Jupiter's* thunderbolts.

21. *dragged into the pit*: The manuscripts are divided on this line. I have translated E's *antro* ('to the pit') because the pit needs to be specified here, especially in view of the next sentence. But A's *retro* (dragged in 'backwards') is attractive given that this is a description of a necromantic ritual in which an inversion of the normal practice of leading the victim in head first would be expected. Note the detail in the next paragraph that Tiresias* uses his *left* hand when making the offering of milk and wine.

22. *possessed by the god*: This refers to the tearing apart of Pentheus* by Agave* and her sisters.

23. *charge is dismissed*: This last sentence, which I attribute to Creon,* is given to Oedipus* in the manuscripts.

24. *a wandering heifer*: Specifically, Cadmus* was ordered to follow the cow until the cow lay down or collapsed from exhaustion, where he was to settle and build a city.

25. *Cow-country*: Boeotia,* the land of Thebes,* is derived from *bous*, the Greek for 'cow' or 'ox'.

26. *pregnant earth gave birth*: Seneca does not directly connect the two interrelated episodes narrated here, but this is probably purposeful since his concern is not the full story (Seneca is heavily dependent here on the beginning of Ovid's *Metamorphoses*, Book 3). Instead, he concentrates on the *supernatural* events in Thebes'* history. To fill in the gap: after Cadmus* slays the giant serpent, he sows its teeth into the earth, which gives birth to the armed men who fight each other. Some scholars believe that something has dropped out of the text either here or a few lines later to connect the two episodes more explicitly, but I find this unlikely given Seneca's aims.

27. *a brood just born*: Not all of the sown men perished in this struggle. Five survived; they and their descendants (the Serpent Race*) were leading citizens of Thebes.* Creon* and Jocasta* were descended from one of them.

28. *the feathers*: This refers to the *formido* ('terror'), a long row of feathers attached to a line, which is set out to scare fleeing prey into the direction of the nets.

29. *bathing her maiden limbs*: The virgin goddess is Diana,* who caused Actaeon's* metamorphosis because he had gazed on the goddess as she bathed (as told in Ovid's *Metamorphoses* 3). Seneca's narrative does not include Actaeon's mistake or his gruesome mauling by his dogs, but focuses rather on his supernatural transformation (keeping with the theme of the ode) and adds the unusual but striking detail of his return to the very spring where his metamorphosis began.

30. *a blow of my staff*: In the final act Jocasta,* seizing Oedipus'* sword, claims that Laius* died by it. In Act II Creon* reported that a group of brigands wielding swords had killed him.

31. *in defence of the king*: Again, Jocasta's* report contradicts that of Creon* in Act II, who stated that all were slain.

32. *disdainful kings faithful*: The text and meaning of this line is uncertain. Interpretation hinges on whether Merope* deceived her husband Polybus* by passing Oedipus* off as her own in order to save her marriage, or whether Polybus, too, was aware that Oedipus was not his own son and passed him off as heir to the throne. In the latter case, the line may mean (with a slight emendation) 'children ensure that kings have their subjects' loyalty'. Both interpretations are possible and supported by early myth, but since Oedipus in the previous line asks specifically what *Merope* hoped to get from passing off the son as her own, I incline to the former interpretation.

33. *the swelling of your feet*: A common Greek etymology for Oedipus'* name: *oidein*, 'to swell', and *pous*, 'foot'.

34. *Jocasta*: These lines and the subsequent lines of Jocasta* in this act are attributed to the Old Man from Corinth* in the manuscripts, but the content of the lines indicates that they belong to Jocasta. She is the only one who has both the knowledge of the whole picture and a reason to urge Oedipus* to give up his pursuit of the truth. The Old Man, who knows only part of the story and cannot connect Oedipus to Laius* and Jocasta, has no cause to speak these lines.

35. *reckless lad . . . Cretan king*: The reckless lad is Icarus,* the son of Daedalus.* Minos,* the king of Crete,* imprisoned them because Daedalus had constructed the infamous hollow wooden cow that allowed Minos' wife Pasiphae* to copulate with a bull and thus conceive the Minotaur.*

36. *gave his name to the sea*: Icarus* was said to have fallen into the

Icarian Sea near the island of Icarus, one of the Sporades in the Aegean Sea* west of Samos.

37. *Fortune's grasp*: A Stoic *bon mot*. The Stoics believed that when Fate had led one to a point of utter misery, one could commit suicide to extract oneself from the difficult straits. The Stoic theme will be continued in the next choral ode.

38. *Fate*: The Stoics believed that the whole universe was interconnected and infused by a rational divine force (called *logos* in Greek, *ratio* in Latin) and that all events were predetermined by Fate (or better, by a benevolent force called Providence) at the beginning of the cycle of time. This causal chain, once begun, cannot be altered even by the Stoic god that permeates everything – as Seneca himself tells us in his treatise *On Providence* (5.9). Here, Seneca merges this philosophical belief with the mythical Lachesis,* who was one of the three Fates who determined human destinies. The myth of Oedipus* is easily merged with the Stoic concept of Fate.

39. *faraway sun*: The Antipodes ('standing opposite') were humans that inhabited the theoretical world on the other side of the earth opposite the Romans, hence the reference to 'different stars' and the 'faraway sun'.

40. *husband and sons*: Unlike Sophocles' play, in which Jocasta* hangs herself offstage, here she uses a more masculine sword (like Phaedra) and kills herself onstage. Her manner of death is strikingly similar to the death of Agrippina* (Nero's mother) as reported in Tacitus' *Annals* (14.8). When confronted by the henchman sent by her son to dispatch her, she is said to have pointed to her womb and cried out, 'Strike my belly!' The historian Dio Cassius adds a detail, 'Strike this, strike this, Anicetus, because it produced Nero!' See also the end of the first chorus of *Octavia*, where Agrippina cries out, 'Stab your sword here [i.e., the womb], yes here,' said she, / 'where I bore such a monstrosity.' Could Seneca here have been making a veiled criticism of Nero's matricide? This is possible, but the stabbing of a woman in the womb to prevent a monstrosity is a common rhetorical motif found in many historical descriptions. It is also possible, though perhaps less so, that the scene in *Octavia*, which is modelled directly on this one, itself influenced later historical accounts of Agrippina's death, especially since no one outside Nero's circle likely knew the precise details of Agrippina's final moments.

THYESTES

1. *Minos will never have rest*: Minos,* one of the judges in the underworld, assigned the dead their allotted punishments; the point here is that the descendants of Tantalus'* son Pelops* are so inherently wicked that Minos* will be continually occupied with assigning them punishments.

2. *In this wicked house . . . all will perish*: I follow Fitch's transposition of these lines ('A hostile wife . . . all will perish') here. In the manuscripts they occur later and follow '. . . mighty leaders of nations'.

3. *in a greater number*: The Thracian crime refers to Procne's* murder of her son Itys, whom she cooks and feeds to her unfaithful husband Tereus* because he had raped her sister Philomela.*

4. *all too familiar to you*: In the most common tradition Tantalus* was punished for killing and feeding his son Pelops* to the gods – foreshadowing the type of revenge Atreus* will exact on his brother.

5. *I will yet voice this warning, too*: Seneca alludes here to an alternate reason for Tantalus'* punishment, namely, that he revealed the gods' secrets to humankind.

6. *primeval drought*: The Argolid* is by nature an arid area and myths about early Argos* reflect this fact; according to one version, Neptune* dried up the area because the river-god Inachus* testified that the land belonged to Juno.* The early king of Argos,* Danaus,* and his daughter Amymone were credited with solving the water problem either by digging wells or by discovering springs that could supply water.

7. *land famed for chariots*: Pisa,* located near its more famous neighbour Olympia* (where in historical times chariots were raced at the Olympic Games), was said to be the location of Pelops'* chariot race against Oenomaus (see Preface to the play).

8. *A little boy*: Pelops,* Tantalus'* son.

9. *what they do not*: Seneca may have been influenced here by the *Atreus* written by the early Roman playwright Accius (*c.* 170–90 BC.), which is preserved only in fragments. In one of these Atreus* utters the famous line *oderint dum metuant* ('let them hate so long as they fear'), which was quoted frequently by Roman authors, including Cicero and Seneca in their philosophical works.

10. *Atreus*: I follow the attribution of these lines found in the E manuscript, which assigns them to Atreus;* the A manuscript family (followed by Zwierlein) attributes them to the Adviser.

11. *heavenly Bears*: The constellations around the North Pole do not sink beneath the horizon (i.e., the sea).

12. *take these innocent children of mine*: The phrase *obsides fidei* 'guarantees (lit. 'hostages') of good faith', recalls the practice of client kings providing family members to the Roman emperor as hostages to ensure their loyalty.

13. *echoes with triple-barkings*: The hounds of Hecate,* the goddess of magic associated with the moon, night and Diana,* were said to bark three times to announce the advent of the goddess.

14. *in a hideous cloud*: The cloud shrouding the household gods is another sign of the gods hiding from the wickedness of the family. Similarly, the smoke from the sacrifice in Act II of *Oedipus* settles down around Oedipus'* eyes and face, indicating his mental blindness and portending his physical blindness.

15. *Thessaly's Mount Pelion*: Phlegra's* armies are the Giants,* who attempted to attack heaven by piling three mountains upon one another.

16. *drifting throughout the spangled sky*: The collapse of the universe here vaguely recalls the Stoic concept of *ecpyrosis*, the cyclical conflagration that consumed the universe, purifying it to begin anew. Here, as is typical in Senecan tragedy, the destruction of the universe (conceived of as a return to the formless Chaos*) is absolute and the chorus does not hint at renewal.

17. *bore young Helle to her horror*: Here the sign Aries* ('Ram') is identified as the golden-fleeced ram that rescued Phrixus* and Helle.* The focus here on Helle is purposeful, as Helle fell from the ram and plunged into the Hellespont ('Helle's Sea'), matching the 'plunging' of the constellation from heaven.

18. *will fall from heaven's heights once more*: According to some accounts the Nemean Lion* was said to have been born of and raised on the moon before being sent to earth. Hercules* defeated the lion, after which it was elevated to the heavens as the constellation Leo.*

19. *the temple doors*: The use of the word temple here for Atreus' house is striking, and it may have to do with his aspirations and claim to divinity through his wicked deed, as is seen at the beginning of this Act.

OCTAVIA

1. *bring me sorrow*: This verse is transmitted in the manuscripts after line 18, where it has caused great consternation among editors; I

have transposed the line here, where it is better suited to context
and produces a more sensible pattern later. See note 5 below.

2. *halcyons, sea-dwellers*: Alcyone, the daughter of Aeolus the
   wind-god, was said to have turned into a sea-dwelling halcyon
   (traditionally a bird of sorrow) while mourning the death of her
   husband Ceyx, who perished at sea.

3. *Pandion's winged daughters*: Procne* and Philomela.*

4. *Mother*: Valeria Messalina,* wife of the Emperor Claudius,* and
   mother of Octavia* and Britannicus; her promiscuity was notorious, and she married Gaius Silius in AD 48 while her husband
   Claudius was away from Rome; Claudius retaliated by executing
   Silius and Messalina and subjecting her to *damnatio memoriae*,
   the removal of her image and name on all statuary and inscriptions.

5. *how sad*: After this line, the manuscripts have a verse which I have
   transposed to after line 4 (see note 1 above). The transmitted text
   would read 'How I wish the aged spinster / Clotho* had snapped
   my life-threads with her hands / before I saw your wounds, your
   face / covered in gruesome gore – how sad! / O light, you always
   bring me sorrow! / Since then the light has been more hateful / to
   me than shadows or darkling night.'

6. *look here*: This 'second prologue' delivered by the Nurse, which
   awkwardly repeats much of what Octavia* has just sung, recalls
   Hecuba's* opening speech in *Trojan Women*, effectively equating
   the fall of Claudius'* house to the destruction of Troy.*

7. *Claudius*: Emperor of Rome AD 41–54, conqueror of the Britons,
   father of Octavia* and Britannicus by his wife Messalina;* after
   Messalina's death he remarried Agrippina, who both secured the
   throne for her own son Nero,* displacing Claudius' biological
   son Britannicus as heir, and murdered Claudius with poisoned
   mushrooms.

8. *her heartless husband*: This passage, equally dense in the Latin
   original, describes in order: 1) Claudius' death by his wife Agrippina;* 2) Agrippina's by her son Nero;* 3) Britannicus' death by
   his stepbrother Nero; and 4) the grief of Octavia,* Britannicus'
   sister and Nero's stepsister and wife. For a detailed discussion of
   the complicated historical background see the preface to the play.

9. *Electra*: The opening of the play, especially Octavia's* ode to dawn,
   is indebted to Sophocles' *Electra*. Here the debt is made explicit
   as Octavia compares her dismal situation to that of Electra.*

10. *An insufferable whore*: Poppaea,* Nero's mistress.

11. *smitten by his niece*: The niece is Agrippina the Younger,* the daugh-
    ter of Claudius' brother Germanicus, a famed general who enjoyed

much popular support. She engineered a marriage between her own
son (the Emperor Nero) by Lucius Domitius Ahenobarbus and
Octavia,* thus thrusting out Claudius' own son Britannicus as heir.

12. *Silanus*: Lucius Silanus, a descendant of Augustus,* was
betrothed to Octavia;* Agrippina,* aiming to make her son
Nero* heir to the throne through a marriage to Octavia, had
Silanus removed from the Senate and started the rumour that
Silanus was engaged in an incestuous relationship with his own
sister; Silanus took his own life on the day of Claudius' and
Agrippina's marriage.

13. *Britannicus*: Claudius Britannicus (AD 41–55), the son of the
Emperor Claudius* and Messalina,* heir to the throne; after the
death of his mother, Claudius married Agrippina,* and Britannicus was displaced by Nero,* Agrippina's biological son, who
poisoned him to eliminate his claim to the throne. The honorific
name 'Britannicus' came from his father's subjugation of Britain.

14. *your husband's slave girl*: Acte,* an imperial freedwoman who
was Nero's mistress from AD 55 onwards.

15. *the wings of a swan*: This catalogue refers to Jupiter's* mortal
affairs with Leda,* Europa* and Danae,* and to his children
Castor* and Pollux* by Leda,* Bacchus* by Semele,* and
Hercules* by Alcmena.*

16. *Emperor's young sister-wife*: The position of Octavia,* stepsister
and wife of Nero,* is equated with that of Juno,* who was sister
as well as wife of Jupiter.* See note 41.

17. *with a blazing trail*: This refers to the comet of AD 60, which,
according to Seneca (*Natural Investigations*, 7.29.2), was visible
for just under six months (Chinese records offer a total of 135 days)
and 'took away the ill repute comets have' (7.17.2), meaning that
in this instance it did not herald a change in rulers. The biographer
Suetonius (*Nero*, 36.1) and the historian Tacitus (*Annals*, 14.22)
record that Nero's* reaction to the comet was to eliminate leading
citizens to prevent a possible overthrow. Tacitus informs us that
one of these was Rubellius Plautus, whose execution Nero will
order as soon as he arrives on stage in Act II (see note 27). As befits
the context of the play, Octavia's* negative interpretation of the
comet differs from that found in Seneca's *Natural Investigations*.

18. *into a fit of mad lust*: Messalina* (see note 4 above).

19. *ill-gotten spoils*: In 450 BC Verginia was famously killed by her
father Verginius to prevent the *decemvir* (member of the Council
of Ten) Appius Claudius from raping her; the subsequent revolt
led to the overthrow of the despotic *decemviri*.

20. *Lucretia*: This virtuous Roman woman was raped by Sextus Tarquinius, the son of the seventh and last king of Rome (Tarquinius the Haughty); after the rape, she summoned her father and husband, revealed Sextus' crime and committed suicide out of shame; her father and husband then led the successful revolt to overthrow the Tarquins and established a new form of government, the Republic, in 509 BC.

21. *Tullia*: Daughter of the sixth king of Rome, Servius Tullius; she, along with her husband Tarquinius, deposed her father, installed Tarquinius as king and, as a final insult, drove a chariot over her father's corpse.

22. *my husband*: Claudius.*

23. *such a monstrosity*: It is difficult to determine here whether the author of *Octavia* is influenced by Jocasta's* similar suicide at the end of *Oedipus*, by a common rhetorical motif, or by the real events of Agrippina's* death as reported by the historians Tacitus and Dio Cassius. See *Oedipus,* note 40.

24. *stony cliffs of the Corsican Sea*: Seneca was exiled to Corsica from AD 41 to AD 49; he was recalled by Agrippina* specifically to act as her son Nero's* tutor.

25. *a new stock of men*: The author of *Octavia* is employing the Senecan (Stoic) idea that the world goes through cyclical renewal and purification. The author may be recalling the fourth ode of *Thyestes* ('The Collapse of the Heavens'), where the heavens plunge into a shapeless mass.

26. *gap in the text*: Given the shortness of the description of the second age of humankind (the Silver Age), something has likely fallen out of the text.

27. *bring me back their heads*: Rubellius Plautus and Faustus Cornelius Sulla, both with distinguished lineages, were exiled by Nero* because they were potential usurpers (Sulla to Gaul in AD 58, Plautus to Asia in AD 60, the latter following the appearance of the comet: see note 17 above). Their deaths and Nero's divorce from Octavia* are also linked in Tacitus' *Annals* (14.57–9).

28. *on kin rashly*: The debate between Nero* and his adviser Seneca is redolent of the similar debate between Atreus* and his unnamed adviser in Act II of *Thyestes*.

29. *The Father of the Country*: (*Pater Patriae* in Latin, abbreviated to PP on coins and inscriptions) This was a common title assumed by emperors as recognition of their role as protectors of citizens. It was first awarded by the senate to Julius Caesar, and in 2 BC to his successor Augustus, who publicly stated that it was his most

treasured honour. Throughout this passage Seneca upholds Augustus as the model emperor.

30. *since I make them*: Nero had his predecessor Claudius* deified through senatorial decree after his death in AD 54.

31. *in an unspeakable crime*: After the battle of Pharsalus in 48 BC, Julius Caesar, known for his clemency towards conquered foes, pardoned Lucius Junius Brutus, who had fought for his rival, Pompey. Later, in 44 BC, Brutus became one of the ringleaders of the senatorial conspiracy that murdered Caesar.

32. *execution in their death-lists*: The triumvirate ('rule of three men') here refers to the so-called Second Triumvirate (Antony, Lepidus and Octavian, later known as Augustus), a military autocracy that was virtually unchecked by the senate and people of Rome. These men revived the brutal policy of proscription lists, public bounties on political enemies and wealthy men, aimed mainly at confiscating their property to finance their own armies. According to some accounts 300 senators and more than 2,000 wealthy landowners were killed. The heads of the slain were publicly displayed in the forum.

33. *Rostra*: The Rostra was a raised speaker's platform in the Roman Forum; this specific detail may be an allusion to the death of the great orator and consul, Marcus Tullius Cicero ('Cicero'), who was put to death in 43 BC as part of the proscriptions. His head and hands were nailed to the front of the Rostra.

34. *Philippi's battleground*: Octavian (later Augustus) and Antony defeated the assassins of Caesar, Brutus and Cassius at the Battle of Philippi in 42 BC.

35. *butchers of their own countrymen*: Octavian fought Sextus Pompey, the son of Pompey the Great, in a massive and deadly naval battle at Naulochus (on the north coast of Sicily) in 36 BC – effectively a civil war.

36. *his weightless shade*: Antony's forces were defeated by Octavian at the battle of Actium in 31 BC; Antony and his consort, the Egyptian Queen Cleopatra, slipped away on ship and escaped back to Egypt, where a year later they committed suicide. The first great leader to fall in Egypt was Pompey, who was treacherously killed when he sought refuge there after being defeated by Caesar at the Battle of Pharsalus in 48 BC.

37. *enshrined in temples*: Augustus was deified after his death in AD 14 and assigned a temple, priests and rites.

38. *born of a god*: Claudius* was deified after his death.

39. *would all admit defeat*: An allusion to the Judgement of Paris,*

the Trojan who chose Venus* over Juno* (Jupiter's* wife) and Minerva* (goddess of war) in a beauty contest and was awarded Helen* as a prize.

40. *You mean Love*: The debate between Nero* and Seneca on the nature of Love, whether it is divine or a human construct, is indebted to the similar debate between Phaedra and her Nurse in Act II of *Phaedra*.

41. *I will be his sister only*: Octavia's* position first as sister-wife, then as sister only, recalls the opening lines of *Hercules Insane*, where Juno complains that she has been displaced by Jupiter's* mistresses.

42. *in mutual harmony*: Despite the positive tone with which the Nurse tells of the wedding of Peleus* and Thetis,* the wedding has grim undertones. It was here that Eris, goddess of discord, threw the golden apple in the middle of the goddesses Juno,* Minerva* and Venus,* which led to the Judgement of Paris,* which in turn led to the Trojan War and all of its horrors – perhaps hinting at the revolt that Poppaea's* wedding to Nero* will precipitate.

43. *Crispinus*: The identity of Poppaea's* former husband is unknown. It may have been Rufrius Crispinus, who was in charge of the Emperor Claudius' bodyguard; later he was implicated in the Pisonian conspiracy against Nero* (AD 65), exiled to Sardinia and forced to commit suicide the next year. But the fact that he welcomes her in the underworld suggests that her husband died before Poppaea; Rufrius (died AD 66) survived Poppaea's death in 65.

44. *buried a cruel sword in his neck*: The Latin here does not clearly specify *whose* neck is stabbed. I have thus translated it ambiguously, but on comparison with Octavia's* dream reported in Act I (in which Nero* bursts in on Octavia and Britannicus* and stabs them) it seems to me that Crispinus' throat is meant here, especially since the author of *Octavia* is particularly fond of symmetry. The ambiguity continues in Poppaea's last line, as well as in the Nurse's interpretation of the dream.

45. *despite his rage*: In the first book of the *Iliad* Achilles* withdrew from fighting because Agamemnon* (Atreus' son) had taken away his war prize, the captive girl Briseis.* When the Greeks were on the brink of disaster because of Achilles' refusal to fight, Agamemnon sent an embassy to appeal to him (Book 9); they found him strumming on a lyre, though not out of love but out of boredom (the author of *Octavia*, like Seneca in *Trojan Women*, follows the post-Homeric tradition in which the relationship between Achilles and Briseis was erotic).

46. *must sink beneath my flames*: An allusion to the great fire of AD 64 (the play is set in AD 62), which destroyed a large part of the city. It is unlikely that Nero* was responsible for the fire, but it must have seemed possible given Nero's immediate construction of 'The Golden House', an enormous palace which was built on the space that had been consumed in the fire. Tacitus, who reports that some sources claimed Nero was responsible for starting the fire, also notes that a rumour circulated in Rome that Nero, dressed in stage costume, sang an aria 'The Sack of Troy', during the fire itself (*Annals*, 15.39).

47. *our fear will not*: The text of this line is corrupt, perhaps beyond repair. In the absence of anything better, I have translated Fitch's emendation.

48. *the Gracchi*: Tiberius (Tribune of the People, 133 BC) and Gaius (Tribune, 123–2 BC) Gracchus were Roman aristocrats famed for their popular land-reform agendas and policies aimed at helping the urban poor – and they were ultimately killed because of them.

49. *Livius*: M. Livius Drusus, like the Gracchi, attempted to push through popular reforms as Tribune of the People (91 BC) and was murdered for it.

50. *daughter of Agrippa*: Agrippina the Elder (*c.* 14 BC–AD 33) was daughter of M. Vipsanius Agrippa and Julia (the daughter of Augustus), and wife of Germanicus. They had seven children, of whom one was the Emperor Gaius (Caligula: reigned AD 37–41), another Agrippina the Younger, Nero's mother. The elder Agrippina was exiled in AD 29 by the Emperor Tiberius to the island of Pandataria* (where her mother was and Octavia* would be exiled), where she experienced brutal conditions and ultimately starved herself to death in AD 33.

51. *Caesar's wife*: The terms 'Augustus' and 'Caesar' here refer to the emperor and his heir, respectively; Agrippina* was married to Germanicus, who was at the time the Emperor Tiberius' heir.

52. *Livia*: Livia Julia (12 BC?– AD 31), sister of the Emperor Claudius, was said to have been seduced by Tiberius' confidant Sejanus and under his influence poisoned her husband Drusus, the Emperor Tiberius' son. She was put to death in AD 31. Her daughter Julia (described in the next three lines) died in 43 through Messalina's* intrigue (Tacitus, *Annals*, 13.32).

53. *your own mother wielded*: Messalina.*

54. *for Pandataria's shores*: I translate Lipsius' emendation *Pandatariae*; the manuscripts read *tandem Phariae* ('We make at last

for Pharia's [i.e., Egypt's] shores'). Lipsius' emendation brings it in line with our main source for Octavia's* exile, Tacitus' *Annals*, but it introduces an apparent metrical anomaly. It is possible, as Boyle (2008) points out at length, that the author of *Octavia* preserves the correct location for Octavia's exile in Egypt.

55. *Aulis or the Taurians*: The Greek port Aulis* and the land of the Taurians are connected in myth. Iphigenia* was sacrificed by her father Agamemnon* at Aulis* before the Trojan War in order to obtain favourable winds. Just before the ghastly sacrifice took place, however, the goddess Diana* (= Trivia) replaced Iphigenia's body with a deer and transported her to the land of the Taurians (the Crimean Peninsula), where as her priestess she performed human sacrifice on all foreigners.

Glossary of Names, Places and Terms

The following glossary is meant to be comprehensive in terms of myth, but it also includes most geographical references and select Latin terms (*aegis*, *thyrsus*, etc.). Information about historical figures in *Octavia* will generally be found in the notes to that play, although I have included entries for the characters; a detailed discussion of the historical background will be found in the preface to Octavia. A (*) denotes a separate entry for that name, place or term. To conserve space, the following abbreviations are used: s. for son; d. for daughter; f. for father; m. for mother; br. for brother; k. for king.

Achaea: Region in the northern Peloponnese.*

Acheron: 'River of Pains', a river in the underworld, or the underworld itself.

Achilles: S. of Peleus* and Thetis,* greatest Greek warrior at Troy;* when he was a boy, his m., fearful of his fated death in Troy, hid him among the daughters of Lycomedes* on Scyros;* while there he fathered Pyrrhus* by Lycomedes' d. Deidamia; at Troy he killed Hector* and was killed by Paris* with Apollo's* help; after his death, he demanded that Polyxena* be sacrificed to his ghost.

Acropolis: The citadel of Athens.*

Actaeon: Theban, s. of Autonoe and Aristaeus; while hunting on Mount Cithaeron* he gazed on Diana* while she bathed; as punishment, she turned him into a stag and he was devoured by his own dogs.

Acte: Slave and mistress of the Emperor Nero.*

Admetus: K. of Pherae;* the god Apollo* shepherded his flocks while enslaved to him; in return for Admetus' good treatment, Apollo granted that someone could take his place in death.

Adriatic Sea: The sea separating Italy from the Balkan peninsula.

Aeacus: S. of Jupiter* and Aegina, f. of Peleus,* grandf. of Achilles,* and great-grandf. of Pyrrhus;* after his death he became a judge in the underworld.

Aegean Sea: Sea between Greece and Asia Minor;* took its name from Aegeus.*

Aegeus: K. of Athens,* mortal f. of Theseus.*

aegis: Protective goat-skin (Greek *aig*- 'goat'), worn by Minerva;* at the centre was the image of a Gorgon, which terrified all who gazed upon it.

Aegyptus: S. of Belus, br. of Danaus;* his fifty sons were betrothed to his brother's fifty daughters (see Danaids*); all but one of them were murdered by their brides on their wedding night.

Agamemnon: K. of Argos* (or Mycenae*), s. of Atreus,* chief commander of the Greek forces at Troy;* before they could sail, he had to sacrifice his d. Iphigenia* at Aulis* in order to procure favourable winds; upon his return from Troy he was murdered by his wife Clytemnestra* and her lover Aegisthus.

Agave: D. of Cadmus,* m. of Pentheus;* she, with her sisters Ino* and Autonoe, tore apart her son while possessed by the god Bacchus,* as revenge for their denial of his divinity.

Agenor: K. of Phoenicia, f. of Cadmus* and Europa.*

Agrippina: The name of two historical figures: 1) the elder Agrippina (*c.* 14 BC – AD 33), d. of Agrippa and Julia, wife of Germanicus, and m. of many children, one of whom was 2) the younger Agrippina (AD 15? – 59), fourth wife of the Emperor Claudius* and m. of the Emperor Nero* by a previous marriage; in AD 54 she poisoned Claudius in order to install her own s. as emperor over Claudius' biological s. Britannicus; in AD 59 Nero had her killed.

Ajax: The name of two Greek warriors at Troy:* 1) the greater Ajax, s. of Telamon, from Salamis, the second greatest warrior after Achilles;* he, Ulysses* and Phoenix* were sent by Agamemnon* to persuade his cousin Achilles to rejoin the war, unsuccessfully; after Achilles' death, Ulysses* was chosen over Ajax to receive Achilles' armour, prompting Ajax to kill himself; 2) the lesser Ajax, s. of Oileus, from Locris; during the fall of Troy he raped Cassandra* while she clung to a statue of Minerva* and he was punished by suffering shipwreck at sea.

Alani: Barbaric people living north-west of the Black Sea.

Alcaeus: S. of Perseus* and Andromeda, f. of Amphitryon* and hence Hercules'* grandf.

Alcmena: M. of Hercules* by Jupiter.*

Alpheus: The river near Olympia* in the Peloponnese.*

Amazons: A female warrior race, known for their aversion to men, dwelling either north of the Black Sea or beside the Thermodon river in northern Asia Minor.*

Amphion: S. of Jupiter* and Antiope 1,* br. of Zethus,* with whom he ruled Thebes;* Amphion built the city's walls by towing stones that followed the sound of his music.

Amphitryon: S. of Alcaeus,* husband of Alcmena,* mortal f. of Hercules.*

Andromache: D. of Eetion, widow of Hector,* m. of Astyanax;* after the fall of Troy* she was awarded to Pyrrhus* as a war prize.

Antaeus: K. of Libya, killed foreigners by forcing them to wrestle him, a difficult task since he grew stronger while in contact with Earth, his m.; Hercules* killed him by lifting him off the ground and crushing him.

Antenor: Trojan, wisest of Priam's* advisers; he was married to Theano, Hecuba's* sister.

Antiope: The name of two women: 1) m. of Zethus* and Amphion* by Jupiter;* 2) Amazon,* m. of Hippolytus* by Theseus.*

Apollo: S. of Jupiter* and Latona,* the god of the sun, music, prophecy and medicine, and the sender of plague; as punishment for killing the Cyclopes,* the makers of Jupiter's thunderbolts, he was forced to serve the mortal Admetus,* whose flocks he shepherded; he also fell in love with the mortal Daphne,* pursued her, but could not catch her before she turned into a laurel tree (Greek '*daphne*').

Aquarius: 'Water Carrier', a constellation.

Aras: Another name for the Araxes* river.

Araxes: A river in Armenia.*

Arcas: See Callisto,* Ursa Minor,* Arctophylax.*

Arctophylax: 'Guardian of the Bear', a constellation in the northern pole, formerly Arcas* the s. of Callisto.* The constellation is also called the Wagoner* or Bootes ('Ox-driver'), when the same seven stars that composed Ursa Major* were seen to form oxen and a cart instead of a bear.

Argolid: The area around Argos* and Mycenae.*

Argos: Major city in the Peloponnese* south of the Isthmus* of Corinth, sacred to Juno.*

Ariadne: D. of Minos* and Pasiphae;* when Theseus* came to Crete* to slay the Minotaur,* he promised her that he would take her back with him to Athens* and marry her if she helped; she did so, providing him a ball of string so that he could find his way out of the labyrinth,* but on the trip home he abandoned her on the island of Naxos;* Bacchus* rescued and married her, making her immortal.

Aries: 'The Ram,' a constellation, formerly the ram that saved Phrixus* and Helle.*

Armenia: Region south-east of the Black Sea.

Asclepius: The god of healing, s. of Apollo.*

Asia Minor: ('Lesser Asia') the Anatolian peninsula (roughly modern-day Turkey).

Assaracus: Trojan, s. of Tros, ancestor of Anchises and Aeneas.

Astyanax: S. of Hector* and Andromache,* thrown from a tower after the fall of Troy.*

Athens: Major city in Attica,* ruled by Aegeus* and Theseus.*

Atlas: S. of Iapetus, held the heavens aloft on his shoulders.

Atreus: S. of Pelops,* f. of Agamemnon* and Menelaus,* k. of Argos;* after his br. Thyestes* seduced his wife and cast him out of Argos, he gained revenge by killing Thyestes' children and feeding them to him.

Attica: Land surrounding Athens.*

Aulis: Port in Greece where the Greeks mustered their forces in preparation for sailing to Troy;* here Agamemnon* sacrificed his d. Iphigenia* in order to secure favourable winds.

Avernus: An entrance to the underworld, or the underworld itself.

Bacchant: Literally, 'Raving One', a female worshipper of Bacchus;* see also Maenad.*

Bacchus: Also called Dionysus, s. of Jupiter* and the mortal Semele;* when he was still in the womb, his m. was killed by the flames of Jupiter's thunderbolt, but he was saved by Jupiter, who stitched him into his thigh until he came to term; he, the god of wine and irrationality, was worshipped by female attendants (Bacchants,* Maenads*) in ecstatic rituals; he was said to have led the citizens of Thebes* on a campaign to the east where he conquered lands as far as India; he visited revenge on all those who opposed him (see Pentheus* and Agave,* Lycurgus*).

Boeotia: Region of Greece where Thebes* is located.

Boreas: The North Wind.

Briseis: Female captive from Pedasus, awarded to Achilles* as a war prize; the great rift between Agamemnon* and Achilles (as told in the *Iliad* 1) occurred when the former took her from the latter.

Bruttian Sea: Another name for the Ionian Sea.*

Busiris: K. of Egypt, ritually sacrificed all foreigners on the altar of Jupiter,* slain by Hercules* upon those very same altars.

Cadmus: S. of Agenor,* br. of Europa;* after unsuccessfully searching for his sister, he, following Apollo's* oracle, founded Thebes* after vanquishing a giant serpent and the soldiers that grew from its teeth; he fathered by his wife Harmonia four daughters, Semele,* Agave,* Ino,* Autonoe and a son, Polydorus; later he and his wife were exiled to Illyria,* where they were transformed into serpents.

Caesar: Gaius Julius Caesar, famed Roman general and dictator, killed by Brutus and other conspirators in 44 BC; later emperors took the name, and it came to designate the successor of the emperor, who was in turn called 'Augustus'.

Caicus: A major river in north-west Asia Minor* flowing into the Aegean Sea.*

Calchas: Greek seer at Troy.*

Callisto: A virgin follower of Diana;* Jupiter* seduced her while disguised as the goddess herself; in anger Juno* turned her into a bear, and when sixteen years later her s. by Jupiter, Arcas,* encountered her and attempted to kill her, Jupiter elevated them both to the stars, her as Ursa Major* (the Great Bear), him as Ursa Minor* (the Little Bear).

Cancer: 'The Crab', a constellation that is associated with summer heat.

Capricorn: 'The Goat', a constellation heralding the winter months.

Caspian Sea: Major sea east of the Caucasus.*

Cassandra: Trojan prophetess, d. of Priam* and Hecuba;* Apollo,* desiring her love, gave her the gift of prophecy; when she refused his advances, he, unable to retract his gift, cursed her with never being believed; on the night of Troy's* fall she was raped by Ajax 2 and the next day was awarded to Agamemnon* as his war prize.

Castalia: The sacred spring at Delphi* where visitors would purify themselves before seeking the god's oracular response.

Castor: Spartan, s. of Tyndareus* and Leda,* br. of Pollux,* famed for his horsemanship; see also Dioscuri.*

Caucasus: Mountain range between the Black and Caspian* Seas.

Cecrops: Mythical k. of Athens.*

Centaur: Mythical horse-like creature with a human head and torso.

Cephallenia: Island near Ithaca,* ruled by Ulysses.*

Cerberus: Three-headed hound that guarded the gates to the underworld, Hercules'* last labour.

Ceres: (Greek Demeter) The goddess of grain and fertility, m. of Proserpina;* when her d. was abducted by Dis,* she searched the world over in great sadness until an agreement was struck allowing her d. to spend part of the year with her; both were celebrated in Eleusinian Mysteries.*

Chaos: Primeval god, Greek 'Gaping Void', but in Seneca it means 'Formless Mass'.

Charon: Boatman who ferried the dead across the rivers of the underworld.

Charybdis: Sea monster that swallowed and disgorged the sea three times a day, located in the Strait of Messina between Italy and Sicily.

Chiron: Centaur* living on Mount Pelion,* tutor of Achilles.*

Chryse: See Chryseis.*

Chryseis: Woman from Chryse (near Troy)* awarded to Agamemnon* as a war prize; when her f. Chryses, a priest of Apollo, supplicated Agamemnon to return her to him, he refused and Apollo sent a great plague that afflicted the Greeks; after Agamemnon did return Chryseis, he then took Briseis* from Achilles,* causing the latter to withdraw from the war.

Chryses: See Chryseis.*

Cilla: City south of the Troad* sacked by Achilles* during the Trojan War.

Cithaeron: Mountain located between Thebes* and Corinth,* where Pentheus* was torn apart by his m. and Oedipus* was exposed.

Clotho: 'The Spinner', one of the three Fates.*

Clytemnestra: D. of Tyndareus,* wife of Agamemnon.*

Cnossus: Major city in Crete,* ruled by Minos.*

Cocytus: 'Wailing', a river in the underworld.

Colchis: Land on the east coast of the Black Sea along the Phasis* river, known in general for its barbaric nature; the sorceress Medea* hailed from there.

Corinth: Major Greek city lying on the west side of the Isthmus.*

Corus: The North-west Wind.

Creon: Br. of Jocasta,* second in command in Thebes* after Oedipus,* f. of Megara.*

Crete: Island to the south of the Peloponnese.*

Cupid: S. of Venus,* also called Amor ('Love, Desire'), the god of sexual attraction.

Cybele: The 'Great Mother' (*Magna Mater*), an earth goddess originating in Asia Minor* and associated with Mount Ida* near Troy.*

Cyclades: A group of islands in the Aegean Sea.*

Cyclopes: Names of originally three distinct gigantic, one-eyed creatures, often conflated in Latin literature: 1) the builders of the giant fortifications of Mycenae; 2) the creatures inhabiting Sicily (famed for Polyphemus' encounter with Ulysses*); 3) the makers of Jupiter's* thunderbolts.

Cygnus: The name of two figures: 1) s. of Neptune,* invulnerable to weapons, strangled to death by Achilles,* the first Trojan casualty in the Trojan War; 2) s. of Mars, killed by Hercules,* whom Seneca conflates with Cygnus 1 (see *Hercules Insane* note 33).

Cyllarus: Famed horse of Castor.*

Daedalus: Athenian inventor exiled to Crete,* builder of the hollow wooden cow for Pasiphae* so that she could copulate with a bull, a union that produced the Minotaur;* for this offence, her husband Minos* first compelled Daedalus to build the Labyrinth* for the Minotaur, then locked him and his s. Icarus* in a high tower; Daedalus contrived artificial wings that allowed them to escape, but Icarus perished over the sea.

Dahae: Nomads, known for their horsemanship, dwelling to the east of the Caspian Sea.*

Danae: D. of Acrisius, destined to give birth to a s. who would kill him; Acrisius locked her up to keep her away from men, but Jupiter* impregnated her by taking on the form of golden rain, fathering Perseus.*

Danaids: The fifty daughters of Danaus* who murdered their husbands (the fifty sons of Aegyptus*) on their wedding night, punished in the underworld with the eternal task of filling a pot full of holes with water; Hypermnestra, the sole daughter not to carry out her task, saved her husband Lynceus and they became the ancestors of the noble line of kings in Argos.*

Danaus: S. of Belus; fleeing his brother Aegyptus,* he came to Argos* with his fifty daughters (Danaids*), where his brother's sons caught up with him and forced him to give his daughters to them as wives; compelled to do so, Danaus instructed his daughters to murder their husbands on their wedding night, which they did, save one; Danaus later found water sources that allowed Argos* to be habitable.

Danube: Major river running from the Alps to the east into the Black Sea.

Daphne: Mortal woman who turned into a laurel tree (Greek *daphne*) as she was chased by Apollo.*

Dardanus: S. of Jupiter* and Electra;* he first settled the site of Troy.*

Delos: Island in the Aegean Sea,* the birthplace of Apollo* and Diana,* and the location of one of Apollo's cult centres.

Delphi: City in Greece where Apollo's oracular seat was located.

Deucalion: S. of Prometheus;* he and his wife Pyrrha alone survived the great flood sent by Jupiter* on an ark and repopulated the Greek lands by throwing over their shoulders stones which turned into humans.

Diana: (Greek Artemis) Virgin goddess of the hunt, also identified with the moon, Hecate,* and Trivia* ('of the three ways').

Diomedes: The name of two separate figures: 1) Greek general in the Trojan War, who with Ulysses* discovered Achilles* hiding among Lycomedes'* daughters on Scyros* and went on a secret night-time raid against the Trojan allies, killing Rhesus;* 2) savage Thracian k. who fed human flesh to his man-eating horses; Hercules* killed him by feeding him to those same horses.

Dioscuri: The collective name for the two sons of Leda,* Castor* and Pollux,* known for their true brotherly love; they appeared to sailors as St Elmo's Fire, which forecast salvation from a storm; upon his brother Castor's death, Pollux, being the immortal s. of Jupiter,* shared his immortality with him and the two were raised into the stars as Gemini.*

Dirce: A spring/river in Thebes* named after the queen who tortured Antiope 1* and was killed by Antiope's sons Zethus* and Amphion,* who tied her by the hair to a wild bull.

Dis: The god of the underworld, the more common name for Pluto* (Greek Hades).

Draco: 'Serpent', a constellation in the northern sky.

Eetion: F. of Andromache,* k. of Thebe.*

Electra: D. of Agamemnon* and Clytemnestra;* she rescued her brother Orestes* from certain death when Clytemnestra and her lover Aegisthus murdered her f.; after spending many years of sadness tormented by her m. and Aegisthus, Electra watched on as Orestes returned and exacted revenge on them.

Eleusinian Mysteries: See Eleusis.*

Eleusis: City north-west of Athens* where the secret rites of Ceres* and her d. Proserpina* were celebrated (the Eleusinian Mysteries); these rites were associated with the agricultural cycle and for its initiates promised life after death; Hercules* was initiated before he made his descent into the underworld.

Elysium: The blessed region in the underworld reserved for virtuous and heroic souls.

Epidaurus: City located across the Saronic Gulf from Athens* where a famous temple to Asclepius* was located.

Erebus: Greek 'Darkness', referring generally to the underworld.

Erinys: An avenging goddess.

Eryx: 1) K. of Sicily who killed foreigners by forcing them to box with him, defeated by Hercules;* 2) a mountain in Sicily where Venus* had a cult centre, named after the king.

Etesians: Cooling northerly winds that blow in the summertime.

Etna: Volcano in eastern Sicily.

Euboea: Large island to the east of mainland Greece.

Euripus: The narrow strait between Chalcis (in Euboea*) and mainland Greece known for its dangerous shifting currents.

Europa: D. of Agenor,* abducted by Jupiter* in the form of a white bull (or by a bull sent by Jupiter; see Taurus*) and whisked away to Crete;* she bore three sons to him: Minos,* Rhadamanthus* and Sarpedon.

Eurus: The East Wind.

Eurydice: See Orpheus.*

Eurystheus: Ruler of Mycenae,* descendant of Jupiter;* on the eve of Hercules'* birth, Juno* tricked Jupiter into swearing that the next descendant of his born would rule over the earth, and he, anticipating Hercules' imminent birth, eagerly swore to it; then Juno delayed Hercules' birth and hastened that of Eurystheus, who thereby had the authority to impose upon Hercules the twelve labours.

Eurytus: K. of Oechalia, f. of Iole; when Hercules* won Iole's hand in marriage by defeating Eurytus in an archery contest, the king refused to give her to him, prompting Hercules to sack Oechalia, kill Eurytus and take Iole by force.

Evenus: A river in Aetolia.

exostra: A platform that was rolled forth in the Roman theatre to produce an interior scene.

Fates: Goddesses, three in number, who determined human destiny.

Furies: Avenging goddesses who cause madness.

Ganges: A river in India.

Geloni: A nomadic tribe north of the Black Sea.

Gemini: 'The Twins', a constellation, formerly the twins Castor* and Pollux* (see Dioscuri*).

Georgia: Region located between the Black and Caspian Seas.*

Geryon: The triple-bodied monster inhabiting the western edge of the world; Hercules'* tenth labour was to fetch his cattle.

Getae: A barbaric nation located to the north of the Danube* river along the Black Sea.

Giants: Literally, 'born of the earth', monstrous offspring of Earth that challenged Jupiter* for the kingship of heaven; in Roman sources they are often conflated with the sons of Aloeus, who attacked heaven by piling Mt Ossa* on Mt Pelion* on Mt Olympus.*

Hebe: Greek 'Youth', d. of Jupiter* and Juno,* goddess of youthful beauty, awarded to Hercules* when he attained immortality.

Hecate: The goddess of magic, associated with the goddess Diana,* the night and the moon.

Hector: S. of Priam* and Hecuba,* husband of Andromache,* f. of Astyanax,* Troy's greatest warrior, killed and mutilated by Achilles.*

Hecuba: D. of Cisseus, wife of Priam,* and queen of Troy,* awarded to Ulysses* as war prize after Troy's fall.

Helen: Spartan, d. of Jupiter* and Leda,* wife of Menelaus;* her seduction by the Trojan Paris* precipitated the Trojan War; after Troy's fall she returned to Menelaus as his wife.

Helenus: Trojan seer, s. of Priam;* angered because he was not awarded

Helen's* hand in marriage after Paris'* death, he left Troy* before it was sacked.

Helle: See Phrixus.*

Heniochi: Barbaric tribe on the eastern banks of the Black Sea.

Hercules: (Greek Heracles) S. of Jupiter* and Alcmena,* persecuted relentlessly by his stepmother Juno;* his twelve labours were: 1) the Nemean Lion;* 2) the Lernaean Hydra,* 3) the Cerynitian Deer; 4) the Erymanthian Boar; 5) the cleaning of Augeas' stables; 6) the Stymphalian Birds; 7) the Cretan Bull; 8) the man-eating horses of Diomedes 2*; 9) the war-belt of the Amazon* Hippolyte; 10) the cattle of three-bodied Geryon;* 11) the golden apples of the Hesperides; and 12) Cerberus.*

Hermione: D. of Menelaus* and Helen,* wife of Pyrrhus.*

Hippolytus: S. of Theseus* and Antiope 2,* devoted to the virgin goddess Diana;* falsely accused of rape by Theseus' wife Phaedra,* he was cursed by Theseus and killed by a sea-bull as he fled Athens.

Hyades: 'the Rainy Ones', a constellation between the horns of Taurus.*

Hyblaea: A city in Sicily.

Hydra: Greek 'Water Snake', the multi-headed monster that inhabited the swamps of Lerna* in the northern Peloponnese,* Hercules' second labour.

Hyrcania: Harsh region located to the south-east of the Caspian Sea.*

Icarus: S. of Daedalus* who perished because he flew too high on artificial wings while escaping from Minos.*

Ida: Mountain outside Troy,* home of young Paris,* where the judgement of the three goddesses by Paris took place.

Ilissus: A river in Attica.*

Ilium: Another name for Troy.*

Illyria: Area to the east of the Adriatic Sea.*

Inachus: A river (and river-god) in Argos.*

Ino: D. of Cadmus,* wife of Athamas; she plotted against her stepchildren, Phrixus* and Helle,* but was foiled; later, because she had raised Bacchus,* Juno* drove her insane, during which time she leapt into the sea with her son Melicertes, where she became the sea-goddess Leucothea, he the sea-god Palaemon.*

Ionian Sea: The sea south of Italy, east of Sicily.*

Iphigenia: D. of Agamemnon,* sacrificed by him at the Greek port of Aulis* to secure favourable winds so that the Greeks could sail to Troy;* in order to lure her there, Agamemnon deceitfully announced that she was to marry Achilles.*

Iris: Goddess of the rainbow.

Ismenus: A river in Thebes.*

Isthmus: Narrow strait between mainland Greece and the Peloponnese* where Corinth* is located.

Ithaca: Island to the west of mainland Greece, ruled by Ulysses.*

Ixion: Mortal who was punished eternally in the underworld for trying to rape Juno* by being bound to a swiftly turning wheel.

Jocasta: Theban, wife of Laius,* m. and later wife of Oedipus.*

Jove: Jupiter.*

Juno: Wife of Jupiter,* queen of the gods, protector of marriage; she often persecuted her husband's illegitimate mortal children, especially Hercules.*

Jupiter: (Greek Zeus) God of the sky, k. of the gods, f. of many gods and heroes; also known as Jove.*

Labdacus: K. of Thebes,* f. of Laius* and so grandf. of Oedipus.*

Labyrinth: A maze-like enclosure with endless twisting passageways built by Daedalus* in order to imprison the Minotaur.*

Lachesis: One of the Fates.*

Laertes: K. of Ithaca,* f. of Ulysses.*

Laius: K. of Thebes,* husband of Jocasta* and f. of Oedipus,* by whom he was killed.

Laomedon: K. of Troy,* f. of Priam,* known for his duplicity; he failed to pay the gods Apollo* and Neptune* what he promised for building the walls of Troy, and later refused to give Hercules* his d. Hesione in marriage, as promised, for saving her life; Hercules sacked Troy because of this.

Latona: M. of Apollo* and Diana* by Jupiter;* when pregnant, she was driven by Juno* to wander over the world looking for a place to give birth, eventually doing so on the island of Delos.*

Leda: Wife of Tyndareus,* seduced by Jupiter* in the form of a swan; their union produced Helen* and Pollux.*

Leo: 'The Lion', a constellation, formerly the Nemean Lion,* Hercules' first labour.

Lerna: A spring in the northern Peloponnese* inhabited by the Hydra.*

Lesbos: An island in the Aegean Sea.*

Lethe: 'Forgetfulness', a river in the underworld, which, when drunk by the dead, caused them to forget their former life.

Leucas: A promontory on the western coast of Greece at the entrance of the Adriatic Sea.*

Liber: Another name for Bacchus.*

Libra: 'The Scales', a constellation.

Lycomedes: K. of Scyros,* hid the disguised Achilles* amidst his daughters.

Lycurgus: K. of Thrace,* opposed the god Bacchus* and was punished with madness, which caused him to kill his own son with an axe, believing he was chopping a vine.

Lydia: Region in central Asia Minor,* known for its luxury.

Lyrnessus: City south of Troy,* sacked by Achilles* during the Trojan War.

Maeander: A river in south-western Asia Minor* known for its winding course (hence the English word 'meander').

Maenads: Literally, 'the mad ones', female worshippers of Bacchus* who raved in a rapturous state while under the influence of the god.

Maeotis: Modern Sea of Azov, a marshy sea north-east of the Black Sea.

Marathon: Plain to the north-east of Athens* in Attica.*

Mars: (Greek Ares) God of war; he had an illicit affair with Venus.*

Massagetes: A barbaric tribe along the Caspian Sea.*

Medea: D. of Aeetes, sorceress from Colchis;* through her magic she helped Jason overcome her father's challenges and steal the Golden Fleece, and after killing her brother she returned to Greece with Jason; when Jason divorced her in Corinth,* she killed his new wife, his new father-in-law and her own two sons by him; she then escaped to Athens,* married Aegeus,* and attempted to kill his son Theseus.*

Medes: Nation living south of the Caspian Sea.*

Megaera: One of the Furies.*

Megara: D. of Creon,* wife of Hercules.*

Memnon: Ethiopian, s. of the goddess Aurora (Dawn) and Tithonus; he came to aid Troy,* but was killed by Achilles.*

Menelaus: K. of Sparta,* s. of Atreus,* br. of Agamemnon,* husband of Helen.*

Merope: Wife of Polybus,* adoptive m. of Oedipus.*

Mimas: One of the Giants.*

Minerva: D. of Jupiter,* goddess of righteous war, invention and weaving.

Minos: S. of Jupiter* and Europa,* k. of Crete, husband of Pasiphae,* f. of Ariadne* and Phaedra by her; when he failed to sacrifice the magnificent bull sent by Neptune, the god struck his wife with an unnatural lust for the animal; she mated with it through Daedalus'* help and gave birth to the Minotaur,* which Minos housed in the Labyrinth* built by Daedalus;* when Minos' son was killed in Athens, he attacked the city and forced it to send seven young men and seven young women yearly to be fed to the Minotaur, until Theseus* arrived and killed the monster; after death Minos became a judge in the underworld.

Minotaur: 'Minos'* Bull', the half-man, half-bull offspring of Pasiphae* and a sacred bull.

Mopsopus: Early mythical k. of Athens.*

Mycenae: City in the Argolid.*

Myrtilus: The charioteer of King Oenomaus of Pisa; bribed by Pelops,*
he rigged the king's chariot to break apart during the race for the
king's daughter's hand in marriage; despite the favour, Pelops later
hurled Myrtilus to his death into the sea east of the Peloponnese*
(called Myrtoan* after him); for this treachery Myrtilus cursed
Pelops' descendants.

Myrtoan: See Myrtilus.*

Mysia: The region to the east of Troy* ruled by Telephus.*

Naiads: Nymphs that inhabit springs and rivers.

Naxos: Island in the Aegean Sea* where Theseus* abandoned Ariadne*
and Bacchus* rescued her.

Nemean Lion: The invulnerable lion born of the Moon, the first labour
of Hercules,* who killed it by strangulation and used its skin for
protection; it became the constellation Leo.*

Neptune: God of the sea, winds and earthquakes, associated with bulls;
f. of numerous heroes, including Theseus.*

Nereids: Daughters of Nereus,* sea divinities.

Nereus: A sea-god, f. of the Nereids.*

Nero: Emperor of Rome (reigned AD 54–68), s. of Gnaeus Domitius
Ahenobarbus and Agrippina;* when his m. married the emperor
Claudius, he was adopted by the emperor and was betrothed to his
d. Octavia;* when Claudius died, Nero assumed the throne and
poisoned Britannicus, Claudius' s. and legitimate heir to the throne;
later (AD 59) he killed his own m., to whom he owed his position
on the throne, divorced Octavia and ordered her death (AD 62), and
committed other heinous acts as emperor.

Nestor: Greek general from Pylos who lived three generations and
fought in the Trojan War.

Nile: Major river in Egypt.

Niobe: D. of Tantalus* who offended the goddess Latona* by boasting
that she was more blessed in children (she had fourteen to Leto's
two); when Leto's children Apollo* and Diana* slew her children in
revenge, Niobe turned to stone and wept eternally.

Notus: The South Wind.

Nysa: Mountain where Bacchus* was raised.

Ocean: Primordial god, conceived of as a giant river encircling the
world.

Octavia: D. of Claudius and Messalina, wife (and stepsister) of
Nero.*

Oedipus: Theban, s. of Laius* and Jocasta,* fated to kill his f. and share his m.'s bed; he was exposed as an infant on M Cithaeron,* but was saved and raised as the child of Polybus,* k. of Corinth,* and his wife Merope;* after receiving an oracle at Delphi about his fate, Oedipus* went to Thebes,* killing his f. on the way, dispatching the Sphinx* when he arrived, and then marrying his m. Jocasta,* the widowed queen of Thebes; when he realized what he had done, he blinded himself and Jocasta committed suicide.

Oeta: A mountain in central Greece; here Hercules* killed himself on a burning pyre.

Olenus: A city in Aetolia in the western part of mainland Greece.

Olympia: City in the western Peloponnese* where the Olympic Games were held.

Olympus: Mountain located in northern Thessaly,* the highest in Greece, home of the gods.

Omphale: Queen of Lydia;* Hercules* was sold into slavery to her and she compelled him to perform womanly work.

Orestes: S. of Agamemnon.*

Orion: Giant* born of a bull's hide and the urine of Jupiter,* Neptune* and Mercury; after his death he was elevated into the stars as a constellation.

Orpheus: S. of Oeagrus or Apollo,* famed musician who accompanied the Argonauts on their voyage; when his wife Eurydice died from a snakebite, he journeyed to the underworld and with the sweetness of his songs convinced Dis* and Proserpina* to release her, which they did, but on the condition that he did not turn back before they reached the world of the living; Orpheus glanced back too soon, and Eurydice returned to the underworld.

Ossa: A mountain in Thessaly.*

Pactolus: Golden river in Lydia.*

Palaemon: The divine name of Melicertes (see Ino*).

Pallas: Another name for Minerva.*

Pallene: A region in Chalcidice (north-eastern Greece) inhabited by the Giants,* also called Phlegra.*

Pan: God of the wild countryside, sometimes conceived of as multiple deities (Pans).

Pandataria: Island west of the Bay of Naples, where Octavia was exiled (though see *Octavia* note 54).

Pandion: See Procne.*

Pangaeus: A mountain in Thrace.*

Paphos: City on Cyprus, where Venus* had a cult centre.

Parian Marble: Brilliant white marble from the island of Paros.

Paris: Trojan, s. of Priam* and Hecuba;* he was exposed when his m.

dreamed that he would bring ruin to his country, but he survived; while living on Mt Ida,* he conducted the famous judgement of the goddesses (Juno,* Minerva* and Venus*); later, he seduced Helen* of Sparta, initiating the Trojan War and bringing his m.'s dream to fulfilment; he killed Achilles* with an arrow.

Parnassus: The mountain on which Delphi* was located.

Parthians: Eastern foes of Rome who were known for their unique cavalry tactics in war, turning and firing arrows as they feigned retreat.

Pasiphae: D. of the Sun, wife of Minos;* she was stricken with an unnatural lust for a sacred bull, copulated with it inside a hollow wooden cow made by Daedalus,* and bore the Minotaur;* to Minos* she bore two daughters, Ariadne* and Phaedra.

Pegasus: Famed winged horse, the offspring of Neptune* and Medusa.

Peleus: S. of Aeacus;* he fathered Achilles* by the goddess Thetis.*

Pelion: A mountain in Thessaly,* home of the centaur Chiron.*

Peloponnese: Literally, 'Pelops'* Island', the large peninsula lying south of the Isthmus of Corinth and mainland Greece.

Pelops: S. of Tantalus;* when he was a boy, his f. killed him and tried to feed him to the gods, who recognized the trick, punished Tantalus, and reassembled the boy; later Pelops came to Greece and defeated king Oenomaus in a chariot race (see Myrtilus*), winning the king's daughter Hippodamia as wife; she bore him two sons, Atreus* and Thyestes;* extending his power wide, he gave the Peloponnese* its name.

Penthesilea: Amazon* who came to aid the Trojans, killed by Achilles.*

Pentheus: S. of Agave,* k. of Thebes* after Cadmus;* when he denied Bacchus'* divinity and attempted to keep his rites out of Thebes, the god convinced him to witness the secret rites on Mount Cithaeron,* where he was torn apart by his m. and aunts.

Pergamum: The citadel of Troy.*

Perseus: S. of Jupiter* and the mortal Danae;* he killed Medusa, and was raised into the stars after his death.

Phaethon: S. of the Sun; when he learned his f.'s identity, he asked that he be allowed to drive the sun-chariot through its course in heaven; he disastrously mishandled the team and plunged to the earth below.

Phasis: See Colchis.*

Pherae: City in Thessaly* ruled by Admetus.*

Philippi: City in eastern Macedonia where Octavian and Antony defeated Brutus and Cassius, the assassins of Caesar.*

Philomela: See Procne.*

Phineus: Blind seer who was tormented by the Harpies ('The Snatchers'), who constantly descended upon his table, snatched his food and fouled whatever they left behind with excrement.

Phlegethon: 'Burning', a river in the underworld.

Phlegra: See Pallene.*

Phocis: Region in Greece in which Delphi* is situated.

Phoebe: 'Shining', an epithet of Diana* in her role as the moon.

Phoebus: 'Shining', an epithet of Apollo* in his role as the sun.

Phoenix: Achilles'* elderly companion in Troy,* part of Agamemnon's* embassy to persuade him to rejoin the war.

Phrixus: Theban, s. of Athamas and Nephele; he and his sister Helle* were saved from death (plotted by their stepmother Ino*) by a golden ram sent by their m.; as the ram was carrying them across the sea to Colchis,* Helle fell off the ram at the Hellespont ('Helle's Sea', the modern Dardanelles); in Colchis Phrixus sacrificed the ram, the pelt of which became the famous Golden Fleece.

Phrygia: Region near Troy;* often means 'Trojan' or more generally 'from Asia'.

Phthia: Region in Thessaly* from which Achilles* hailed.

Pindus: A mountain in northern Thessaly.*

Pirithous: Close friend of Theseus;* the two of them travelled to the underworld to abduct Proserpina* for Pirithous; the expedition ended disastrously and the two were imprisoned in the underworld.

Pisa: City in western Peloponnese.*

Pisces: 'The Fish', a constellation.

Pittheus: K. of Troezen, famed for his wisdom; his d. Aethra was seduced by Poseidon and bore Theseus.*

Pleiades: A constellation, formerly the daughters of Atlas* by Pleione, three of whom Jupiter* seduced, fathering children: Mercury by Maia, Dardanus* by Electra,* and Lacedaemon by Taygete; the rising of this constellation heralds the stormy season.

Pluto: See Dis.*

Pollux: S. of Jupiter* and Leda,* br. of Castor,* famed for his boxing; see also Dioscuri.*

Polybus: K. of Corinth,* husband of Merope,* adoptive f. of Oedipus.*

Polyxena: Youngest d. of Priam* and Hecuba,* sacrificed to Achilles'* ghost.

Pontus: Literally, 'sea', but refers specifically to the Black Sea; in Roman times, Pontus referred to a province along the south-east shores of the Black Sea.

Poppaea: Noble Roman woman who married Nero,* displacing Octavia.*

Priam: S. of Laomedon,* k. of Troy* during the Trojan War, husband of Hecuba* and f. of Hector,* Paris,* Polyxena,* among others.

Procne: D. of the Athenian king Pandion,* wife of the Thracian king Tereus;* when her husband raped her sister Philomela,* cutting off her tongue and imprisoning her, Procne gained her revenge by killing their s. Itys and feeding him to Tereus; as Tereus pursued the sisters, he turned into a hoopoe, they into a nightingale and swallow (who became which varies according to the account).

Procrustes: Villainous monster living outside Athens* who killed travellers by putting them on a bed that did not fit, lopping off the excess or pounding out the flesh to make his victim match the length of the bed.

Proetus: K. of Argos;* his daughters rejected Bacchus'* rites, and for that they were driven mad by the god and ran wild throughout the Peloponnese.*

Prometheus: S. of the Titan Iapetus, champion and/or creator of humans; he angered Jupiter* by stealing fire for humans and by refusing to reveal certain prophecies; in return he was punished by being bound to Mount Caucasus and having his liver eaten out daily by an eagle; Hercules* freed him.

Proserpina: D. of Ceres,* goddess of the underworld.

Proteus: A sea-god.

Pyrenees: Mountain range between Spain and France.

Pyrrha: See Deucalion.*

Pyrrhus: S. of Achilles* and Deidamia, the d. of Lycomedes;* he killed Priam* on the altar of Jupiter* and Polyxena* on his f.'s tomb.

Rhadamanthus: S. of Jupiter* and Europa,* one of the judges in the underworld.

Rhesus: Thracian k. who came in aid of the Trojans, killed on the night of his arrival by Diomedes* and Ulysses* in a night-time raid.

Rhine: Major river running from the Alps north to the North Sea.

Rhoeteum: A promontory north of Troy on the Dardanelles.

Sarmatians: A nomadic people living to the north-east of the Black Sea.

Saturn: S. of Uranus (Sky), f. of Jupiter,* leader of the Titans* in their war against Jupiter and the other Olympians; they were defeated and bound in Tartarus; Saturn was k. of heaven during the Golden Age on earth.

Sciron: Monster dwelling along the cliffs of Megara who used to make passing travellers wash his feet and, while they did so, kicked them into the sea, where a giant sea-turtle would devour them; Theseus* killed him in the same fashion.

Scylla: Sea monster with the face and torso of a woman, but with six dogs around her waist and twelve dog feet below; located in the strait between Italy and Sicily, Scylla would snatch sailors as they passed by.

Scyros: Island in the Aegean Sea where Achilles* was raised while disguised as a young girl.

Scythians: A nomadic tribe occupying the area to the north and north-east of the Black Sea.

Semele: Theban, d. of Cadmus* and Harmonia, impregnated by Jupiter;* when she was pregnant with Bacchus,* Juno* convinced her to ask Jupiter to visit her in his full glory, and Semele made Jupiter swear an oath to do so; when he did, she was consumed by the fire of his thunderbolts, but Jupiter saved the foetus and stitched it into his thigh until it came to term; later, Bacchus rescued Semele from the underworld and made her immortal under the name Thyone.

Seres: The Chinese, 'famed for silk', with whom the Romans had limited commercial relations.

Serpent Race: The people of Thebes* who were born from one of the serpent's teeth sown by Cadmus,* or their descendants.

Sidon: A Phoenician city north of Tyre* (in modern-day Lebanon), often associated with Tyre as the homeland of Cadmus* and Europa.*

Sigeum: Promontory to the west of Troy.*

Silenus: A follower of Bacchus,* usually depicted as fat and grotesque and riding a donkey.

Sinis: A monster dwelling on the Isthmus of Corinth* who tied passing travellers to two pine trees which he had bent down; when released, the trees tore them in two; Theseus* killed him in the same fashion.

Sinon: Greek warrior who allowed himself to be captured by the Trojans, convinced them that the Greeks had abandoned the war, and persuaded them to bring the fateful Trojan Horse inside the city walls, which led to the fall of Troy.*

Sipylus: Mountain in west-central Asia Minor* where Niobe* turned to stone.

Sisyphus: S. of Aeolus, founder and k. of Corinth;* he revealed Jupiter's* secrets and was punished eternally in the underworld by having to constantly carry (or push) a large boulder to the top of a hill, only to have it roll back down just before reaching the top – the origin of our word 'Sisyphean'.

Sparta: City in southern Peloponnese,* land of Tyndareus,* Menelaus,* and Helen.*

Sphinx: Offspring of Typhon* and Echidna, a monstrous creature with a woman's head, a lion's body and a bird's wings; she terrorized Thebes* by posing a riddle and killing those who could not answer it; Oedipus* dispatched the Sphinx by solving the riddle.

Strymon: A river in Thrace.*

Stygian: See Styx.

Stymphalian Birds: A large flock of birds that had infested the Stymphalian marsh in Arcadia, Hercules'* sixth labour.

Styx, Stygian: The river in the underworld on which the gods swore inviolable oaths, or more generally the underworld itself.

Sunium: Promontory in southern Attica.*

Syrtes: A pair of shifting sandbars north of Africa that were notoriously dangerous to ships.

Taenarum: The cape at the southern end of the Peloponnese* where there was a cave that led to the underworld.

Tagus: River in Spain, known for its gold.

Tanais: The modern Don River, which flows through the Russian steppes into the Maeotis.*

Tantalus: S. of Jupiter;* he killed his s. Pelops* and attempted to feed him to the gods; for this he was punished with eternal thirst and hunger while residing in a pool of water and surrounded by trees with low-hanging fruits, which would recede and retreat whenever he tried to drink or eat them – the origin of our word 'tantalize'.

Tartarus: The location in the underworld reserved for the punishment of the wicked, or more generally the underworld itself.

Taurians: A people living on the Crimean peninsula who practised human sacrifice.

Taurus: ('The Bull') A constellation, formerly the bull that carried Europa* from Tyre* to Crete.*

Taygetus: Mountain near Sparta.*

Telephus: S. of Hercules,* k. of Mysia* in northern Asia Minor;* on their first attempt to attack Troy,* the Greeks got lost and invaded Mysia instead, where Achilles* wounded Telephus in the thigh; when the wound would not heal and Telephus learned from an oracle that he could be cured only by the weapon that had wounded him, he went to Argos* and threatened to kill Agamemnon's* son Orestes unless the Greeks helped him; Achilles eventually healed Telephus, and in return Telephus showed the Greeks the way to Troy.

Tempe: Narrow valley in Thessaly between Mt Ossa* and Mt Olympus* through which the Peneus river flows, created by Hercules.*

Tereus: See Procne.*

Tethys: 'The Nourisher', a primeval sea-goddess, married to Ocean.

Thebe: City in Asia Minor,* ruled by Eetion,* father of Andromache.*

Thebes: Major Greek city in Boeotia,* land of Cadmus,* Zethus,* Amphion,* and Oedipus.*

Thermodon: A river in north-east Asia Minor* along which the Amazons* dwelled.

Theseus: S. of Neptune* and Aethra, raised by his mortal f. Aegeus;*

after killing the Minotaur* on Crete,* he abandoned Ariadne* on the island of Naxos;* he later journeyed to the underworld with his friend Pirithous* to abduct Proserpina,* but failed and was bound there until Hercules* freed him.

Thessaly: Region in the eastern part of mainland Greece.

Thetis: A Nereid,* m. of Achilles.*

Thrace: Land to the north of the Aegean Sea* known for its uncivilized nature.

Thyestes: S. of Pelops;* he seduced his br. Atreus'* wife and took control of Argos;* in retaliation, Atreus butchered Thyestes' sons, cooked them, and fed them to him; later, Thyestes slept with his own daughter, Pelopia, and produced a son, Aegisthus, who would exact revenge on both Atreus and his son Agamemnon.*

thyrsus: A staff wielded by Bacchus* and his worshippers, usually depicted as a spear with a large pine cone and ivy covering the tip.

Tigris: Major river in the Near East, running through modern day Iraq.

Tiresias: Famed Theban seer.

Tisiphone: One of the Furies.*

Titans: Originally the generation of gods prior to the Olympians, the children of Uranus and Earth, who were defeated by the Olympians in a mighty battle termed the Titanomachy ('Battle of the Titans'); in Seneca's plays they are conflated with other primeval gigantic beings such as the Giants* and the sons of Aloeus, all of whom revolted against Jupiter* and the Olympian gods.

Tityus: Monstrous giant who tried to rape Latona* and was punished for it in the underworld, where his liver (or heart) was eaten out each day by a vulture, only to have it grow back at night.

Tribune of the People: An office in Rome that served to protect the interests of the people.

Triptolemus: S. of Celeus, k. of Eleusis who was given grain by Ceres* to spread to mankind; grain is thus called 'the gift of Triptolemus'.

Triton: A sea god, the s. of Neptune* and Amphitrite; the plural (Tritons) is used for a group of sea deities.

Trivia: Another name for Diana.*

Troad: Area around Troy.*

Troy: City in north-west Asia Minor,* location of the Trojan War.

Tyndareus: Spartan, husband of Leda,* mortal f. of Helen,* Clytemnestra,* Castor* and Pollux* (Helen* and Pollux* were Jupiter's children).

Typhon: Gargantuan fire-breathing offspring of Earth and Tartarus* with 100 dragon heads and viper coils below the waist; he challenged Jupiter* for the kingship of heaven, but was defeated and pinned beneath Mount Etna* in Sicily, where he was said to continually spew eruptions of fire from the mountain.

Tyre, Tyrian: A Phoenician city that produced famed scarlet dyes; as an eastern city, Tyre was a symbol of wealth, luxury and excess; Cadmus* and Europa* hailed from here.

Tyrrhenians: A people in Italy, the Etruscans.

Ulysses:(Greek Odysseus) K. of Ithaca,* s. of Laertes,* Greek general in the Trojan War, known for his ingenuity and cunning.

Ursa Major, Minor: The constellations 'The Greater Bear' and 'The Lesser Bear', formerly Callisto* and her s. Arcas.

Venus: Goddess of sexuality and passion (Greek Aphrodite), m. of Cupid.*

Vesper: The evening star.

Virgo: A constellation, formerly the goddess Dike ('Justice'), who in the Golden Age descended from heaven to dwell with humans, but when wickedness on earth became rife, she abandoned them and ascended into the stars.

Vulcan: God of fire and metal-working, husband of Venus.*

Wagon, Wain: A constellation; the same stars that composed the constellation Ursa Major* were also seen to form a cart or wagon; when seen thus, Ursa Minor is seen as the Wagoner (see next entry).

Wagoner: The northern constellation Bootes (Ox-driver); see also Arctophylax.*

Xanthus: A river (and river-god) in Troy.*

Zephyrs: Gentle western breezes that blow in the springtime.

Zethus: S. of Jupiter* and Antiope,* br. of Amphion,* an early ruler of Thebes;* with his brother he killed Dirce,* who had been torturing their m., by tying her by her hair to a wild bull.

PENGUIN CLASSICS

THE ODYSSEY
HOMER

'I long to reach my home and see the day of my return. It is my never-failing wish'

The epic tale of Odysseus and his ten-year journey home after the Trojan War forms one of the earliest and greatest works of Western literature. Confronted by natural and supernatural threats – shipwrecks, battles, monsters and the implacable enmity of the sea-god Poseidon – Odysseus must test his bravery and native cunning to the full if he is to reach his homeland safely and overcome the obstacles that, even there, await him.

E. V. Rieu's translation of *The Odyssey* was the very first Penguin Classic to be published, and has itself achieved classic status. For this edition, his text has been sensitively revised and a new introduction added to complement E. V. Rieu's original introduction.

'One of the world's most vital tales. *The Odyssey* remains central to literature'
Malcolm Bradbury.

Translated by E. V. Rieu
Revised translation by D. C. H. Rieu, with an introduction by Peter Jones

PENGUIN CLASSICS

THE ILIAD
HOMER

> 'Look at me. I am the son of a great man. A goddess was my mother.
>   Yet death and inexorable destiny are waiting for me'

One of the foremost achievements in Western literature, Homer's *Iliad* tells the story of the darkest episode in the Trojan War. At its centre is Achilles, the greatest warrior-champion of the Greeks, and his refusal to fight after being humiliated by his leader Agamemnon. But when the Trojan Hector kills Achilles' close friend Patroclus, he storms back into battle to take revenge – although knowing this will ensure his own early death. Interwoven with this tragic sequence of events are powerfully moving descriptions of the ebb and flow of battle, of the domestic world inside Troy's besieged city of Ilium, and of the conflicts between the gods on Olympus as they argue over the fate of mortals.

E. V. Rieu's acclaimed translation of Homer's *Iliad* was one of the first titles published in Penguin Classics, and now has classic status itself. For this edition, Rieu's text has been revised, and a new introduction and notes by Peter Jones complement the original introduction.

Translated by E. V. Rieu

Revised and updated by Peter Jones with D. C. H. Rieu

Edited with an introduction and notes by Peter Jones

PENGUIN CLASSICS

THE RISE OF THE ROMAN EMPIRE
POLYBIUS

> 'If history is deprived of the truth,
> we are left with nothing but an idle, unprofitable tale'

In writing his account of the relentless growth of the Roman Empire, the Greek statesman Polybius (*c.* 200–118 BC) set out to help his fellow-countrymen understand how their world came to be dominated by Rome. Opening with the Punic War in 264 BC, he vividly records the critical stages of Roman expansion: its campaigns throughout the Mediterranean, the temporary setbacks inflicted by Hannibal and the final destruction of Carthage in 146 BC. An active participant in contemporary politics, as well as a friend of many prominent Roman citizens, Polybius was able to draw on a range of eyewitness accounts and on his own experiences of many of the central events, giving his work immediacy and authority.

Ian Scott-Kilvert's translation fully preserves the clarity of Polybius' narrative. This substantial selection of the surviving volumes is accompanied by an introduction by F. W. Walbank, which examines Polybius' life and times, and the sources and technique he employed in writing his history.

Translated by Ian Scott-Kilvert
Selected with an introduction by F. W. Walbank

PENGUIN CLASSICS

THE POLITICS
ARISTOTLE

'Man is by nature a political animal'

In *The Politics* Aristotle addresses the questions that lie at the heart of political science. How should society be ordered to ensure the happiness of the individual? Which forms of government are best and how should they be maintained? By analysing a range of city constitutions – oligarchies, democracies and tyrannies – he seeks to establish the strengths and weaknesses of each system to decide which are the most effective, in theory and in practice. A hugely significant work, which has influenced thinkers as diverse as Aquinas and Machiavelli, *The Politics* remains an outstanding commentary on fundamental political issues and concerns, and provides fascinating insights into the workings and attitudes of the Greek city-state.

The introductions by T. A. Sinclair and Trevor J. Saunders discuss the influence of *The Politics* on philosophers, its modern relevance and Aristotle's political beliefs. This edition contains Greek and English glossaries, and a bibliography for further reading.

Translated by T. A. Sinclair
Revised and re-presented by Trevor J. Saunders

Penguin Classics

THE BIRDS AND OTHER PLAYS
ARISTOPHANES

The Knights/Peace/The Birds/The Assemblywomen/Wealth

> 'Oh wings are splendid things, make no mistake:
> they really help you rise in the world'

The plays collected in this volume, written at different times in Aristophanes' forty-year career as a dramatist, all contain his trademark bawdy comedy and dazzling verbal agility. In *The Birds*, two frustrated Athenians join with the birds to build the utopian city of 'Much Cuckoo in the Clouds'. *The Knights* is a venomous satire on Cleon, the prominent Athenian demagogue, while *The Assemblywomen* considers the war of the sexes, as the women of Athens infiltrate the all-male Assembly in disguise. The lengthy conflict with Sparta is the subject of *Peace*, inspired by the hope of a settlement in 421 BC, and *Wealth* reflects the economic catastrophe that hit Athens after the war, as the god of riches is depicted as a ragged, blind old man.

The lively translations by David Barrett and Alan H. Sommerstein capture the full humour of the plays. The introduction examines Aristophanes' life and times, and the comedy and poetry of his works. This volume also includes an introductory note for each play.

Translated with an introduction by David Barrett and Alan H. Sommerstein

---

PENGUIN CLASSICS

THE PERSIAN EXPEDITION
XENOPHON

'The only things of value which we have at present are our arms and our courage'

In *The Persian Expedition*, Xenophon, a young Athenian noble who sought his destiny abroad, provides an enthralling eyewitness account of the attempt by a Greek mercenary army – the Ten Thousand – to help Prince Cyrus overthrow his brother and take the Persian throne. When the Greeks were then betrayed by their Persian employers, they were forced to march home through hundreds of miles of difficult terrain – adrift in a hostile country and under constant attack from the unforgiving Persians and warlike tribes. In this outstanding description of endurance and individual bravery, Xenophon, one of those chosen to lead the retreating army, provides a vivid narrative of the campaign and its aftermath, and his account remains one of the best pictures we have of Greeks confronting a 'barbarian' world.

Rex Warner's distinguished translation captures the epic quality of the Greek original and George Cawkwell's introduction sets the story of the expedition in the context of its author's life and tumultuous times.

Translated by Rex Warner with an introduction by George Cawkwell

---

PENGUIN CLASSICS

ELECTRA AND OTHER PLAYS
SOPHOCLES

Ajax/Electra/Women of Trachis/Philoctetes

> 'Now that he is dead,
> I turn to you; will you be brave enough
> To help me kill the man who killed our father?'

Sophocles' innovative plays transformed Greek myths into dramas featuring complex human characters, through which he explored profound moral issues. *Electra* portrays the grief of a young woman for her father Agamemnon, who has been killed by her mother's lover. Aeschylus and Euripides also dramatized this story, but the objectivity and humanity of Sophocles' version provided a new perspective. Depicting the fall of a great hero, *Ajax* examines the enigma of power and weakness combined in one being, while the *Women of Trachis* portrays the tragic love and error of Heracles' deserted wife Deianeira, and *Philoctetes* deals with the conflict between physical force and moral strength.

E. F. Watling's vivid translation is accompanied by an introduction in which he discusses Sophocles' use of a third actor to create new dramatic situations and compares the different treatments of the Electra myth by the three great tragic poets of classical Athens.

Translated with an introduction by E. F. Watling

PENGUIN CLASSICS

THE GREEK SOPHISTS

'In the case of wisdom, those who sell it to anyone who wants it are called sophists'

By mid-fifth century BC, Athens was governed by democratic rule and power turned upon the ability of the individual to command the attention of the other citizens, and to sway the crowds of the assembly. It was the Sophists who understood the art of rhetoric and the importance of being able to transform effective reasoning into persuasive public speaking. Their inquiries – into the gods, the origins of religion and whether virtue can be taught – laid the groundwork for the next generation of thinkers such as Plato and Aristotle.

Each chapter of *The Greek Sophists* is based around the work of one character: Gorgias, Prodicus, Protagoras and Antiphon among others, and a linking commentary, chronological table and bibliography are provided for each one. In his introduction, John Dillon discusses the historical background and the sources of the text.

Translated by John Dillon and Tania Gergel with an introduction by John Dillon

---

PENGUIN CLASSICS

LA VITA NUOVA (POEMS OF YOUTH)
DANTE

> 'When she a little smiles, her aspect then
> No tongue can tell, no memory can hold'

Dante's sequence of poems tells the story of his passion for Beatrice, the beautiful sister of one of his closest friends, transformed through his writing into the symbol of a love that was both spiritual and romantic. *La Vita Nuova* begins with the moment Dante first glimpses Beatrice in her childhood, follows him through unrequited passion and ends with his profound grief over the loss of his love. Interspersing exquisite verse with Dante's own commentary analysing the structure and origins of each poem, *La Vita Nuova* offers a unique insight into the poet's art and skill. And, by introducing personal experience into the strict formalism of Medieval love poetry, it marked a turning point in European literature.

Barbara Reynolds's translation is remarkable for its lucidity and faithfulness to the original. In her new introduction she examines the ways in which Dante broke with poetic conventions of his day and analyses his early poetry within the context of his life. This edition also contains notes, a chronology and an index.

Translated with a new introduction by Barbara Reynolds

PENGUIN CLASSICS

THE DECAMERON
GIOVANNI BOCCACCIO

'Ever since the world began, men have been subject to various tricks of Fortune'

In the summer of 1348, as the Black Death ravages their city, ten young Florentines take refuge in the countryside. They amuse themselves by each telling a story a day for the ten days they are destined to remain there – a hundred stories of love, adventure and surprising twists of fate. Less preoccupied with abstract concepts of morality or religion than earthly values, the tales range from the bawdy Peronella hiding her lover in a tub to Ser Cepperallo, who, despite his unholy effrontery, becomes a Saint. The result is a towering monument of European literature and a masterpiece of imaginative narrative.

This is the second edition of G. H. McWilliam's acclaimed translation of *The Decameron*. In his introduction Professor McWilliam illuminates the worlds of Boccaccio and of his storytellers, showing Boccaccio as a master of vivid and exciting prose fiction.

Translated with a new introduction and notes by G. H. McWilliam

Penguin Classics

HOMERIC HYMNS

'It is of you the poet sings ...
at the beginning and at the end
it is always of you'

Written by unknown poets in the sixth and seventh centuries BC, the thirty-three *Homeric Hymns* were recited at festivals to honour the Olympian goddesses and gods and to pray for divine favour or for victory in singing contests. They stand now as works of great poetic force, full of grace and lyricism, and ranging in tone from irony to solemnity, ebullience to grandeur. Recounting significant episodes from mythology, such as the abduction of Persephone by Hades and Hermes' theft of Apollo's cattle, the *Hymns* also provide fascinating insights into cults, rituals and holy sanctuaries, giving us an intriguing view of the ancient Greek relationship between humans and the divine.

This translation of the *Homeric Hymns* is new to Penguin Classics, providing a key text for understanding ancient Greek mythology and religion. The introduction explores their authorship, performance, literary qualities and influence on later writers.

'The purest expressions of ancient Greek religion we possess ... Jules Cashford is attuned to the poetry of the Hymns' Nigel Spivey, University of Cambridge

A new translation by Jules Cashford with an introduction by Nicholas Richardson

---

THE STORY OF PENGUIN CLASSICS

Before 1946 ... 'Classics' are mainly the domain of academics and students; readable editions for everyone else are almost unheard of. This all changes when a little-known classicist, E. V. Rieu, presents Penguin founder Allen Lane with the translation of Homer's *Odyssey* that he has been working on in his spare time.

1946 Penguin Classics debuts with *The Odyssey*, which promptly sells three million copies. Suddenly, classics are no longer for the privileged few.

1950s Rieu, now series editor, turns to professional writers for the best modern, readable translations, including Dorothy L. Sayers's *Inferno* and Robert Graves's unexpurgated *Twelve Caesars*.

1960s The Classics are given the distinctive black covers that have remained a constant throughout the life of the series. Rieu retires in 1964, hailing the Penguin Classics list as 'the greatest educative force of the twentieth century.'

1970s A new generation of translators swells the Penguin Classics ranks, introducing readers of English to classics of world literature from more than twenty languages. The list grows to encompass more history, philosophy, science, religion and politics.

1980s The Penguin American Library launches with titles such as *Uncle Tom's Cabin*, and joins forces with Penguin Classics to provide the most comprehensive library of world literature available from any paperback publisher.

1990s The launch of Penguin Audiobooks brings the classics to a listening audience for the first time, and in 1999 the worldwide launch of the Penguin Classics website extends their reach to the global online community.

The 21st Century Penguin Classics are completely redesigned for the first time in nearly twenty years. This world-famous series now consists of more than 1300 titles, making the widest range of the best books ever written available to millions – and constantly redefining what makes a 'classic'.

The Odyssey continues ...

The best books ever written

PENGUIN CLASSICS

SINCE 1946

Find out more at www.penguinclassics.com